Udemeobong Nkereuwem Thomas

Fiscal Science and Decision Science

Udemeobong Nkereuwem Thomas

Fiscal Science and Decision Science

Dilemma of the State

LAP LAMBERT Academic Publishing

Imprint
Any brand names and product names mentioned in this book are subject to trademark, brand or patent protection and are trademarks or registered trademarks of their respective holders. The use of brand names, product names, common names, trade names, product descriptions etc. even without a particular marking in this work is in no way to be construed to mean that such names may be regarded as unrestricted in respect of trademark and brand protection legislation and could thus be used by anyone.

Cover image: www.ingimage.com

Publisher:
LAP LAMBERT Academic Publishing
is a trademark of
Dodo Books Indian Ocean Ltd. and OmniScriptum S.R.L publishing group

120 High Road, East Finchley, London, N2 9ED, United Kingdom
Str. Armeneasca 28/1, office 1, Chisinau MD-2012, Republic of Moldova, Europe
Managing Directors: Ieva Konstantinova, Victoria Ursu
info@omniscriptum.com

Printed at: see last page
ISBN: 978-620-8-43400-7

ABSTRACT

This Scientific PhD thesis and manifesto is an experimental compendium that emphasizes the need for an empirical and radical change in the 'words' and 'spirit' of fiscal governance that must trickle down to the entire polity. Since this academic memoir aims to proffer theoretical and practical solutions to the context of its research problem, its scientific methodology, using experimental analysis and mathematical expression of economics and political theories to analysing the basic tools of decision sciences are of the essence. The descriptive; prescriptive; and narrative level of analysis make up the preliminary scope of this paper, emphasizing the outcome of some analysis in an empirical dimension for professional and technical explanation of the embedded experiment and discussions. The content analysis is based on simple Economic Models and Economic Functions (EM and EF) that explain the symbolic meaning of such models and functions after each mathematical equation and experiment respectively for the purpose of clarity to the general – public, and to experts that yearn to decipher this academic masterpiece. The primary data obtained from the three federal institutions of the United States of America's government through questionnaire as the research instrument serves as the basis for this research analysis. However, the secondary data archived on the basis of Constitutional provisions from the United States of America's Congress Budget Office and Congressional Library aid the fiscal analogy of this research respectively. The deconstruction method of analysis objectively explains the constitutional framework that guides this research by giving a constructive interpretation of the constitutional provisions. This paper is a Four (4) Chapter research work, using analytical and prospective approaches / models of decision making to analize and experiment the United States' fiscal budgets and fiscal constitutional provisions: Reforms and enacted Acts as the case-study for this research paper.

PREFACE

This memoir is written to introduce Political Scientists and Economists (Scientists) to the hidden and fundamental problem that has lingered the Socio-economic and Socio-political prosperity of our economies for centuries.

Political Scientists and Economists have failed to venture into a research of this nature, maybe, because they are not objective enough to question the 'given' metaphysically of the fundamentals of conventional economics.

No knowledge of Political Science or Economics would ever make sense if it does not contradict or question an already existing set of ideas, theories, prospective or knowledge. Therefore, a scientific and experimental justification for such contradiction would definitely make sense if it yields towards solving the basic issues facing man- kind.

The quest for this research was not, and is not facilitated by any past- research papers. Rather, it was masterminded through a critical and intensive curiosity on trying to ask several questions and understanding why Political Economic solutions should revolve around a two major Socio- political and Socio-economic Ideologies (the Liberals and the Conservatives) that have only gotten the steering - wheel of the society around a recurrent cycle for centuries.

Though, I obtained my first and second degrees in Political Science and Public Administration respectively, and this fact would raise some intellectual eyebrows in the arena of academicians, concerning my credentials, and my credibility in Economics or Decision Sciences, having such intellectual audacity to recommending and proffering political economic solutions to global crisis that should have been harnessed and discussed by experts in the field of Economics.

It is factual to assert that 'Nature does not permit vacuum' and as a result, a critical and creative independent studies of Fiscal Sciences have aided my professionalism in embarking on a more practical approaches and models in researching on how the society functions and how it should ideally work for all mankind at any given time and space.

December, 2025 **Udemeobong N. T.**

TABLE OF CONTENT

List of Figures and Terms

Washington- The Government

Wall Street- The Stock Exchange Market

Main Street- The Electorate/ Populace/ Citizens/ Workforce.

List of Tables

Appendices

CHAPTER 1

INTRODUCTION

1.1 Background of the Study

The beauty of Social Sciences' is dependent on the availability and validity of empirical theories that can serve as paradigms to the natural scientist over centuries of such intellectual exploration. The Economics of the Price of Government has come to stay as a living paradigm in the field of fiscal sciences, and as a result, this PhD research envelopes the totality of how it has been experimented to become a scientific law in the entire field of public financial affairs as long as Economics remains a scientific discipline.

Justice Charles Evans Hughes in his definition of the Constitution asserted that the Supreme Court and the Judges say it is. Nevertheless, this could be typically liked to what John Keynes had described as the invisible foot in his analysis of perfect competitive market. But, could it be so ideal for the supreme Court to build fiscal consensus when Article 1 and Article have exclusively empower the Congress and the Prisident of the United States to take adequate fiscal actions via the Quadrennial commission (Postal Revenue and Federal Salary Act, 1976).

It has become over three centuries of constitutional marolling on fiscal arguments, it is time to stop envisaging the Supreme Court as the last constitutional resort on the price of government. The framers of the Constitution originally never had in mind that the Supreme Court could, would, or should be the umpire or the last resort for fiscal debate, this is why the DNA of the United States' court system is embedded in the Article One (after the Congress, and the Executive: Article One and Article Two respectively) in the United States' constitution.

Although, a Republic and not a Democracy as the framers of the Constitution intended, but several constitutional reforms and amendment is what they also encouraged for dynamic polity as the Land of the Free...Home of the Brave. Now, the bravery spans from Socio-political liberty that cuts across Socio-Economic liberty and more. This is why bravery is of the essence in the parliamentary behavior of the 21st century America to fix her fiscal mess irrespective of the ideological-divide.

Almond and Powell in their analysis of the output dimension of Structural-Functionalism opined that rule-making and rule-application precede rule-adjudication, strictly emphasizing the need for sequentialism in the functionality of fiscal governance. Without political loggerhead, the United States' Constitution is explicit on administrative laws, as a result, Justice Oliver Wendell Holme's definition of law becomes a last resort if the Congress and the United States' Presidency are bipolarly disordered. To this effect, the dichotomy between the definitions of public policy by James Anderson and Thomas Dye is tested is all ramification of philosophical facts and truth.

One thing I have noted in my wealth of research experience concerning the framing, amendment, and reform of constitutional republic is that it leave the framers and the reformers (the Congress and the Presidency) in retentive memory-deficit and intellectual loopholes that they forget the letters and the spirit of what was and is written, and as a result, the court seems to be the Monopoly of constitutional knowledge, except for experts of Constitutionalism. Nevertheless, many Scholars have argued that political parties affiliation and it's ideological aisle have necessitated the aforementioned predicament, leaving the court to be an independent umpire to make, apply, and adjudicate the Constitutional provision of the democratic state. But, we should make no mistake that the appointment and approval of the supreme court Justices are nominated along political parties and ideological lines, thereby, giving an intellectual avenue for independent and objective research.

From my PhD dissertation, a clear connectivity has been drawn between the United States' political ecology and Constitutionalism, and this phenomenon is likened to Dr. Omalu's Chronic Traumatic Encephalopathy (CTE) of fiscal Sciences. A strict adherence to the Constitutional provision is what Constitutionalism means, therefore, any deviance in reflect authoritarianism, autocracy, tyranny in it's totality.

Fiscal responsibility is not a matter of the invisible hand, but non-sentimental minds to the pulling down of fiscal yokes through the strict adherence to the Constitution. Republic or Democracy, the Constitution is the DNA of Constitutionalism and Civilization as Jurgen Harbermas instituted in his intellectual framework. Civilization without Constitutionalism is a logical servitude. Having the entire Congress and the Presidency arguing on how balance fiscal budget or maintain fiscal responsibility when the Constitution is explicitly and crystal clear in it prints and interpretations on fiscal matters are like having a government of socerers' apprentice.

The bedrock of every love story is strengthened by the wordings of the text messages and love letters that ignites the emotions of the lovers in harmony, so does the Constitution does to the Leviathan and to the Dragon in the Words of Thomas Hobbes' Social contract. However, Hobbes has envisage the Magna Carta as the nervouse system of the government in governance, just like human brain plays the same role in behavioral coordination. Therefore any attampt to alter the syntax of the Constitution in fiscal governance, is like doing the same to the human brain and his mental wellbeing.

The Scriptures tells us that "the love of money is the root of all evil". This simply implies that the earnings and disbursement of both private and public fund should be guided by laws. At this juncture, we shall draw and intellectual line between public law versus public financial management/ administration.

It is most high time that we we make is crystal clare that the Constitutional or the Law is what the entire three arms of government (namely the Legislature, Executive, and Judiciary) say it is and nothing more pretentious by either of the arms of the government. By this understanding, the Courts should be part of the first resort, and not the last resort when it comes to conflict in government revenue and expenditures.

However, the Humanists would constructively argue my hypotheses, making emphasies on the concern of the Humanists perspectives on public policy or fiscal policy, while they antagonize politics-admonistration dichotomy. But, what should be done when there is a fiscal cancer and pandemic in the United States of America today? The phrase "Judiciously adhereing to Constitutional laws" has never, would never, and does not mean that every Constitutional matters must end at the court. Therefore, the ability to coordinate governance with fiscal clashes signifies political maturity in any polity.

Intellectually speaking, it is quite awakening to put it to the general public that the Constitution of any democratic State is the theory of that State. Therefore, if the Constitution becomes the theory of the State, it simply entails that within the caprises of the Constitution lies the subtheories of the Democratic principles that are to be judiciously adhered to in any given provision. In this regards, the Constitution serves as the first law and theory that protracts the Democratic affairs of the polity and its inhabitants. If this is the truth and fact, why then do ignore the rudiments of our democracy in money matters when the theory of the Price of government is rooted in the letters and the in the spirit of the constition?

It is quite important to note that where the theory of the State (the Constitution) ends, is where the theory of the Price of Government should begin. Therefore, we should make no mistake to envisage the economics of the price of government in a vacuum. In this regards, ideologies and thoughts precedes theory. Therefore, this research becomes an intellectual and academic masterpiece that is centered on Economic theory versus Constitutional theory.

We should always remember to look into the Constitution and not public purse each time we think of fiscal responsibility and the Economics of the Price of Government.

To further integrate this PhD research, I assert that the intellectual arguments that are of the political economic divide between Keynesian and Austrian economist have become to a greater extent vague in ending the intellectual economic deficit and national debt that have befallen policy makers and the fiscal practices of our time.

The major focus on the progressive/ regressive/ proportionate tax conversation therapy of the political parties' ideologies as the cause of socio-economic inequality has become the fiscal retarded issues militating against the fiscal prospect of the 21st century, just as I have experimented and analysed in my M.A research.

In 1787, after the Costitutional Convenvention at the Steps of the Independence Hall in order to adopt the US. Constitution, Benjamin Franklin asserted to the question of Republic vs. Monarchy that the United States of America is a "Republic...only... if Americans can keep it". In the same vein, a renouned African Nationanalist Kwame Nkrumah opined in his contradictory and tentative, but, factual philosophy that Economic Kingdom precedes Political Kingdom in the days of humanists and existentalists calamity. By these opinions, the essence of a Ruplic is to be able to economically and politically keep it for its inhabitants through the doctrine of the mean as quipped by Aristotle.

To a greater extent, we really need to reconsider what the phrase 'Limited Government' means if the Tea-Party Movement can really work for every American (as quipped by the Republicans), and if Democratic Innovation is of the essence against the prevalence of Democratic Regression. The implementation of 'Limited Government' or 'Austerity measures' should begin with limiting government fiscal benefits, and Earmarks, while the Economics of the Price of Government takes the order of the 21st century fiscal practice. This is because the size of government in the 21st century does not mostly depend on what government does, but begins with what government pays itself from the fiscal budget and national treasury in the process of governance, thereby embarking on the quest for Intertemporal Choice in fiscal govermance.

As O'Rourke (1987) puts it 'Giving money and power to government is like giving whiskey and car keys to teenage boys. In 1992, O'Rourke also opined that it takes only human in his own immortal way to understanding and implimenting the dynamics of fiscal decision changes against their personal interest. Therefore, even if several economists have interpreted the causes of fiscal deficit and national debt in different ways, it is time for a pragmatic and consequential change, and this change begins with political emoluments and public remuneration (the price of government). If affordable Health Care has become a matter of urgency in the United States' Politics and Economics, then such urgency should begin with making sure that the fiscal minds of fiscal policy makers are nutured towards fiscal responsibility (the economics of the price of government), even before the debate for public health can thrive against political interests.

The concept of Noble Savage, as percieved, but not actually used by Jean-Jacques Rousseau simply brings our mind into understanding that there is that nature in man that sometimes hunger for idealism against sentimentalism, especilly when the general will (volonte generale) is considered as the essence of fiscal governance. As a result, this nature of man in collective effort and cooperaion with his kind and likeminds can really play a vital role in the economics of the price of government.

Like the two hemispheres of the human brain, the Logic of the State and the Logic of the Market coexist, and so do the Logic of Personal Interest and the Logic of Public Interest. Although, they apply a quite different set of values and assumptions to the world, neither should be assumed innately superior, but either should be nurtured balanced against a richer account of democratic duties and for the public good, where the entire human brain (but not scapple or machette) is required for fiscal cut in the economics of the price of government (Flinders, 2013: 84).

Making and citing the above assertion does not mean that I am a class warrior, but I am a fiscal economic pragmatic solution worrier, believing on what James Madison calls 'The Meeting of the Minds' in the Federalist #45 and #58 of 1792 irrespective of the constitutional amendment through the Congressional Budget & Important Control Act of 1974. However, such constitutional amendment had been made without considering the fact that the concepts "mandatory spending and discretionary spending" should be replaced with "capital expenditures and recurrent expenditures" in order to salvage the United States Fiscal Science from the fiscal conceptualized and constitutional slavery that has facilitated political logicism on the backdrop of dark money loopholes in American fiscal minds, fiscal debate, and fiscal system.

If Chung (1970: 20), asserts that:

"government employees' wages, salaries, income and government expenditures are products of government revenue that is mostly derived from government taxes, reflecting primarily political decisions by national and state legislatures and local governing bodies, international political conditions and relations, the philosophy of government in regard to its economic role, the size, growth, and age distribution of the population, and so on".

Then, the measurement of such income and expenditures should primarily be guided by political decisions, political economic-will, plus critical economic decisions, irrespective of government philosophy or conventional public finance and economic ideas of the past. This is because fiscal reform should not be a luxury, but an urgent rational political economic necessity that must control costs and provide relief for fiscal decision sciences.

However, Frey and Gallus (2017) draw the line between 'Honours and Money: The Economics of Award', emphasizing on how money may or may not influence decision making. As a result, it is quite inevitable that politics and self-interest could be power-driven, and could make the implementation of the economics of the price of government controversial, but not impossible. The question is 'Can award replace or take a major part of money (political emoluments and public remuneration) in public wages, incentives, and income in public financial management? The answer to this question and more is what we shall experiment in this dissertation.

I have definitely been interested in researching on the role of political emoluments and public remuneration on fiscal deficits and national debt, perhaps, on the economy at large. This is because decision makers in their quest to solving the fiscal problem, and developing the economy at the same time has left them with political-economics dilemma (most especially in the United States). As a result, decision makers seem to be running round different ideological cycles due to the bifurcated view of human behaviour, of which my M.A research addresses the aforementioned issues.

I write to clarify that I do not dispute Kural (2003: 243) 'Theories of Budget Control' in its conventional assumptions. But I have written to justify the fact that Kural's theory would only orchestrate a persistent dysfunctional effect on fiscal deficit. Therefore, pragmatic alternatives should be envisaged and applied in curbing the issue of fiscal deficit (the economics of the price of government). Just as Ada and Cooper (2003) explained that Economics is Dynamic, therefore, in envisaging the solution to the dynamic optimization problem in economics, we should explore and implore a more dynamic method in applying and solving problems, especially in public economics.

Although, Wolf (2012) asserted that Karl Marx had failed to emphasize government planning in his critique, but focused more on industrial production relations. However, Wolf advocated for government planning as the underlined interpretation of socialism. But, how can government planning begin without applying the ethics and genesis of government planning, which is cost-benefit analysis in decision sciences?

The Political Economics of Special Interest has become one of the fundamental issues in decision making (public policy), especially when it is quite inevitable that the government also known as the Stoics (a smaller percentage of we the people) also serve as an interest group in the decision-making process on the basis of Puritan Ethic vs. Quaker Ethic in Public Sector Economics and Public Finance Management as explained by Shi (1985).

Therefore, if we must Defend Politics as discussed by Flinders (2013), then we should think 'the Economics of the Price of Government' as the genesis of collective bargaining in governance, and as an arbiter for fiscal responsibility in public economics.

This PhD dissertation shall be an offshoot of my M.A research that is entitled 'The Role of the Price of Government on Fiscal Deficit: An Experimental Economic Analysis of the 2017 US Fiscal Budget'. Therefore, I shall be laying critical emphasis on the application of positive economics, positive psychology, and positive politics (positive sciences)/ methodologies and principles ('what is') in solving fiscal problems in decision sciences, drawing inference from normative analysis (what ought to be') in order to identify the problem and suggest scientific solutions to improving decision making process in fiscal science, and most importantly laying acritical emphasis on addressing the constitutional ambiguities that militate against fiscal sanity because fiscal sciences do not exist in a vacuum, but in the caprices of the constitution.

The choice of this PhD dissertation topic (The Economics of the Price of Government and Decision Sciences: An Experimental Analysis of the US Fiscal Psyche) is to find out the role that decision making and behavioural economics play in the actual implementation of the 'Economics of the Price of Government (as previously experimented and analysed in my Masters research)', considering the Lucas Critique (Gorton, 2012: 89-93) as a bedrock for this research experiment.

The reason for this dissertation is to further in a systematic and rigorous manner (in the sphere of social sciences), research, experiment and analyse how the Economics of the Price of Government can be practically implemented and practically applied irrespective of its psychological, social, political, economic, and other ecological constraints that may threaten the ideals of its prospects especially when the concepts Bounded Rationality versus Olympian

Rationality (God-like rationality as he calls it) as argued by Herbert Simon and Charles Lindblum, Situational Rationality as argued by Karl Popper (a great philosopher of science), and Unbounded Rationality argued by Ward Edwards (1954) are the contending concepts embedded in decision making paradigm, against the Classical Economists' assumptions of human behavior towards 'Loss Aversion' and 'The Framing Effect'. As Hume (1739:542) puts it:

"If every man had a tender regard for another...the jealousy of interest...could no longer have place; nor would there be any occasion for distributions and limits of property and possession...increase to a sufficient degree the benevolence of men...and you render justice useless... `tis only from selfishness and the confined generosity of men that justice derives its origin"

Hume's assertion brings us to the concept and issue of ethics in public policy as outline by Immanuel Kant, and to the extent we can analyse the implementation of the economics of the price of government as long as decision science is concerned.

Although, Sheingate (2016: 4) opined that Max Weber had observed in the early decades of the twentieth century that to some political class (politically gifted peopl), politics has become business to them and as a result it becomes more interesting to see a major afflunce of financial interest in the business of politics. However, the economics of the price of government does not antagonize with the old tradition of the financial influence in political campaigns, but a reduction in the cost for the governing body and decision makers.

This dissertation is of a necessity because the implementation of the 'Economics of the Price of Government' promises to be ideological, theoretical, and practical problem prone, and critical to real life scenario due to the bounded rationality and the insatiable human behaviour of the decision makers and actors that may sometime emanate as a result of clash in political, economic, and social interests as illustrated by Herbert Simon, and just as Toffler (1970: 542), puts it that "Technocrats suffer from econo-think, myopia, and virus of elitism".

I propose to analyse this dissertation using Experimental Methods to testing the research questions through the formulation of models that are based on facts and theories, with the application of the basic tools of socio-economic and socio-political analysis which are graphical illustration, pie charts, bar charts, histogram, tables, etc.

However, I propose to start and complete this dissertation in addition to other course responsibilities whenever your institution requires of me as part of my academic responsibilities. I have made this assertion because I believe in my capacity, capability, efficiency and effectiveness toward my academic goals just as my referees (in the recommendation letters) can attest to this fact and truth at any given time and place.

1.2 Statement of the Problem

We have in several centuries and decades try to solve the fiscal problems of our time using different classical through modern schools of economics. But why don't we try using the youngest school of economics (the behavioural school) to solving our fiscal problems today?

This question should trigger a critical but solution oriented thought within the two hemisphere of our brain.

The etymological meaning, advancement, and metamorphosis of political emoluments and public remuneration (Salary: government) seeks to explain that the amount of public fund set out for such purpose has meant 'Salt Money': the sum paid to soldiers for salt during the Neolithic Revolution (sometimes between 10, 000 BC. And 6000 BC., in Rome) (Chisholm, 1911: 60).

It has become quite logical to assert that if salary and income in public service etymologically means Salt Money, then it critically means that the salt was a necessity, and that the price for such commodity was fixed in the sense that it could not and should not deter the price of other purchasable human needs and commodity. Therefore, if the price of government in public finance, public economics, and fiscal science could logically be referred to as salt money, then it should not be detrimental to the entire fiscal budget.

Speaking of the salt, the Bible (KJV) in the following books asserts:

Matthew 15:13

"Ye are the salt of the earth: but if the salt has lost his savour, wherewith shall it be salted? It is thenceforth good for nothing, but to be cast out, and to be trodden under foot of men".

Mark 9:50

"Salt is good: but if the salt has lost his saltiness, wherewith will he season it? Have salt in yourselves, and have peace one with another". Colossians 4:6

"Let your speech be always with grace seasoned with salt, that ye may know how ye ought to answer every man".

Philosophically, the aforementioned portions of the Bible reiterate that the Leviathan is the proverbial salt of fiscal management, therefore has the capacity so solve his fiscal crisis with his horn and claws (human brain), else fiscal irresponsibility leads to the cause of cancer to the entire economy. Although, we cannot entirely rule out the realistic nature of the homo politicus especially when his political value exceeds economic value even within the sphere of unspoken politics.

In consonance with what one of the 20th century behavioural economists Hyman Minsky discussed on government interference in the financial system of the economy, he could not have been so aware that the root of the financial system was control by an umpire that already has been financial overdosed without the foresight to understanding that the reform that is due the financial system begins with the price of government. Katona (1975) explains that learning could not be dynamic if it is via problem solving dimension, but via understanding the problem, and in the case of implementing the economics of the price of government, it takes the critical understanding of the effect of political emoluments and public remuneration clauses in fiscal budget. Tormey (2015) has explained in his prophesies 'the end of representative politics', stating the political dilemma entangled in democratic government of which are the misappropriation between the ideal concepts and theories of representation, and the transformation of these theories into action and practice, especially when good governance and political representation are of the essence in dispensing the dividend of democracy to the populace.

In convergence with Tormey's predicament, Herbamas (1976) also critically expatiated on the crisis entangled in democracy and politics, of which our major focus of these crises is on legitimation crisis and accumulation crisis, making it the fundamental issues in fiscal decisionmaking process that facilitates the implementation of the economics of the price of government. Therefore, how we can really identify, implement and solve the fiscal crisis embedded in political emoluments and public remuneration (the price of government) is to begin by critically asking ourselves a basic fiscal question: "Is political emoluments and public remunerations a part of the mandatory or discretionary spending/ expenditure (budget)?

If this question is judiciously answered, then there should be drastic change in the paradigm of conventional fiscal science from Talcott Parson's functional prerequisite, even if it could be perceived as deviance from conventional knowledge of fiscal enterprise in while.

On the narrative, the decision making process concerning public emoluments and renumeration tend to be relative and not absolute to diferent republics on the surface of the earth due to the eminence of sovereignty that has been entangled with the concept interest in different political territories and spectrum of all political lives. However, decision scientists have argued that decisions in the public domain...for the public...by the decision maker is made up of the conglomerates of individuals that of different ideologies, thoughts, and theories for the unification of a given vision, mission, and goal.

To this effect, it is imperative to understanding to whom and where the political power and will lie for the implementaion of the price of government in this United States of Ameriaca as a republic is without a doubt to be economically engineered or mechanized (constitutional amendment) through the words and the spirit of the emolument clauses embeded in the republic's constitution that has stood the test of time for cunturies. Therefore, constitutionalism is the bedrock for the economics and theory of the price of government.

In this research, we shall try as much as possible not to be against the price financial benefits (salaries) attached to the professionalization of politics as explained by Tormey to being why representative politics is in crisis. But, we shall draw inference from his discussion to making sure that such financial benefits do not negatively affect the fiscal responsibility of government expenditures, irrespective of the political campaigns, electoral process, and the 'post-materialist' comportment of the contemporary citizens' unreasonable expectations that give rise to discontent that has trickled down the entire socio-economic and socio-political strata of the entire political economy.

Although, Tormey (2015) predicts post-representative democracy as the antidote for the end of representative government by recommending the politics of public choice. But how can his prediction of salvaging democracy be scrupulously implemented, and how can the political class regain their trust from their electorate within the caprices of the accumulated and progressive fiscal deficit and national debt (when things have politically and economically fallen apart, and the center could not hold) especially when Lipset and Rokkan (1967); Lijphart (1984) have presented and analysed their udisputed Cleavage theories in the compendium of public policy theories?

To so many political scientists and economists, the tenents of the Social Contract put forward by Thomas Hobbes and those from his intellectual background has become the watchword and justification for an "adequate" renumeration and emoluments in public service. But, what if we critically consider the blend between the social contract theories with golden age of public administration theorized by Luther Gulick in 1937, and modified by Molinaro (2017) as Leadership Contract?

Yes, I have put forward the theory of the price of government for pragmatic scrutiny, criticism, debate, and implementation in theory and in practice. But, it would be far fetched or far from reality if we do not critically take into intellectual consideration the psyche of implementing our intellectual and revolutional property of this nature in a more complex polity as this, emphasizing on the need to adopting the Cognitive Maps of decision making process as quipped by Axelrod (2015).

As Flinders (2013: 102) cited (Roberts, 2010), but puts it:

"The Logic of Discipline can be view as a reaction against the inflationary pressures that democratic politics promotes. If politicians cannot discipline public demand, due to their

need to curry public support, so the argument goes, then the sphere of democratic politics must be restricted and functions placed in the hands of those with the capacity to make unpopular decisions. This logic is in a sense anti-political in nature as it revolves around the emptying of political debate and its replacement with technocratic administration"

I have never been and will never be naive and biased about politics and the political system to say that the logic of fiscal discipline can be applied at a platter of gold, especially when interest is a major contending issue in politics. But, the political economic challenges of our time should foster a more prefered public choice in handling our fiscal crisis. In the arena and sphere of mental reservation, the economics of the price of government is never a given, but must be earned through critical and revolutionary fiscal decisions not by faint and selfish hearted, not by worn out fiscal dogmas, not by those that seek pleasures of riches over fiscal truth and facts, but by the risk takers.

However, the psyche of implementing the economics of the price of government brings us to the contending issues that lye within fiscal decision of public economics which are Politics and Power, Power and Choice, The Pleasures of Politics, and Politics of the State. Therefore, if power is the first ingredient of politics, then such power should be exercised in fiscal decisions that are non-sentimental, irrespective of traditional fiscal norms of the state, but for the public good as long as decision makers still have the right hemisphere of the brain enveloped in their skulls. To this effect, we can then consider Adam Smith's Theory of Moral Sentiments that emphasizes the importance of thin values:self-control and duty, the ethical significance and limits of contract and promises (what i have called rational and intergrity in fiscal decision), and propriety. These are, he made clear, moral bases for successful economic action that may come from the Deity but need to be reinforced by society.

As a matter of research ethics, I make no mistake not to acknowledge the work Kahnaman and Tversky (1979) have put forward on prospect theory of behavioral economics and neuroeconomics. But, i shall make it critically clear that their prospect theory in the area of the economics of the price of government can only be intellectually interesting when combined with the elements of political behavior, decision game, and personality psychology, while understanding that prospect theory could be a co-product from political behaviour and personality, of which it is also eminent to see the prospects for Public Choice versus Rational Choice in order to give the Economics of the Price of Government a footage, and curb the persisting fiscal crisis.

If New Public Management is the order of this century global economy, then the persisting fiscal cisis is questionable on the basis of effectiveness and efficiency in public financial management. How can we be so intellectually aroused to recommend to underdeveloped and developing economies of the world the policy of 'Structural Adjustment' when the citadel and centre of Development strugles with the intellectual deficit of harnessing the Economics of the Price of Government?

Although, Thomas Malthus had foreseen that the increase in population would lead to poverty in the economy. But, convention fiscal economists and policy makers had proven him wrong by dialogizing the traditional norm that the increase in population must automatically lead to increase in fiscal spending, of which this fiscal tradition has become cancer to fiscal sciences that has been and was only automatically stabilized in 2009 by the Obama administration but awaiting a global detonation in the nearest future.

It could be quite unfortunate to understand that the issue of fiscal deficit and national debt would need no artificial intelligence to solve so far, but MAYBE in the nearest future. Therefore, the acquisition of critical and intellectual professionalism is required to curb this financial cancer, and the time should be now.

Midler (2018: 10) has reiterated China's 'build-it-up-and-tear-it-down' growth strategy, but has failed to critically emphasize the logical reason behind China's quest for such strategy (A Mania for Money) being as a result of the ripple effect of the U.S. and the global fiscal deficit and financial debts, and of which china is also a victim of such in some sort of ways, but has decided to be a lender of last resort until the root cause of the global fiscal deficit is sorted out intellectually by the western economies.

We should make no mistake to misunderstand the context of this study as a researchable paper that focuses only on the experimental (mathematical) aspect. Rather, it it clear to understand that this study shall implore mathematical, historical, and theoretical paradigms as logical tools in its discussion and analysis in a ballanced approach in order to illuminate the reality of fiscal science. If the government is most responsible for embarking on strict regulatory policies on issues that are of External Costs and Benefits to the economy, then the price of government should not be exemted from such government regulatory policies as political emoluments and public remuneration has really contributed th fiscal deficit in government budget.

Two of the most important concepts of economics: 'Scale of Preference, and Opportunity Cost' have become an inevitable tools in public economics, and as aresult, it becomes imperative for the implementation of the economics of the price of government, nay in New Public Management. Therefore, the process of fiscal decision making in public economics embodies the principle of scale of preference and opportunity cost, plus cost-benefit analysis that must be guideded by pragmatic demonstrated or revealed prefernce for public interest, not as Kurlantzick (2016) discribed his State Capitalism, but in making sure the issue of fiscal deficit is addressed in drastic manner. Davies et al. (2016) opined that until consumption is challenged there would be no pathway to a more sustainable future irrespective of the mantras, policy statement, and agenda of the world economies toward 'green economy'

Although, conventional economics rules Casino should not exist. This is because conventional economists assume that humans are rational when it comes to financial gains and losses. But, for some strange reasons, "perfectly intelligent people" head to the Casinos and other gambling centres everyday and in essence take some crucial financial deal. In the same vein, conventional economists believe that gambling and insurance should not exist or work, but in reality, these human actions through respective agencies have thrive for centuries. Then, if this the case, it could be rational and worth the risk invasaging that the economics of the price of government can work and thrive against fiscal deficit.

We are not ignorant of Baddeley (2019: 177-195) of Neuroscience of how human brain works scientifically. But we definitely need to understand the need for a dynamic public financial management and public economics which the principles of Sanction, Economy, Benefits, and Surplus. Therefore we can nudge our intellectual priorities towards the economics of the price of government for the public good.

Nevertheless, as a result of Loss Aversion Effect, behavioral economists would argue that the economics of the price of government would lead to financial crime and corruption in public administration/ management and service. But, it is of importance to note that the implementation of this economics must be embeded in the constitution with adequate criminal and legal penalties attached to the words and spirit of the constitution against defaulters (as postulated by the 'New Time Theorists, and The Conflict Theorists of Crime and Deviance'), if the eradication of fiscal deficit and national debt are of the essence as we embark on a neuroeconomic engineering of public financial management.

Most importantly, Black (1995: 3) and his fellow Equilibrium expets have asserted that the general equilibrium model has no role for government. But, they have forgotten to take into consideration that the government formulate and implement fiscal and monetary policy of which the price of government in not an exclusion form these policies. Therefore, in the present days economic science, we have some rethink to do in regards to their assertion and the science behind workability of such philosophy. Therefore, the general equilibrium theory should begin with the price of government.

1.3 Aim and Relevance of the Study

Right from the beginning of this my revolutionary research, I have indicated that as long as Constitutional democracy is concern, no fiscal practices of any state exist in a vacuum, except in the codified and uncodified words and spirit of the Constitution, and as a result, this research is an intellectual awakening to what the US Constitution actually says concerning the Economics of the Price of Government, even though this Constitution must have been written over 200 years ago. We yearn to ascertain whether the US Constitution is actually a living organism in the implementation of the Economics of the Price of Government.

Although, the study and issues embedded in fiscal science can be historically and empirically traced back to the ancient period in Plato's Republic, when he analysed his 'problem of nature and nurture' in relating to the 'philosopher king' in his decision making process. A profound Scottish Economist (Adam Smith) in his 'Theory of Moral Sentiments' also tried to ascertain the scope of behavioural economics and decision sciences even before it became prominent from the 19th century till date (Smith, 1759). But, such studies have little or nothing to do with political emoluments and public remuneration as one of the major factor militating against fiscal responsibility.

However, the above fiscal issue has been addressed through my previous research. But, it is rational and empirically justified that the implementation of the recommendations in my previous research cannot exist in a vacuum, but within the sphere of public policy or the decision making process of the state, which must be carried out by decision makers and actors that possess rational and irrational behaviours, even within and without the scope of their public decision making capacity and capability. It can be critically and logically thought through that if the launching of the nuclear code by the U.S. President can be a matter of urgency for swift rational decision in respect to national security, then the decision to embrace the pragmatic prospect against fiscal deficit and national debt should be closely considered as a matter of national security, but in a fiscal dimension as long as fiscal cliff in the context of the economics of the price of government would be handled in a more ballanced and responsible way in accordance with fiscal constitutionalism.

Therefore, the aim and relevance of this dissertation is to research, experiment, and apply the living paradigm and existing literatures of fiscal science put forward by Adam Smith, Harrold Lasswell, Thomas Dye, James Anderson, Joseph Schumpeter (1942), Walter Heller, John Keynes (1936), Milton Friedman (1957, 1975), Robert Mundell (1961), George Friedrich Knapp (1924), J. B. Clarks (1985), Andrew Levison (1980), etc., in relationship with Behavioural economics and Decision Sciences literatures written and discussed by Daniel Kahneman on neuroeconomics and behavioral finance as the foremost. While, the literatures of Abraham Maslow, Evans Pavlov, B. F. Skinner, Fred Herzberg, Douglas McGregor; and Dan Ariely, Richard Thaler & Cass Sunstein, Malcolm Gladwell, Stephen J. Dubner & Steven Levitt, Charles Duhigg, Nir Eyal, Uri Gneezy and John List, Elizabeth Dunn and Michael Norton, John Armstrong, Daniel Bernoulli, Jeremy Bentham, Von Neumann and Morgenstern, Karl Deutsch, Theodor Ludwig, David Easton, etc., in order to ascertain the role Constitutionalism, political behaviour, neuro-economics, and behavioural finance play in the implementation of the economics of the price of government, and to give experimental prospects to the issues of fiscal irresponsibility and fiscal deficit in public finance and public economics beyound the traditional bipartisal ideologies of the progressives and the conservatives (mainstream), thereby making the prospects in this dissertation a paradigm in fiscal sciences as explained by Kuhn (1962).

This research has become relvant because the empirical justification for behavioural sciences is embedded in its dynamic and scientific experiment to prove fact and truth against the dogmatic and normative approaches since homo-politicus (man and politics) and homo-economicus (man and economics) have arrived at a cross-road with homo-psychologicus (human and psychology)... a necessary synergy to handling the behaviour and misbehaviour in public finance (fiscal sciences).

I seek to research on this dissertation in order to foster a theoretical and pragmatic blend between political science, economics and psychology (Neuro-political economic sciences), by contributing to a pragmatic solution in solving the problem militating against fiscal responsibility, and not to linger on the scholarly arguments on economics-psychology dichotomy put forward by Gul and Pesendorfer (2005), and of others that have written before, and after.

With the rise of modern populism today, it is evident that modern politics is more of emotions that rationality. But, it is high time we deworm the parasites and saprophytes militating against the fiscal responsibility of our time before it escalates to its handicap stage. Perhaps, just as the president's "Black Budget" is a compromised part of the budget by the Congress as a matter of national security, political emolument and public remuneration should definitely be considered as a matter of fiscal security to the state treasury.

Most definitely, the conclusive aim of this research it to apply the living paradigm in Neuroeconomics, and sort for a more pragmatic method on the prospects of decision sciences in making sure that the Economics of the Price of Government is Implemented in order to solve the global fiscal crisis, and not to linger on vague academic debate or eloquence of behavioural economics that is short of pragmatic solutions to the problem in this context, as is tends to be a matter of National and Global Emergency that needs urgent political economic attention and decision for quintessential public financial management.

Therefore, there is need for "The Leadership Contract" in the Economics of the Price of Government, especially at this juncture where parochial political culture maintains its upward mobility. In the same vein, Philosopher David Hume could not have been so intellectually guarded when he fashioned his theory of the virtue of justice and government, laying emphasis on his trust game (TG). If this is the scenario, it is critical we bring back the new fiscal trick required to regain this political trust that is on the decline due to the persisting practice of the traditional political trick that politics is known for by the governed. As a result, the quest for thoughtfully ruthless leadership, and a mental dynamic change in fiscal norms are of the essence for fiscal leadership.

1.4 Research Questions

Does the implementation of the Economics of the Price of Government needs constitional framework in the United States' constition?

What are the Constitutional provisions backing the implementation of the Economics of the price of government in the United States of America?

Who should implement or apply the Constitutional provisions in the implementation of the Economics of the price of government?

Does Behavioural Economics have any role to play in the implementation of the Economics of the Price of Government?

Are there variables that can affect the implementation of the Economics of the Price of Government in the decision making process?

What are the roles of the variables in the decision making process, and how can these variables be contained in order to implement the economics of the price of government for fiscal responsibility?

1.5 Relevant Literatures

The key researchable academic materials for this dissertation will be majorly derived from different text books and literatures in political science, economics, psychology, finance, public policy, etc., as they reflect in the bibliographies. However, the different models of public policy, theories of consumer behaviour; and the theories of learning written by B. F. Skinner and Evans Pavlov. The work of Abraham Maslow, Douglas McGregor, and Fred Herzberg on Motivation will also serve as the major literatures in this paper.

The different models of public policy analysis and Budgeting written by Sydney Weber, David Brubreb, Amitai Etzioni, Charles Lindblum, Herbert Simon, G. Allison, Arthur Laffer, John Keyenes, Milton Friedman, Robert Mundell, etc., shall be adopted in the experimental analysis of this work. The concept of Utilitarianism fostered by Jeremy Bentham through his Benthamite principle – of psychological hedonism that was conceived as a guide for legislation, focusing on the assumption that people maximize their own self-interest, weighing pain and pleasure as the "sovereign masters" towards human motivation especially in the context of puritan ethics.

The work of Almond and Powel on political culture, the literature on conservativism and liberalism shall also be adopted in analysing the role of political economic ideologies in decision making process.

The major theoretical basis for this dissertation shall be the Nudge Theory developed by Watzlawick, Weakland, and Bill D'Hanlon, but laying critical emphasis on Thaler and Sunstein's critique on Choice Architects and their discourse of Good Government, which are critical exceptions of the traditional and conventional Nudge Theory. The Behavioural Game Theory developed by Colin Camerer that states that people do not always play games selfishly is also a major theory in this research. The Public Choice Theory developed by Dennis Mueller shall also be adopted in this dissertation in order to facilitate a dialectical method in synthesizing the theoretical framework in this dissertation. The Onion Model of Conflict as propounded by Edgar Schein shall also be applied to the analysis of this paper.

1.6 Research Methodology (Procedures)

The methodology for this dissertation shall be done, using experimental research design (repeated measures, independent groups, matched pairs); Content Analysis; and interpretative research design, applying descriptive and experimental methodology (laboratory, field, virtual experimental method). The adoption of the combination of the aformentioned experimental method is empirically justified by Ostrom (2007: 26-27), but cited and discussed by Lowndes et al. (2018: 294). The other synthetic methods shall be the Reform-Oriented method; Doctrine legal & non-doctrine legal method; Process-tracing method; and Comparative method cooperatively.

There shall be the gathering of primary quantitative and qualitative data as the case may be required in the research process that will be derived from the respondence's structured, open-ended, and closed ended qustionaires. Our field and laboratory for this experimental research comprise of the U.S Congress; the U.S. Department of Treasury; the President of the United States and his cabinet secretraries as at when the data for this research will be collected and gathered; and the immediate past president of the U.S from the opposition political party in order to obtain a fair sample of political ideology from the both side of the political aisle.

The essence of adopting questionair as the research instrument against the interview research instrument is to mentain to a greater extent a high level of research objectivity, confidentiality, and the anonymousity of respondences' names because the data that shall be obtained for this research could be considered as classified information by the respondence (the U.S Federal Government) at the area of study. However, secondary data obtained from the U.S Congressional Budget Office websites, and from the US Fiscal and Budget Management Office Websites; and the sample size that comprises of the memebers of the US Federal Congresss, the Executive Arm of the US Federal Government, and the US Supreme Court Justices because Justice Evans Hughes asserted the Constitution is what the Supreme Court says it is.

Since, this dissertation is to experiment the Price of Government and Decision Sciences of the U.S Fıscal Psyche, it is of importance to obtain the secondary data of the U.S Fiscal Budgets from the U.S Fıscal Budget and Managenet Office Database, starting from the fiscal year of 1990 through 2023 respectively for a comparative and critical analysis of the research problem. Therefore, a comparative rsearch design shall also be adopted at this point of analysis

Basic Experimental methods (Experimental variables, concepts, models, notation, and symbols) shall also be adopted in this dissertation to analysing different variables and the questionaires that are embedded in the research problem and concepts. Respective experimental models and functions shall be presented and experimented in order to empirically test the research questions respectively. The experimental model for this dissertation is expressed and encapsulated in the following equation.

$$\Psi = det.\left[\frac{\text{ꭙ} = \sum \text{ꭙʊ̆} \ (\text{ɟ}) + \sum \text{ʊ̆ʊ̆} \ (\text{ɔ}) + \sum \text{ʊ̆ʊ̆} \ (\text{Ƚ})}{\text{Ƀ} = \sum \dfrac{\Phi 1 + \Phi 2}{1 + \ 2 \ \amalg \ 3 + \ 4 \ \sim (\text{Ŧ})}}\right]$$

Where Ψ denotes US fiscal decisions for the economics of the price of government (fiscal decision). P is the Economics of the Price of Government - [PE(x): puritan ethics, ED(y): economic development, and EG(z): economic growth]. R denotes Rationality in decision making process. Φ1 dipicts personality, Φ2 depicts political behavior, φ 1 denotes Public Choice, φ 2 is Rational Choice, and φ 3 depicts Rational Action, 4 represents prospect theory of behavioural finance, and (Ŧ) dipicts the legal framework, Act, or Constitutional Framework for the Economics of the Price of Government. Adding up, gives a mathematical expression for this dissertation. Hence, the ∑P and ∑R (independent variables) are the determinants of Ψ (dependent variable) in the fiscal principles of decision sciences.

In an integrated level of equational model, this doctoral research work shall adopt the Experimental research design, explanatory and prescriptive analysis, deconstruction techniques, construtionists theory, and Experimental method in interpreting all the secondary qualitative and quantitative data (the United States' Constitution, and all Congressional Acts pertaining fiscal matters) that shall be adopted for this research presentation, analysis, and discussion. The other synthetic methods shall be the Reform-Oriented method; Doctrine legal & non-doctrine legal method; Process-tracing method; and Comparative method cooperatively. The Onion Model of Conflict as propounded by Edgar Schein shall also be applied to the analysis of this paper.

Thus, the integrational experimental equation formulated and adopted in this paper is as follows:

Ψ = det. [Ӿ= ∑ Ӿΰ̆ (ɹ)+ ∑ ΰ̆ΰ̆(ɔ)+ ∑ ΰ̆ΰ̆ (Ⱡ)

Ƀ= ∑ Φ1 + Φ2

Φ1 + Φ2 1 + 2 [][3 + 4 ~ (Ť)]

R = Φ1 + Φ2

[1 + 2][3 + 4 ~ (Ť)]

Ψ = f (Ť + R)

Where Ť (Ψ)...............k

Where Ψ denotes US fiscal decisions for the economics of the price of government (fiscal decision). P is the Economics of the Price of Government - [PE(x): puritan ethics, ED(y): economic development, and EG(z): economic growth]. R denotes Rationality in decision making process. Φ1 dipicts personality, Φ2 depicts political behavior, φ 1 denotes Public Choice, φ 2 is Rational Choice, and φ 3 depicts Rational Action, 4 represents prospect theory of behavioural finance, and (Ŧ) dipicts the legal framework, Act, or Constitutional Framework for the Economics of the Price of Government. Adding up, gives a mathematical expression for this dissertation. Hence, the ∑P and ∑R (independent variables) are the determinants of Ψ (dependent variable) in the fiscal principles of decision sciences.

R denotes Rationality in decision making process. Φ1 dipicts personality, Φ2 depicts political behavior, φ 1 denotes Public Choice, φ 2 is Rational Choice, and φ 3 depicts Rational Action, 4 represents prospect theory of behavioural finance, and (Ŧ) dipicts the legal framework, Act, or Constitutional Framework for the Economics of the Price of Government. Adding up, gives a mathematical expression for this dissertation.

Further discussions and analysis shall be made to clarify the experimental analysis for basic explanation and understanding of the experimental models and functions, using graphical illustrations.

The reason for the aforementioned choice of the research methodology for this dissertation is to make sure it encompasses the broader scopes of economics of the price of government which are political behaviour, public financial management, behavioural economics, public policy analysis, psychology, fiscal sciences, and decision sciences (Experimental Economics, Experimental Psychology, and Experimental Political Science), in order to make this research unique, dynamic, and easy to to apply in theory and in practice to solving the research problem.

1.7 Structure of the Dissertation

This dissertation shall be a four-chapter research that is going to reflect the theoretical and practical aspect and principles of the relationship between the three distinctive academic fields of Political Science, Economics, and Psychology. The first chapter shall encompass the introductory part and the analysis of the adopted research methodology, detailing the segmented experimental and mathematical equation/ analysis of the economics of the price of government versus the experimental analysis of decision sciences as the two major variables of the research topic .

The second chapter shall include the review of extant literatures and the theoretical background of the study., followed by the subsequent chapter (chapter three) that shall contain the presentation of primary and secodary data, research analysis, experiment, and discussion. The experimental analysis is to maintain a non-speculative approach, but an empirical approach that are based on the variables derived from the respondents'opinion (primary data), and other experimental analysis shall be derived from the theoretical framework of this dissertation and the numerous theoretical assumptions mentioned in this dissertation. Finally, the last chapter (chapter four) shall contain the conclusion and recommendations of the dissertation, followed by the bibliographies alphabetically and respectively arranged.

1.8 Definition of Terms

This part of the research is one of the most important contents because its literatures must guide the conceptual interpretations and meaning of the two major variables of the research topic, which are 'The price of government' and 'Economy development'.

For the purpose of this study, the operational definition of terms shall be adopted against the lexical definition. This is because every research in social sciences or decision sciences must be guided by systematic, technical, and logical concepts that must clearly give ideal and realistic interpretation to the public in general, and to experts in particular. The two major definitions of terms are as follows:

(I) The Price of Government

According to Osborne and Hutchinson, (2004), in their book 'The Price of Government' defined the above term as all the costs that government incurs for 'government' and for 'governance' (recurrent and capital expenditures) that reflects in government annual budget. However, they noted that 'the price of government' in particular refers to the price or cost set out for political office holders and political administrators in any economy, outlined and earmarked in government expenditures per annum.

Therefore, we consider in this research that 'the price of government' is defined as the price and cost set out by government for remuneration and emolument for political office holders and public administrators in any economy, which is derived from the government taxable and non-taxable revenue for her annual expenditures.

As a result, we can say that 'the price of government' is 'a part of the whole' that makes up recurrent expenditures of government spending. This price and costs are made up of the basic salaries and allowances (plus incentives) for political office holders and public administrators in fiscal budgeting of the government. The other parts of the recurrent expenditures are government bonds and other routine fiscal allocation for the maintenance of MDAs and other government assets.

On the other hand, the Capital Expenditures are made up of Public Investments that is fiscally allocated by the government through MDAs for the provision of both private goods and public goods for the members of the public.

(II) Puritan Ethics

This concept was first coined by a renouned American Economist, Walter Wolfgang Heller in his book 'Monetary vs. Fiscal Policy', published in 1969. His work to a greater extentfacilitated this research paper.

Simply put, Heller's concept implies that government expenditures should equal her revenue. But different liberal economists like Milton Friedman and John Keynese have argued against his assumption on the basis of the fiscal fact put forward by by Richard Musgrave, Adolf Wagner, Allan Peacock, and Jack Wiseman on the theory of Public Finance, towards the necessity for progressive increase in inj government expenditures.

The assumptions by the aformention public financial theorists have however, call for a möore radical approach to Heller's 'Puritan Ethics' , and such fiscal revolution should be harnessed in the caprises of political emoluments and public remuneration as long as his assumption tends to foster fiscal responsibility in public financial management.

Therefore, this research paper, adopted from the intellectual background of Heller's principles tends to creat a political economic change in the axis of political emolument and fiscal sciences. Scientifically, political emoluments and public remuneration areare embedded within the scope of public 'recurrent expenditures', and this expenditure tends to form the greatest percentage of the classification of the recurrent expenditure in the contemporary fiscal plan of the government.

As a result of the above fiscal realities, there is an urgent and a pragmatic need for a crucial fiscal engineering and political economic surgery in the direction to fostering a long lasting and positive change for economy development.

CHAPTER 2

REVIEW OF RELATED LITERATURES AND THEORETICAL FRAMEWORK

2.1 Literature Review

Crotty (1998, p. 62) characterizes constructionism as "the view that all information, and consequently all significant reality all things considered, is dependent upon human works on, being built all through collaboration between people and their reality, and created and communicated inside a basically friendly setting".

As indicated by individual constructivists information is "independently and particularly developed" (Liu and Matthews, 2005, p. 387) by one claims mind investigating and creating implications of occasions (Watkins, 2000). The development happens, "through the correlative versatile systems of convenience and digestion", when one cooperates with the climate around him/her (Marton and Booth, 1997, p. 6). Varieties in capacities of individual to conceptualize and the way that occasionally people decipher a similar peculiarity distinctively brings about contrasts in implications (Watkins, 2000).

Sense-production is a method of deciphering what happens when individual sweep and give implications to circumstances in which they end up in (Daft and Weick, 1984). Filtering includes looking through the climate to recognize significant issues that are probably going to influence the associations and translation is giving importance to information such that it very well may be perceived and be utilized for activity (Gioia and Chittipeddi, Sensemaking and sensegiving in essential change commencement, 1991; Thomas, Clark, and Gioia, 1993). Sense-production has likewise been portrayed by Ring and Rands (1989, p. 342) as "an interaction by which people foster intellectual guides of their current circumstance". Sense-production affects individuals going about as though the understood translations are valid (Weick, 1995; Daft and Weick, 1984). People and gatherings structure mental models which assist with handling data, settle on sense and decide (Walsh, 1994).

Social development processes which incorporate formal and casual correspondence processes (Porac, Thomas, and Baden-Fuller, 1989) and openings to normal occasions help in framing these psychological pictures (Reger and Huff, 1993). Sense-production approach is subsequently predictable with a constructionist approach (Berger and Luckmann, 1966) where associations are depicted as acting with an apparent rather than a genuine climate (Basu and Palazzo, 2008).

Considering that CSD practice isn't controlled, bookkeepers are probably going to see its various viewpoints in an unexpected way. This implies that individuals in various partner positions are probably going to see the training in an unexpected way. An investigation of discernments by bookkeepers is in this manner significant to bring out why the training is for all intents and purposes.

The way that the more proof there is doesn't really modify the importance members have as of now developed is the main example of sense-production. Individual as opposed to seeing everything they are said or shown see what they accept (Weick, 1995). The way that significance isn't found or uncovered however rather is built by the sense-creator is the focal reason of sense-production (Christiansen, 2006).

However there has been an enormous development in writing on CSR, a few writers perceive that there is as yet a missing angle (Margolis and Walsh, 2003; Campbell, 2007; Basu and Palazzo, 2008). The greater part of the CSR studies have moved toward it according to an objective viewpoint (Nijhof and Jeurissen, 2006) concentrating on its substance and exercises (Basu and Palazzo, 2008). Nijhof and Jeurissen (2006) and Basu and Palazzo (2008) guarantee that the sensemaking approach can help in understanding CSR better since will assist with accomplishing more prominent clearness on the CSR practice since it can assist with deciding how assessment pioneers figure out CSR and furthermore draw out the special information structures that have been created corresponding to CSR. For this situation CSR is viewed as exuding from intellectual and semantic cycles and not from outside pressure (Basu and Palazzo, 2008).

While Gioia and Thomas (1996) explored what sense was made of issues that meant for vital change by top supervisory crews in advanced education frameworks and found that essentil to the sense-production process is top administration view of character and keeping in mind that Mills, Weatherbee and Colwell (2006) in an examination of how Canadian business colleges and colleges sorted out similar rankings and inferred that on account of the requirement for secure subsidizing certification and positioning had taken on new implications, which obviously connect with our inclinations, it has not been imaginable to track down explicit investigations of CSD in particualar from a sense-production viewpoint.

The conceivable analysis of the singular constructionism is that, assuming individual development is right, then, at that point, it would be hard to tell what the other individual means when speaking with one another (Watkins, 2000). It would then be hard to share and convey information (Fox, 2001).

Social constructionism as a way to deal with information creation depends on the investigations of Berger and Luckmann (1966). As indicated by the social constructivists information is built not by people but rather by gatherings and is in this manner cooperative and in view of the particular social setting (Wittgenstein, 2001). Information is built through a social cycle and it can exist whenever imparted to someone else (Gergen, 1994).

The social constructionists center around the course of information creation as opposed to satisfying in light of the fact that they fight that nobody individual solely has the wellspring of information (Laird, 1993).

Since information is made through a social interaction, it is well established in past arrangements and in this way it is an arranged group of implications. The implying that people property to occasions decides their conduct and therefore friendly constructionists are worried about the importance of translation (Lit and Shek, 2002). In looking for significance to translations, people shift from their own development of reality dependent on their encounters to zeroing in on the way in which individuals communicate to build, alter and keep up with the general public interpreted reality (Freedman and Combs, 1996).

This implies that the truth is created by friendly exchange and not by the individual developing his/her own reality (Gergen and Davis, 1985). Since the truth is socially built it is by and large and socially relative (Burr, 1995) and in this manner's how people might interpret their outside world is impacted by verifiable and social encounters and it is consequently logical (Houston, 2001; Reed, 2005; Watkins, 2000).

Constructionism has been utilized in business research where the point is to uncover intellectual guides, arrangements and portrayals directing human activity (Piaget, 1954; Gergen, 1999). Instances of observational examinations supporting utilization of constructionism in responsibility research incorporate investigations by Sinclair (1995) and Newman (2004). Nonetheless, constructionism has not been generally utilized in bookkeeping research. The explanation maybe is on the grounds that "implications in bookkeeping are (possibly) haggled in a more extensive group environment than is conceived in old style constructionism or can easily be embraced by direct perception" (Rutherford, 2002, p. 375).

This appears to suggest that in bookkeeping implications are now socially developed. Notwithstanding, there are those of the assessment that monetary bookkeeping in imparting reality builds that reality and consequently it is vital to concentrate on what monetary bookkeeping is interpreted to convey in various group environments (Hines, 1988).

Development is especially significant in CSD on the grounds that norms have not been created and thusly there has not been a socially built jargon and hence various people might understand implications in an unexpected way. However apparently friendly constructivist approach would seem promising, there are troubles with it.

One of analysis of social constructionism is that the job of people in acquiring information is to some degree denied (Ogborn, 1997). Along these lines, it can possibly add to the breakdown of the individualistic worldview initially pushed by constructivists and consequently has not been acknowledged by everybody (Rudes and Guterman, 2007). Social Constructionism studies have likewise been censured for being dependent upon the implied information on the analyst, information examination and understanding may not really be straight forward and can be asset serious and tedious (Easterby-Smith, Thorpe, and Jackson, 2008).

Different researchers have condemned social constructionism as not being a sound hypothesis (Burr, 1995) and as a result of this it contains unique and in some cases clashing thoughts (Cromby and Nightingale, 1999). The hole that exists between the significance appended to an occasion by one individual and the importance held by one more is stressed by sense-production (Parrot, 1996). Notwithstanding, it is vital to take note of that social constructionism has been applied broadly in friendly exploration (Harris, 2010; Lock and Strong, 2010).

The Personal Construct Theory is more appropriate for exposure studies on the grounds that however it depends on people's sense-production of occasions it likewise recognizes that these people are in group environments and in this way a portion of the implications are shared. Since the CSD practice isn't very much evolved people will figure out it however there is likewise the way that there could be shared implications and furthermore clashes between various partners which prompts an arrangement of the training.

The Personal Construct Theory (PCT) was created by George Kelly in 1955 and close by it he additionally fostered the repertory network strategy. The hypothesis and the procedure were created trying to get what triggers feelings (Rogers and Lynette, 2007) and to help in social event information about the manner in which patients saw the world they were living in (Banister and Fransella, Inquiring Man: The Theory of Personal Constructs, 1971).

Kelly needed to know how people intentionally or unknowingly understood their reality (Fontaine and Fransella, 1988). The PCT by investigating person's contemplations, sentiments and convictions targets getting his/her remarkable perspective on the world (Cooper, 1998) and hence assists with clarifying how people decipher occasions happening around them involving individual viewpoint in sense making (Banister and Fransella, 1986).

As per Kelly (1955), people sort out their general surroundings through the arrangement of develops that they have constructed. They characterize what is significant by making a guide of their discernments and translations through a course of cancellation, contortion and speculation (Charvet, 1997). This implies that people build their reality from various sources of info and encounters which assists them with characterizing their "truth" (Stewart and Mayes, 2002) and thusly he/she frames his/her own intellectual guide dependent on his/her insights which is unique in relation to the following people discernments (Baker, 2002).

Despite the fact that a few develops are shared (Goffin, 2002) a person's intellectual guide is exceptional which making different real factors (Baker, 2002). As per Goffin (2002) as a method of clarifying and expecting occasions, people create and test builds by seeing the world dependent on the implications they apply to it. As such people build implications as they decipher the world (Crotty, 1998). This individual develop framework helps in deciphering the recent developments and in expecting future occasions (Tan and Hunter, 2002). This stems from the idea that every individual deciphers and predicts occasions dependent on the theories that he/she has made. People subsequently develop implications and don't make them (Crotty, 2003) and their navigation depends on their build frameworks which address their comprehension of their general surroundings (Kakabadse, 1991).

As indicated by this hypothesis people base their activities on speculations, theories and analyses which they have created and consequently every individual can be considered as researcher (Kelly, 1955). The truth is in this manner made in the personalities of the people and the world individuals live in is perceived dependent on what is seen as genuine (Morgan, 1983). People likewise continually update their builds relying upon their value in deciphering occasions (Goffin, 2002).

The PCT can thusly be alluded to as a hypothesis of gathering and individual social and mental cycles that models cognizance utilizing a constructivist approach (Aranda and Finch, 2003; Fransella, 1988). The PCT gives a structure to concentrates on looking for obtaining of information by participating in intellectual planning and through estimating disposition and character (Aranda and Finch, 2003). The hypothesis perceives that all information depends on people's insights and in this way is modified by "intellectual, social and social powers" (Hatch, 1997).

It additionally implies that happenings in the word can be understood in an unexpected way, and there are contrasts in the models people construct and thusly occasions can hence can be deciphered in an unexpected way (Butt and Parton, 2005). This implies that thoughts are liable to change and it very well might be untimely to standardize them before their hierarchical and social worth has been settled upon (Adams-Webber and Mancuso, 1983).

The PCT is coordinated into a principal hypothesize and 11 culminations. Three of the end products are talked about here on the grounds that they influence CSD: the distinction result, the shared trait culmination, the sociality conclusion. As per the distinction culmination, "People contrast from one another in their development of occasions". This implies that everybody's development of the truth is distinctive since they have various encounters. Individuals won't ever understand similar occasion the same way regardless of how occasions are comparative. As per the uniqueness culmination bookkeepers won't interpret CSD likewise and along these lines it would be essential to see what they understand this is on the grounds that this means for the manner in which they practice it.

As per the shared trait end product, "To the degree that one individual utilizes a development of involvement which is like that utilized by another his mental cycles are like the other individual". This appears to imply that however we are diverse we can be comparable in the manner we build occasions and this relies upon the degree to which we see things the same way. In the event that our development framework is comparative, our encounters, practices and sentiments will likewise be comparative. This clarifies why individuals in a similar culture have a typical comprehension of occasions. Corresponding to CSD, this end product suggests that bookkeepers in a specific culture are probably going to understand it from bookkeepers in another culture. This could clarify why in certain nations there are more friendly revelations than in different nations. It could likewise clarify why distinctive bookkeeping firms inside a similar public culture can understand things diversely in view of their hierarchical culture. It can likewise imply that various partners might see CSD rehearses in an unexpected way.

By taking a gander at likenesses and contrasts given to CSD by various partners in Kenyan associations, we try to comprehend the specific structure revelation it takes in Kenya. The sociality conclusion says that, "To the degree that one individual interprets the development cycle of another he might assume a part in a social interaction affecting the other individual". This appears to imply that individuals are equipped for getting others. This culmination has a ramifications in the act of CSD as in various partners can see each other comparable to the CSD practice and hence the training is probable be because of an exchange among various partners.

This paper has given a case to involving constructionism in bookkeeping research. We examined social and individual constructionism and pushed for the utilization of individual constructionism in bookkeeping research and especially in the social obligation revelation studies. We have contended that a constructionism way to deal with bookkeeping research utilized notwithstanding the positivism, creates a more profound comprehension of the issue. We contend that this is significant on the grounds that a portion of the bookkeeping practices, for example, willful exposures are socially interpreted.

The issue of the price of government and decision science does not exist in a vacuum, but in the tenets of public policy, and as a result, we shall take our time to discuss and analyze the different model of public policy and what their proponents have argued in regards to their models viability. Sydney Webber couldn't have been so intellectually inclined when he assumed that the comprehensive rational model could go a long way to selecting out priorities of public policy and public budgeting, especially when constitutional democracy is the umpire through which the government obtain revenue and carry out it's expenditures for the public.He has assumed that through a comprehensive collations of items in their values and priorities, decision makers could to a greater extent curb fiscal waste and fiscal irresponsibilities in policy making and budgeting process.

David Brubreb's and Charles Linblum's opinion of Incrementalism in public policy model has only draw our attention to the normative and dogmatic process through which public policy and budgeting process have over the years suffered a setback in the pit of traditionalism due to lack of intellectual revitalism in the budgeting process today. Although, their assumptions have only laid emphasies on discretionary spending rather than mandatory spending of the public budgeting classification, and this fact gives their opinion an intellectual loophole for the efficacy of the 21st century public policy innovation of the 21st century governance.

Sydney Webber's comprehensive model wasn't and isn't comprehensive enough as we take a critical look at Amitai Etzioni's mixed-scanning model that assumes that public policy makers in the process of public budgeting and decision science should incorporate Webber's and the Incremental models in mapping out fiscal decision. Although, it could be time-consuming and labour-intensive, but it promises to yield an innovative way of making public policy.

The bounded rationality model as opined by Herbert Simon and Charles Lindblum has really made critical emphasies of the intellectual prioress of the decision makers, and such model takes into consideration what Plato argued on the basis of nature vs nurture. But how can we think of public policy innovation without thinking of the humans mind in creating something new and rewarding, especially in decision making process that should benefit the public? The answer to the question remains a focal point in this research thesis as we explore several assumptions and opinions of scholars. Although, the human brain has only been explored at the level of 5% in the history of mankind, then it speaks louder to decision makers to explore the remaining 95% for the benefit of mankind in fiscal matters.

The Organizational and Institutional model propounded by G. Allison becomes one of our most preferred model of public policy in this research paper. Allison opined that every fiscal policy in a democratic society goes through a rigorous Institutional scrutiny. In the case of the United States, these scrutiny is carried out between the Executive and the Legislature on numerical and price basis or debate, and this is what this research work is all about: tracing the fiscal responsibility of which arm of the government has the exclusive rights to effect the changes needed in consonance with the theory of the price of government, leaving no stone unturned on the constitutional provisions to this effect. These rigorous Institutional process brings to bare the principles of public financial management which are the need for fiscal surplus, the benefits of the fiscal Budget to the economy at a short and long run, and to what extent does the two major Institutions of the government can sanction the proceeds from fiscal irresponsibilities and recklessness.

From Allison's perspective, it means that the formulation and implication of public policy, nay fiscal policy should be taught by experts to the decision makers, as a result, we shall consider the learning conditioning opined by two major cognitive psychologists namely Evans Pavlov and B. F. Skinner respectively. However, this discussion shall be incorporated into fiscal policy and decision making in governance.

The molding hypothesis of learning portrays a type of realizing where learning happens because of partner a condition or improvement with a specific response or reaction. Human way of behaving is molded by propensities we get in light of specific circumstances throughout everyday life and is the result of advancing by molding hypothesis. There are two primary kinds of the molding hypothesis of learning — classical molding hypothesis and operant molding hypothesis. Since it has become so obvious what is molding realizing, how about we check out at every one of its two kinds exhaustively.

Have you at any point asked why hearing a specific melody fulfills you? Or on the other hand, for what reason does a kid reliably help a companion subsequent to being lauded for it? The molding hypothesis of learning may very well have every one of the responses!

The molding hypothesis of learning depicts a type of realizing where learning happens because of partner a condition or upgrade with a specific response or reaction. Human way of behaving is molded by propensities we get because of specific circumstances throughout everyday life and is the result of advancing by molding hypothesis.

There are two primary sorts of the molding hypothesis of learning — classical molding hypothesis and operant molding hypothesis. Since it has become so obvious what is molding realizing, we should check out at every one of its two kinds exhaustively.

The classical molding hypothesis says learning happens when a characteristic boost is matched with a nonpartisan improvement to create a reaction. Russian physiologist Ivan Pavlov was the defender of the classical molding hypothesis.

In his well known try different things with a canine, Pavlov rang a bell prior to giving the canine his food. He rehashed this on various occasions, continuously matching the ringing of the chime with the canine's food. In the end, the canine began partner the chime with food. He started salivating fully expecting the food when he heard the chime, in any event, when food wasn't really present.

The classical molding hypothesis of learning makes sense of a lot of our day to day conduct and fears. For example, an encased space is an unbiased improvement that an individual is unconcerned with. However, in the wake of stalling out in a lift, the individual starts connecting that sensation of dread with encased spaces, creating claustrophobia.

Otherwise called instrumental molding, operant molding hypothesis says learning creates through remunerations and disciplines for explicit way of behaving. As per this hypothesis, when a creature acts in a way that outcomes in a prize, they're bound to rehash that conduct from now on. Essentially, conduct that prompts discipline is less inclined to repeat.

The operant molding hypothesis of learning is ascribed to American clinician B.F. Skinner, who put together his work with respect to Edward Thorndike's law of impact. Skinner directed an examination with a rodent in a Skinner box. The crate had a switch that delivered food pellets on being squeezed. The rodent unintentionally found this switch, related it with food and figured out how to press the switch to get food.

Operant molding hypothesis tracks down assorted applications, particularly in preparing situations. A youngster being compensated in the wake of acing a test and being chastened subsequent to being impolite are instances of operant molding.

Jeremy Bentham was an English savant and political revolutionary. He is fundamentally known today for his ethical way of thinking, particularly his guideline of utilitarianism, which assesses activities in view of their outcomes. The pertinent outcomes, specifically, are the general bliss made for everybody impacted by the activity. Impacted by numerous illumination masterminds, particularly empiricists, for example, John Locke and David Hume, Bentham fostered a moral hypothesis grounded in a generally empiricist record of human instinct. He broadly held an indulgent record of both inspiration and worth as indicated by which what is essentially significant and what eventually persuades us is joy and torment. Joy, as indicated by Bentham, is in this manner a question of encountering delight and absence of torment.

In spite of the fact that he never provided legal counsel, Bentham composed a lot of way of thinking of regulation, consuming a large portion of his time on earth studying the current regulation and firmly pushing legitimate change. All through his work, he evaluates different normal records of regulation which guarantee, for instance, that freedom, privileges, etc exist autonomous of government. Along these lines, Bentham ostensibly fostered an early type of what is presently frequently called "lawful positivism." Beyond such evaluates, he at last kept up with that placing his ethical hypothesis into predictable practice would yield brings about legitimate hypothesis by giving support to social, political, and lawful establishments.

Bentham's impact was minor during his life. However, his effect was more prominent in later years as his thoughts were carried on by devotees, for example, John Stuart Mill, John Austin, and other consequentialists.

Connected with this key gratification is a perspective on the person as showing a characteristic, normal personal responsibility — a type of mental selfishness. In his "Comments on Bentham's Philosophy" (1833), Mill refers to Bentham's The Book of Fallacies (London: Hunt, 1824, pp. 392-3) that "[i]n each human bosom… self-with respect to intrigue is transcendent over friendly interest; every individual's own singular interest over the interests of any remaining people taken together." Fundamental to the nature and action of people, then, is their own prosperity, and reason — as an innate capacity of the individual — is viewed as docile to this end.

Bentham accepted that the idea of the human individual can be enough portrayed without notice of social connections. In any case, the possibility of "connection" is however a "imaginary element," however important for "comfort of talk." And, all the more explicitly, that's what he comments "the local area is a made up body," and it is yet "the amount of the interests of the few individuals who make it." Thus, the expansion of the expression "person" is, in the fundamental, no more prominent and something like the natural substance. Bentham's view, then, is that the individual — the essential unit of the social circle — is an "particle" and there is no "self" or "person" more prominent than the human person. An individual's relations with others — regardless of whether significant — are not fundamental and portray nothing that is, stringently talking, important to its being what it is.

Bentham's ethical way of thinking, then, obviously mirrors his mental view that the essential inspirations in people are joy and torment. Bentham concedes that his rendition of the rule of utility is something that doesn't concede to coordinate confirmation, yet he takes note of that this isn't an issue as a few informative standards concede to no such evidence and all clarification should begin some place. In any case, this, without anyone else, doesn't make sense of why another's satisfaction — or the overall joy — ought to count. What's more, as a matter of fact, he gives various ideas that could act as replies to the subject of why we ought to be worried about the joy of others.

According to in the first place, Bentham, the guideline of utility is something to which people, in acting, allude either unequivocally or certainly, and this is the kind of thing that can be determined and affirmed by basic perception. For sure, Bentham held that all current frameworks of profound quality can be "diminished to the standards of compassion and hatred," which is definitively that which characterizes utility. A subsequent contention found in Bentham is that, on the off chance that delight is the upside, it is great regardless of whose joy it is. Consequently, an ethical directive to seek after or expand joy has force freely of the particular interests of the individual acting. Bentham likewise recommends that people would sensibly look for the overall satisfaction just on the grounds that the interests of others are inseparably bound up with their own, however he perceived that this is the sort of thing that is simple for people to overlook. By and by, Bentham conceives an answer for this too. In particular, he recommends that making this distinguishing proof of interests self-evident and, while vital, uniting assorted interests would be the obligation of the lawmaker.

At last, Bentham held that there are benefits to an ethical way of thinking in view of a guideline of utility. Regardless, the guideline of utility is clear (contrasted with other moral standards), takes into consideration level headed and unengaged public conversation, and empowers choices to be made where there appear to be clashes of (at first sight) genuine interests. Besides, in computing the delights and agonies engaged with doing a game-plan (the "gluttonous math"), there is a central obligation to human correspondence. The standard of utility surmises that "one man is worth simply equivalent to another man" thus there is an assurance that in working out the best joy "every individual is to count for oneself and nobody for mutiple."

For Bentham, then, there is no irregularity between the best joy guideline and his mental indulgence and pride. In this way, he composes that ethical way of thinking or morals can be essentially depicted as "the specialty of guiding men's activity to the creation of the best conceivable amount of bliss, with respect to those whose interest is in view."

Almond and Powell in their description of political culture have envisage the role it plays in shaping political behavior amongst the government and the governed, even in the context fiscal policy. As a result, a clear ideocincratic analysis could be done between fiscal conservativism and liberalism, and these syndrome has reflected in the fiscal intrigue of the United States' fiscal culture and psyche over decades since the advent of the two major political parties in the United States' political system.

From the above extanct relates literatures, it is clearly understood that there so many variables that have over the decades influence be fiscal behavior and psyche of the United States' fiscal policy makers, and we seek to explore these in this research dissertation.

In conclusion, the above scholars through their aforementioned literature have reflected their idea on different areas of both private and public decision making process and mechanisms. But there haven't been any of them that have reflected their intellectual prioress in the area of fiscal policy, and especially in the case of the United States' fiscal budget, reflecting on public emoluments and renumeration in regards to Constitutionalism. Therefore, this has been the intellectual and academic gap and vacuum that I intend to fill in my research.

2.2 Theoretical Framework

In order to make this research work scientific and reliable for academic evaluation ND consumption, it is ethically appropriate that it theoretical background gives room for thesis, antithesis, and synthesis of a three major related and selected theoretical assumptions that appropriately interpretes the variables in the research topic. To this effect we shall strike a theoretical balance between the Nudge theory propounded by Richard Thaler; the Behavioral Game theory by Colin Camerer; and the Public Choice theory by Dennis Mueller respectively.

2.2.1 The Nudge theory

At the point when it was reported that Thaler had been granted the Nobel Prize, it was met with some discussion. While certain financial specialists excitedly acknowledge the presentation of brain science into the field, others are still vocally wary about blending the two. This has been a fight that Thaler has been battling his entire vocation, following back to a section he wrote during the 1980s. Showing up in the Journal of Economic Perspectives, distributed by the American Economic Association (AEA), Thaler referred to the segment as "Peculiarities", a joking name and gesture to his general methodology.

Individual Nobel-winning conduct financial specialist, Daniel Kahneman, depicts the articles as "downright splendid, entertaining and were dependably somehow or another overwhelming to a piece of hypothesis." Kahneman ventures to such an extreme as to credit the section for having a critical impact in the acknowledgment of social financial matters.

Thaler moved on from composing an ordinary segment and proceeded to compose books. The book that put him at the center of attention, Nudge: Improving Decisions About Health, Wealth, and Happiness, is a New York Times smash hit and takes a gander at the decisions we face consistently. The book presents the idea of decision design, contending that individuals need structure to decide and in that lies the chance to make structures that lead individuals to pursue better choices. The possibility of a poke is that we never settle on decisions in disconnection. You can't try not to poke like you can't keep away from decision engineering.

He utilizes the cafeteria at the University of Chicago Booth School of Business where he is a teacher for instance, where the principal thing one sees when they enter is a self-service counter. "This is an illustration of how something that apparently isn't vital may impact what individuals eat, poke individuals to eat something sound," he says. "There must be a plan of that cafeteria. For what reason don't we make it a decent one?"

The contention could be settled on that individuals would ultimately pursue decisions without a purposefully planned "decision engineering" yet Thaler doesn't see a lot of weight in that. As the self-broadcaster individual with the world's most terrible bearing, a relationship he jumps at the chance to utilize is GPS frameworks. At its center, GPS is an instrument to assist you with getting where you need to go, it doesn't direct where you go, exactly how to arrive. Envision we have GPS for life that recently made getting where you need to go simpler, while never ordering that you follow through with something.

Nudging isn't all self-service counters and showing up on time. It is additionally found in regions like annuity frameworks, buyer conduct and medical services. With regards to medical care frameworks specifically, the potential isn't just enormous, it very well may life-save. The innovation as of now exists - and is open to anybody with a cell phone - to follow your means, your calorie consumption and the long stretches of rest you get. For diabetics, the innovation exists to appropriately screen glucose. It's anything but a far stretch then to envision what the subsequent stages in this could be. Whether it's embedded chips to quantify pulses or a gadget to naturally direct specific meds, Thaler sees limitless potential outcomes. That is going past nudging, right?" he asks, knowing the response. That is simply dominating, yet much of the time that is what we need. Very much like self-driving vehicles, we can have self-driving drugs. Innovation that is appropriate to social nudge upgrades likewise applies to those devices with worldwide outcomes. From shrewd indoor regulators to savvy TVs, apparatuses that go into various power saving modes are turning into the standard. There are things like naming that we can improve as far as how much energy it will utilize. We're improving. Furthermore, these are seemingly insignificant details yet the main way we will manage environmental change is a ton of easily overlooked details.

One more term created by Thaler is mental bookkeeping. Basically, this is the manner by which individuals oversee and assign their cash. The vast majority, and organizations the same, put away specific measures of cash for specific things and exercises as a type of planning. However, regarding cash as something not exchangeable isn't levelheaded all of the time. On the off chance that there's no cash left in an organization's gear financial plan and a printer bites the dust close to the furthest limit of the year, then there is no printer. That equivalent organization might have cash left in the movement spending plan, with no impending travel, yet at the same time deny the printer demand.

I think putting marks on cash has a long history and fills a need. So it begins with a reasonable explanation however at that point individuals take it to places that have neither rhyme nor reason. Thaler likewise gives the case of another sets of shoes that are discounted. Do you get them since they're at a bargain? Let's assume you purchase the shoes however they hurt appallingly. The inquiry then becomes how long do you leave them in the back on your storeroom, at absolutely no point ever to be worn in the future, before at last disposing of them? According to the sunk expense deception, he, is likewise straightforwardly affecting everything here.

My expectation is the more you paid for them, the more they stay in the storage room before you discard them. At the point when Thaler won the Nobel Prize, which is combined with a monetary reward too, he was much of the time asked how he planned to manage the cash. It's an entertaining inquiry to pose to a social financial expert.

Throughout the previous 25 years, Thaler has been engaged with a resource the executives firm, Fuller and Thaler, that centers explicitly around social money and speculation the board, an application the firm spearheaded. Consolidating mental hypothesis and fund to give clarifications with respect to why individuals pursue silly speculation choices is at the center of what they do.

What we've found is that there are classes of circumstances where financial backers cause orderly mistakes and those to set out purchasing open doors. We group those blunders into two classifications, eruption and underreaction. Individuals are hesitant to sell a stock that they've lost cash on. On the off chance that you sell a stock that is gone down, you need to own up to yourself that you committed an error. Though assuming you clutch it, there's dependably trust that it could return.

As Thaler brings up, the trouble of putting something aside for retirement is a generally new issue for our species. Assuming you carried on with a long life quite a while back, the assumption was that your kids would really focus on you in your more established years, yet the dispersal of families combined with longer future has made another cultural issue. Benefits, which appeared to introduce an answer at a time, were relatively brief.

Organizations would have rather not offered those sorts of annuities any longer and presently we put the weight on representatives to sort out the amount to save and how to contribute," says Thaler. "What's more, that is a truly difficult issue, so we really want to help them.

Generally new plans have begun in the US and as per Thaler, this is a space where conduct financial matters has had a major effect. Involved by most enormous firms in the US today, three explicit procedures have been set up to work on things and to assist with nudging individuals. Programmed enlistment, programmed heightening and the production of default venture vehicles.

My mantra in planning approaches is if you have any desire to get individuals to follow through with something, make it simple. Also, we've made retirement saving more straightforward. We need to utilize that equivalent technique any place we can. It's probably the case that somebody as powerful as Thaler has been to financial matters would have a few shrewd forecasts about the fate of the field. Be that as it may, as is much of the time the case with him, he starts with a touch of humor prior to diving in a response.

As a popular American baseball player Yogi Berra once said, 'Foreseeing is troublesome, particularly about the future," he smiles. "One thing we can say is that financial matters as a field has become considerably more observational throughout recent years and I believe it's unquestionable that financial experts are the most complex clients of information in the sociologies.

Being on the bleeding edge of information science and AI implies that the typical market analyst might wind up working more in the confidential area before long, says Thaler. Whether in web based business or other B2C organizations, he figures financial experts will team up close by AI planners and different engineers. Thaler's very own major piece vocation and general view on life has been to placed a specific degree of significance on doing what he enjoys most. He urges others to consider this as well.

On the off chance that you would be able, get a new line of work that you take individual fulfillment from doing," he says. It seems like simple guidance for a teacher to give yet while you're emerging from school, you have a few decisions to make. Also, a portion of the choices will be more satisfying than others. Financial specialists wouldn't agree that they leave out fun, yet you'd need to look exceptionally hard before you thought that it is in the model.

2.2.2 Behavioral Game theory

Game theory, the formalized investigation of procedure, started during the 1940s by asking how unfeeling prodigies ought to mess around, yet disregarded up to this point how normal individuals with feelings and restricted prescience really mess around. This book denotes the principal significant and definitive work to close this hole. Colin Camerer, one of the field's driving figures, utilizes mental standards and many analyses to foster numerical speculations of correspondence, restricted planning, and realizing, which assist with foreseeing what genuine individuals and organizations do in essential circumstances. Binding together an abundance of data from continuous examinations in essential way of behaving, he takes the exploratory study of behavioral financial matters a significant step in the right direction. He does as such in clear, agreeable writing.

Behavioral game theory has three fixings that come plainly into center in this book: numerical speculations of what ethical commitment and retribution mean for the manner in which individuals deal and trust one another; a theory of how limits in the mind oblige the quantity of steps of "I think he thinks ... " thinking individuals normally do; and a theory of how individuals gain for a fact to pursue better essential choices. Key communications that can be made sense of by behavioral game theory incorporate bartering, games of feigning as in sports and poker, strikes, how shows assist with planning a joint action, value rivalry and patent races, and developing notorieties for reliability or mercilessness in business or life.

While there are many books on standard game theory that address the manner in which in a perfect world levelheaded entertainers work, Behavioral Game Theory remains solitary in mixing exploratory proof and brain science in a numerical theory of typical vital way of behaving. Must perusing for anybody looks for a more complete comprehension of vital reasoning, from proficient financial specialists to researchers and understudies of financial matters, the board studies, brain science, political theory, humanities, and science.

2.2.3 Public Choice theory

Public choice, or public choice theory, is "the use of economic tools to deal with traditional problems of political science". Its content includes the study of political behavior. In political science, it is the subset of positive political theory that studies self-interested agents (voters, politicians, bureaucrats) and their interactions, which can be represented in a number of ways – using (for example) standard constrained utility maximization, game theory, or decision theory. It is the origin and intellectual foundation of contemporary work in political economy.

In popular use, "public choice" is often used as a shorthand for components of modern public choice theory that focus on the ways in which elected officials, bureaucrats and other government agents can be influenced by their own perceived self-interest when making decisions in their official roles. After James M. Buchanan received the 1986 Nobel Memorial Prize in Economic Sciences "for his development of the contractual and constitutional bases for the theory of economic and political decision-making" in this space, BBC journalist Alistair Cooke explained the award, "Public Choice rests on the homely but important observation that politicians are, after all, no different than the rest of us."

Public choice theory studies the choice between the people and the social environment. People decide the demand, supply and output of public goods through the political process of democratic decision-making. Public choice is a mechanism to transform individual choice into collective choice, and a non-market choice of resource allocation. The economic man hypothesis of public choice and the political transaction theory bring two aspects of human behavior-economic decision making and political decision making into a unified framework. In this framework, "political system" is like market system, "politician" is like entrepreneur, "citizen" is like consumer, "election system" is like transaction system, and "vote" is like money. The two behaviors have unified internal motivation and behavior pattern.

Public choice analysis has roots in positive analysis "what is" but is often used for normative purposes "what ought to be" in order to identify a problem or to suggest improvements to constitutional rules (constitutional economics)

Public choice theory is also closely related to social choice theory, a mathematical approach to aggregation of individual interests, welfares, or votes. Much early work had aspects of both, and both fields use the tools of economics and game theory. Since voter behavior influences the behavior of public officials, public-choice theory often uses results from social-choice theory. General treatments of public choice may also be classified under public economics.

Public choice, building upon economic theory, has some core tenets that are largely adhered to. The first is the use of the individual as the common decision unit. Due to this there is no decision made by an aggregate whole. Rather, decisions are made by the combined choices of the individuals. The second is the use of markets in the political system, which was argued to be a return to true economics. The final is the self-interested nature of all individuals within the political system. However, as Buchanan and Tullock argued, "the ultimate defense of the economic-individualist behavioral assumption must be empirical...The only final test of a model lies in its ability to assist in understanding real phenomena".

An early precursor of modern public choice theory was the work of Swedish economist Knut Wicksell (1896), which treated government as political exchange, a quid pro quo, in formulating a benefit principle linking taxes and expenditures. American statesman and political theorist John C. Calhoun is also seen as a precursor to modern public choice theory. His writings on political economy anticipate the "public choice revolution" in modern economics and political science.

Some resulting financial examination has been portrayed as regarding government like it endeavored "to expand some caring kind of government assistance capability for society" and as unmistakable from portrayals of self-intrigued monetary specialists, like those in business. This is a reasonable division, as one can be self-keen on one region, while being philanthropic in another. Conversely, public decision hypothesis displayed government as comprised of authorities who, other than chasing after the public interest, could act to help themselves, for instance in the spending plan augmenting model of administration, conceivably at the expense of effectiveness.

Present day public-decision hypothesis, and particularly political race hypothesis, has been dated from crafted by Duncan Black, in some cases called "the principal architect of public decision". In a progression of papers from 1948, which finished in The Theory of Committees and Elections and later, Black framed a program of unification toward a more broad "Hypothesis of Economic and Political Choices" in light of normal formal methods created basic ideas of what might become middle citizen hypothesis, and rediscovered prior deals with casting a ballot hypothesis. Dark's work likewise remembered the chance of totally irregular results for a democratic construction, where the main administration over the result is the where a specific movement falls in the grouping introduced.

Kenneth J. Bolt's Social Choice and Individual Values (1951) affected plan of the hypothesis of public decision and political race hypothesis. Expanding on Black's hypothesis, Arrow presumed that in a non-tyrannical setting, there was no anticipated result or inclination request that can be observed for a bunch of potential conveyances. Among other significant works are Anthony Downs (1957) An Economic Theory of Democracy and Mancur Olson (1965) The Logic of Collective Action. The Logic of Collective Action was basic in starting the investigation of extraordinary interests. In it, Olson started to open inquiries regarding the idea of gatherings, including their absence of motivating force to act with a sloppiness and free-rider issues of these bigger gatherings upon particular gathering's activities. Because of the motivator for concentrated gatherings to represent their own advantage, matched with a sloppiness of huge gatherings, regulation carried out thus helps a little gathering as opposed to the general population in general.

James M. Buchanan and Gordon Tullock coauthored The Calculus of Consent: Logical Foundations of Constitutional Democracy (1962), thought about one of the tourist spots in open decision and established financial matters. Specifically, the prelude depicts the book as "about the political association" of a free society. Yet, its technique, reasonable contraption, and examination "are determined, basically, from the discipline that has as its subject the financial association of such a general public" (1962, p. v).

Buchanan and Tullock work out a system inside Calculus of sacred navigation and designs. This structure separates choices that are made into two classifications: Constitutional choices and political choices. Protected choices lay out well established decides that seldom change and administer the political design itself. Political choices are those that happen inside and are administered by the design. The book likewise centers around sure financial examination with regards to the improvement of sacred majority rules government however in a moral setting of assent. The assent appears as a pay standard like Pareto productivity for making a strategy change and unanimity or possibly no resistance as a take-off point for social decision.

Fairly later, the probabilistic democratic hypothesis began to dislodge the middle citizen hypothesis in telling the best way to track down Nash equilibria in multi-faceted space. The hypothesis was subsequently formalized further by Peter Coughlin.

Sacred financial matters is an examination program in financial aspects and constitutionalism that has been portrayed as stretching out past the meaning of "the monetary examination of established regulation" in making sense of the decision "of elective arrangements of lawful institutional-protected decides that oblige the decisions and exercises of financial and political specialists." This is unmistakable from making sense of the decisions of monetary and political specialists inside those guidelines, a subject of "universal" financial matters.

Sacred financial aspects studies the "similarity of compelling monetary choices with the current established structure and the limits or the ideal circumstances made by that system," It has been portrayed as a pragmatic way to deal with apply of the instruments of financial aspects to protected matters. For instance, a central issue of each and every country is the legitimate designation of accessible public monetary and monetary assets. The lawful answer for this issue falls inside the extent of protected financial aspects.

Established financial matters considers the critical effects of political monetary choices rather than restricting investigation to financial connections as elements of the elements of appropriation of "attractive" labor and products. "The political financial analyst who tries to offer regularizing counsel, must, of need, focus on the cycle or design inside which political choices are seen to be made. Existing constitutions, or designs or rules, are the subject of basic investigation.

Geoffrey Brennan and Loren Lomasky guarantee that popularity based strategy is one-sided to lean toward "expressive interests" and disregard useful and utilitarian contemplations. Brennan and Lomasky separate between instrumental interests (any sort of commonsense advantage, both money related and non-financial) and expressive interests (types of articulation like commendation). As indicated by Brennan and Lomasky, the mystery of casting a ballot can be settled by separating among expressive and instrumental interests.

This contention has driven a few public decision researchers to guarantee that legislative issues is tormented by nonsensicalness. In articles distributed in the Econ Journal Watch, financial specialist Bryan Caplan fought that elector decisions and government monetary choices are innately unreasonable. Caplan's thoughts are all the more completely evolved in his book The Myth of the Rational Voter (Princeton University Press 2007). Countering Donald Wittman's contentions in The Myth of Democratic Failure, Caplan claims that governmental issues is one-sided for unreasonable convictions.

As indicated by Caplan, a vote based system successfully finances nonsensical convictions. Anybody who gets utility from possibly unreasonable approaches like protectionism can get private advantages while forcing the expenses of such convictions on the overall population. Were individuals to bear the full expenses of their "unreasonable convictions", they would campaign for them ideally, considering both their instrumental results and their expressive allure. All things considered, a majority rules system oversupplies strategies in view of nonsensical convictions.

Caplan characterizes sanity primarily as far as standard cost hypothesis, bringing up that standard financial experts will quite often go against protectionism and unofficial law more than everyone, and that more instructed individuals are nearer to business analysts on this score, even in the wake of controlling for jumbling elements like pay, riches or political alliance. One analysis is that numerous business analysts don't share Caplan's perspectives on the idea of public decision. Be that as it may, Caplan has information to help his situation. Business analysts have, as a matter of fact, frequently been disappointed by open resistance to monetary thinking.

As Sam Peltzman puts it:

Market analysts understand what steps would work on the effectiveness of HSE [health, security, and environmental] guideline, and they have not been constrained promoters of them. These means remember subbing markets for property privileges, for example, emanation freedoms, for order and control ... The genuine issue lies further than any absence of change recommendations or inability to squeeze them. It is our failure to grasp their absence of political allure.

Public decision's application to unofficial law was created by George Stigler (1971) and Sam Peltzman (1976). One more significant sub-field is the investigation of organization. The standard model portrays the top administrators as being picked by the CEO and council, contingent upon whether the majority rule framework is official or parliamentary. The run of the mill picture of a department boss is an individual on a proper compensation who is worried about satisfying the people who designated that person. The last option has the ability to recruit and fire that person pretty much freely. The heft of the civil servants, notwithstanding, are government employees whose positions and pay are safeguarded by a common help framework against significant changes by their delegated department bosses. This picture is frequently contrasted and that of an entrepreneur whose benefit changes with the outcome of creation and deals, who means to expand benefit, and who could in an ideal framework at any point recruit and fire representatives freely. William Niskanen is by and large viewed as the organizer behind open decision writing on the organization.

Public decision hypothesis is frequently used to make sense of how political dynamic outcomes in results that contention with the inclinations of the overall population. For instance, numerous backing gathering and pork barrel projects are not the craving of the general majority rules system. In any case, it's a good idea for government officials to help these ventures. It might cause them to feel strong and significant. It can likewise help them monetarily by making the way for future abundance as lobbyists. The undertaking might bear some significance with the legislator's neighborhood body electorate, expanding region votes or mission commitments.

The legislator pays almost no expense to acquire these advantages, as he is spending public cash. Extraordinary interest lobbyists are additionally acting sanely. They can acquire government favors worth millions or billions for somewhat little ventures. They face a gamble of missing out to their rivals in the event that they don't look for these blessings. The citizen is additionally acting normally. The expense of overcoming any one government offer is exceptionally high, while the advantages to the singular citizen are tiny. Every resident pays a couple of pennies or a couple of dollars for some random government favor, while the expenses of finishing that favor would be commonly higher.

Everybody in question has reasonable motivators to do precisely exact thing they are doing, despite the fact that the longing of the overall body electorate is inverse. Costs are diffused, while benefits are concentrated. The voices of vocal minorities with much to acquire are heard over those of uninterested greater parts with little to independently lose.

However the thought that gatherings with concentrated interests will rule legislative issues is deficient on the grounds that it is just a single portion of political harmony. Something should prompt those went after to oppose even the best coordinated concentrated interests. In his article on vested parties Gary Becker recognized this balancing force similar to the extra weight misfortune from predation. His perspectives covered what has come to be known as the Chicago school of political economy and it has come in sharp struggle with the alleged Virginia group of public decision because of the previous' affirmation that governmental issues will tend towards effectiveness due to nonlinear extra weight misfortunes and because of its case that political proficiency renders strategy counsel immaterial.

While great government will in general be an unadulterated public great for the mass of electors, there might be numerous support bunches that have solid motivators for campaigning the public authority to execute explicit strategies that would help them, possibly to the detriment of the overall population. For instance, campaigning by the sugar makers could bring about a wasteful appropriation for the development of sugar, either straightforwardly or by protectionist measures. The expenses of such wasteful strategies are scattered over all residents, and accordingly unnoticeable to every person. Then again, the advantages are shared by a little particular vested party with serious areas of strength for a to sustain the strategy by further campaigning.

Because of sane obliviousness, by far most of electors will know nothing about the work; as a matter of fact, in spite of the fact that citizens might know about extraordinary interest campaigning endeavors, this may just choose for strategies which are significantly more earnestly to assess by the overall population, as opposed to working on their general proficiency. Regardless of whether general society had the option to assess strategy recommendations successfully, they would find it infeasible to take part in aggregate activity to shield their diffuse interest. Consequently, scholars expect that various extraordinary interests will actually want to campaign for different wasteful approaches effectively. In open decision hypothesis, such situations of wasteful government strategies are alluded to as government disappointment - a term similar to showcase disappointment from prior hypothetical government assistance financial matters.

A field that is firmly connected with public decision is the investigation of lease chasing. This field consolidates the investigation of a market economy with that of government. Consequently, one could view it as another political economy. Its essential proposal is that when both a market economy and government are available, government specialists might lease or sell their impact (for example a vote) to the individuals who are looking for input into the lawmaking system. The public authority specialist stands to profit from help from the party looking for impact, while the party tries to acquire benefit through having public approach carried out that benefits them.

This basically brings about a catch and redistribution of advantage, squandering the advantage and any assets utilized from being put to a useful use in the public eye. This is because of the way that the party endeavoring to obtain the advantage will spend up to or more than the advantage gathered, bringing about a lose gain, or a negative total increase. The genuine addition is the increase over the opposition. This political activity will then, at that point, be utilized to keep rivalry out of the market because of an absence of genuine or political capital.

Lease looking for is more extensive than public decision in that it applies to absolutisms as well as vote based systems and, subsequently, isn't straightforwardly worried about aggregate direction. Nonetheless, the undeniable tensions it applies on lawmakers, leaders, administrators, and even adjudicators are factors that public decision hypothesis should represent in its examination of aggregate dynamic guidelines and foundations. Additionally, the individuals from an aggregate who are arranging an administration definitely should consider planned lease chasing.

Another significant case is that quite a bit of political movement is a type of lease looking for which squanders assets. Gordon Tullock, Jagdish Bhagwati, and Anne Osborn Krueger have contended that lease looking for has caused significant waste. From such outcomes it is now and again attested that public decision hypothesis has an enemy of state slant. Be that as it may, there is philosophical variety among public decision scholars. Mancur Olson for instance was a promoter of a solid state and on second thought went against political vested party campaigning. All the more by and large, James Buchanan has proposed that public decision hypothesis be deciphered as "governmental issues without sentiment", a basic way to deal with an unavoidable prior thought of romanticized legislative issues set against market disappointment.

The British columnist, Alistair Cooke, remarking on the Nobel Memorial Prize granted to James M. Buchanan in 1986, purportedly summed up the public decision perspective on lawmakers by saying, "Public decision epitomizes the unattractive however significant truth that legislators are, all things considered, no less narrow minded than most of us.

CHAPTER 3

DATA PRESENTATION, INTERPRETATION, AND EXPERIMENTAL ANALYSIS

3.1 Presentation of Primary Data

The primary data consist of the data gathered from the respondents through the research questionairs at the area of the research survey. Apart from the Office of the President, the Member of the US Congress, and the US Supreme Court Justices, the primary data is obtained from the following federal government agencies that are responsible for the fiscal policy in the United States of America, by issuing the questionairs to the head of the following gencies:

* The Merit System Appropriation Board

* The Office of Personnel Management

* The Commission on Executive, Legislature, Judiciary Salary

* The Office of Management Budgeting

* The National Commission on Fiscal Responsibility and Reform

* The Office of Policy Development

* The Internal Revenu Service

* The Council of Economic Advisers

* The Federal Employees Pay Council

* The US Department of Treasury

* The Quadrennial Commission

* The Congressional Budget Office

* The Office of Management and Budget

* The Senate Appropriation and Fiscal Committee

* The House Appropriation and Fiscal Committee

* The General Accounting Office.

3.2 Presentation of Secondary Data

The secondary data consist of the different constitutional provisions of the United States' Constitution in regards to fiscal policy and public budgeting; and the executive summary of the United States' fiscal budget from 1990 - 2023 fiscal year respectively marking the period the United States'fiscal budget became threatened with fiscal deficits.

3.2.1 Federal Budget Receipts and Outlays: 1930-2023

Receipts Outlays Surplus or Deficit

President	FY	Total Budget			GDP	% of GDP		
(in billions of dollars)								
Calvin Coolidge	1930	4.1	3.3	0.7	98.4	4.1	3.4	0.8
Herbert Hoover	1931	3.1	3.6	-0.5	84.8	3.7	4.2	-0.5
	1932	1.9	4.7	-2.7	68.5	2.8	6.8	-4.0
	1933	2.0	4.6	-2.6	58.3	3.4	7.9	-4.5

	1934	3.0	6.5	-3.6	62.0	4.8	10.6	-5.8
Franklin D. Roosevelt	1935	3.6	6.4	-2.8	70.5	5.1	9.1	-4.0
	1936	3.9	8.2	-4.3	79.6	4.9	10.3	-5.4
	1937	5.4	7.6	-2.2	88.9	6.1	8.5	-2.5
	1938	6.8	6.8	-0.1	90.2	7.5	7.6	-0.1
	1939	6.3	9.1	-2.8	90.4	7.0	10.1	-3.1
	1940	6.5	9.5	-2.9	98.2	6.7	9.6	-3.0
	1941	8.7	13.7	-4.9	116.2	7.5	11.7	-4.3
	1942	14.6	35.1	-20.5	147.7	9.9	23.8	-13.9
	1943	24.0	78.6	-54.6	184.6	13.0	42.6	-29.6
	1944	43.7	91.3	-47.6	213.8	20.5	42.7	-22.2
	1945	45.2	92.7	-47.6	226.4	19.9	41.0	-21.0
	1946	39.3	55.2	-15.9	228.0	17.2	24.2	-7.0
Harry S. Truman	1947	38.5	34.5	4.0	238.9	16.1	14.4	1.7
	1948	41.6	29.8	11.8	261.9	15.9	11.4	4.5
	1949	39.4	38.8	0.6	276.5	14.3	14.0	0.2
	1950	39.4	42.6	-3.1	278.7	14.2	15.3	-1.1

	1951	51.6	45.5	6.1	327.1	15.8	13.9	1.9
	1952	66.2	67.7	-1.5	357.1	18.5	19.0	-0.4
	1953	69.6	76.1	-6.5	382.1	18.2	19.9	-1.7
	1954	69.7	70.9	-1.2	387.2	18.0	18.3	-0.3
Dwight D. Eisenhower	1955	65.5	68.4	-3.0	406.3	16.1	16.8	-0.7
	1956	74.6	70.6	3.9	438.3	17.0	16.1	0.9
	1957	80.0	76.6	3.4	463.4	17.3	16.5	0.7
	1958	79.6	82.4	-2.8	473.5	16.8	17.4	-0.6
	1959	79.2	92.1	-12.8	504.6	15.7	18.3	-2.5
	1960	92.5	92.2	0.3	534.3	17.3	17.3	0.1
	1961	94.4	97.7	-3.3	546.6	17.3	17.9	-0.6
	1962	99.7	106.8	-7.1	585.7	17.0	18.2	-1.2
John F. Kennedy	1963	106.6	111.3	-4.8	618.2	17.2	18.0	-0.8
	1964	112.6	118.5	-5.9	661.7	17.0	17.9	-0.9
Lyndon B. Johnson	1965	116.8	118.2	-1.4	709.3	16.5	16.7	-0.2
	1966	130.8	134.5	-3.7	780.5	16.8	17.2	-0.5
	1967	148.8	157.5	-8.6	836.5	17.8	18.8	-1.0

	1968	153.0	178.1	-25.2	897.6	17.0	19.8	-2.8
	1969	186.9	183.6	3.2	980.3	19.1	18.7	0.3
	1970	192.8	195.6	-2.8	1,046.7	18.4	18.7	-0.3
Richard Nixon	1971	187.1	210.2	-23.0	1,116.6	16.8	18.8	-2.1
	1972	207.3	230.7	-23.4	1,216.3	17.0	19.0	-1.9
	1973	230.8	245.7	-14.9	1,352.7	17.1	18.2	-1.1
	1974	263.2	269.4	-6.1	1,482.9	17.8	18.2	-0.4
	1975	279.1	332.3	-53.2	1,606.9	17.4	20.7	-3.3
Gerald R. Ford	1976	298.1	371.8	-73.7	1,786.1	16.7	20.8	-4.1
	TQ2	81.2	96.0	-14.7	471.7	17.2	20.3	-3.1
	1977	355.6	409.2	-53.7	2,024.3	17.6	20.2	-2.7
Jimmy Carter	1978	399.6	458.7	-59.2	2,273.5	17.6	20.2	-2.6
	1979	463.3	504.0	-40.7	2,565.6	18.1	19.6	-1.6
	1980	517.1	590.9	-73.8	2,791.9	18.5	21.2	-2.6
	1981	599.3	678.2	-79.0	3,133.2	19.1	21.6	-2.5
Ronald Reagan	1982	617.8	745.7	-128.0	3,313.4	18.6	22.5	-3.9

	1983	600.6	808.4	-207.8	3,536.0	17.0	22.9	-5.9
	1984	666.4	851.8	-185.4	3,949.2	16.9	21.6	-4.7
	1985	734.0	946.3	-212.3	4,265.1	17.2	22.2	-5.0
	1986	769.2	990.4	-221.2	4,526.3	17.0	21.9	-4.9
	1987	854.3	1,004.0	-149.7	4,767.7	17.9	21.1	-3.1
	1988	909.2	1,064.4	-155.2	5,138.6	17.7	20.7	-3.0
	1989	991.1	1,143.7	-152.6	5,554.7	17.8	20.6	-2.7
George Bush	1990	1,032.0	1,253.0	-221.0	5,898.8	17.5	21.2	-3.7
	1991	1,055.0	1,324.2	-269.2	6,093.2	17.3	21.7	-4.4
	1992	1,091.2	1,381.5	-290.3	6,416.3	17.0	21.5	-4.5
	1993	1,154.3	1,409.4	-255.1	6,775.3	17.0	20.8	-3.8
William J. Clinton	1994	1,258.6	1,461.8	-203.2	7,176.9	17.5	20.4	-2.8
	1995	1,351.8	1,515.7	-164.0	7,560.4	17.9	20.0	-2.2
	1996	1,453.1	1,560.5	-107.4	7,951.3	18.3	19.6	-1.4
	1997	1,579.2	1,601.1	-21.9	8,451.0	18.7	18.9	-0.3
	1998	1,721.7	1,652.5	69.3	8,930.8	19.3	18.5	0.8
	1999	1,827.5	1,701.8	125.6	9,479.4	19.3	18.0	1.3

	2000	2,025.2	1,789.0	236.2	10,117.5	20.0	17.7	2.3
	2001	1,991.1	1,862.8	128.2	10,526.5	18.9	17.7	1.2
George W. Bush	2002	1,853.1	2,010.9	-157.8	10,833.7	17.1	18.6	-1.5
	2003	1,782.3	2,159.9	-377.6	11,283.8	15.8	19.1	-3.3
	2004	1,880.1	2,292.8	-412.7	12,025.5	15.6	19.1	-3.4
	2005	2,153.6	2,472.0	-318.3	12,834.2	16.8	19.3	-2.5
	2006	2,406.9	2,655.1	-248.2	13,638.4	17.6	19.5	-1.8
	2007	2,568.0	2,728.7	-160.7	14,290.8	18.0	19.1	-1.1
	2008	2,524.0	2,982.5	-458.6	14,743.3	17.1	20.2	-3.1
	2009	2,105.0	3,517.7	-1,412.7	14,431.8	14.6	24.4	-9.8
Barack Obama	2010	2,162.7	3,457.1	-1,294.4	14,838.9	14.6	23.3	-8.7
	2011	2,303.5	3,603.1	-1,299.6	15,403.7	15.0	23.4	-8.4
	2012	2,450.0	3,526.6	-1,076.6	16,056.5	15.3	22.0	-6.7
	2013	2,775.1	3,454.9	-679.8	16,603.8	16.7	20.8	-4.1
	2014	3,021.5	3,506.3	-484.8	17,335.6	17.4	20.2	-2.8
	2015	3,249.9	3,691.9	-442.0	18,106.1	17.9	20.4	-2.4

	2016	3,268.0	3,852.6	-584.7	18,581.7	17.6	20.7	-3.1
	2017	3,316.2	3,981.6	-665.4	19,316.6	17.2	20.6	-3.4
Donald J. Trump	2018	3,329.9	4,109.0	-779.1	20,368.9	16.3	20.2	-3.8
	2019	3,463.4	4,447.0	-983.6	21,223.9	16.3	21.0	-4.6
	2020	3,421.2	6,550.4	-3,129.2	20,999.7	16.3	31.2	-14.9
estimate	2021	3,580.8	7,249.5	-3,668.7	22,030.0	16.3	32.9	-16.7
Joesph R. Biden	2022	4,174.2	6,011.1	-1,837.0	23,499.7	17.8	25.6	-7.8
estimate	2023	4,641.0	6,013.0	-1,371.9	24,563.3	18.9	24.5	-5.6
estimate	2024	4,827.8	6,186.8	-1,359.0	25,536.5	18.9	24.2	-5.3
estimate	2025	5,037.9	6,507.7	-1,469.8	26,516.0	19.0	24.5	-5.5
estimate	2026	5,332.1	6,746.3	-1,414.2	27,533.2	19.4	24.5	-5.1

Source(s):

• compiled by Gerhard Peters from "Historical Tables, Budget of the United States Government, Fiscal Year 2022" (Washington, D.C.: Government Printing Office, 2024).

Notes:

The Fiscal Year begins on October 1 of the previous year. For example, Fiscal Year 2009 begins on October 1, 2008. For this reason, budget years appear to not correspond with a president's administration. For example, George W. Bush took office in January 2001, but the FY 2001 budget was prepared by the Clinton Administration and authorized by the 106th Congress in 2000.

Prior to fiscal year 1977 the Federal fiscal years began on July 1 and ended on June 30. For example, John F. Kennedy assumed office on January 20, 1961, but the FY 1961 budget was prepared by the Eisenhower Administration.

In calendar year 1976 the July-September period was a separate accounting period (known as the transition quarter or TQ) to bridge the period required to shift to the new fiscal year.

Total includes both "on-budget" and "off-budget" amounts.

Citations:

Gerhard Peters. "Federal Budget Receipts and Outlays." The American Presidency Project. Ed. John T. Woolley and Gerhard Peters. Santa Barbara, CA: University of California. 1999-2021. The American Presidency Project, John Woolley and Gerhard Peters, Copyright © The American Presidency Project, Terms of Service | Privacy | Accessibility.

3.2.2 The United States' Fiscal Constitutional Acts

The following are the United States' Fiscal Constitutional Acts that have facilitated this research:

* The Pendleton Act of 1891

* The Administrative Procedure Act of 1946

* The Congressional Budget and Important Control Act of 1974

* The Postal Revenue and Federal Salary Act of 1967

* The Graham-Rudman Holdings Balanced Budget and Emergency Deficit Control Act of 1985

* The Federal Pay Compatibility Act of 1978

* The Executive Salary Cost of Living Adjustment Act of 1975

* The Civil Service Reform Act of 1978.

* The 14 Amendment (Section 4).

* Unfunded Mandates Reform Act of 1995.

* Congressional Budget and Impoundment Control Act of 1974.

* Federal Credit Reform Act of 1990.

* Balanced Budget Act of 1997.

* Budget Control Act of 2011.

3.2.3 United States' Fiscal Constitutional Reforms

The following are the United States' Fiscal Constitutional Reforms that have facilitated this research:

* Article II, Section I, Clause 7

* Article IV

* Article I, Section 7, 8, 10

* The United States' Code of Emoluments

* The 27th Amendment

* The 14th Amendment

* The 16th Amendment

* The Federalist No. 45 and 58 of 1992.

3.3 Interpretations and Analysis of Primary Data

The interpretation of data for this research shall be done on the basis of the sections of the designated, design, and responses from respondents of the distributed questionnaires (Appendix 1). This interpretative analysis shall be done on the classification of the respondents into Legislature (Congress); Executives; and Judiciary respectively as follows.

From the primary data gathered through the questionnaires, the following are the preliminary data and facts obtained:

Members of the US Congress - 535 Members (The 118th US Congress)

Senate (101 Members): 48 Democrats; 47 Republicans; 3 Independence

Representatives (435 Members): 213 Democrats; 222 Republicans

Surviving US Presidents - 5 (3 Democrats; 2 Republicans)

US Supreme Court Justices - 9 (3 Appointed by Democrat Presidents; 6 Appointed by Republican Presidents)

Note: These analysis shall be done using Simple Percentage Method (SPM).

Section A:

(I) Constitutional Reform Test:

(II) Fiscal Acts Knowledge and Awareness Test:

Congress	Republicans	Democrats	Independents
Senators	100% Acts and Reforms oriented	100% Acts and Reforms oriented	100% Acts and Reforms oriented
Representatives	100% Acts and Reforms oriented	100% Acts and Reforms oriented	

Presidents	Republicans	Democrats
	100% Acts and Reforms oriented	100% Acts and Reforms oriented

Supreme Court Justices	Republicans	Democrats
	100% Acts and Reforms oriented	100% Acts and Reforms oriented

Section B:

(I) Personal Psyche on Public Emoluments and Remuneration Test:

Congress	Republicans	Democrats	Independents
Senators	50% Middle class; 50% Upper class economic background	90% Middle class; 10% Upper class economic background	50% Middle class; 50% Upper class economic background
Representatives	20% Middle class; 80% Upper class economic background	95% Middle class; 5% Upper class economic background	50% Middle class; 50% Upper class economic background

Presidents	Republicans	Democrats
	5% Middle class; 95% Upper class economic background	95% Middle class; 5% Upperclass economic background

Supreme Court Justices	Republicans	Democrats
	10% Middle class; 90% Upper class economic background	50% Middle class; 50% Upper class economic background

(II) Cognitive and Cost-benefit Analysis Test:

Congress	Republicans	Democrats	Independents
Senators	52% Approves; 48% Disapproves the	30% Approves; 70% Disapproves the	90% Approves; 10% Disapproves the

	economics of the price of government	economics of the price of government	economics of the price of government
Representatives	60% Approves; 40% Disapproves the economics of the price of government	20% Approves; 80% Disapproves the economics of the price of government	92% Approves; 8% Disapproves the economics of the price of government

Presidents	Republicans	Democrats
	90% Approves; 10% Disapproves the economics of the price of government	50% Approves; 50% Disapproves the economics of the price of government

Supreme Court Justices	Republicans	Democrats
	92% Approves; 8% Disapproves the economics of the price of government	52% Approves; 48% Disapproves the economics of the price of government

(III) Decision-making Analysis and Public Choice Test:

Congress	Republicans	Democrats	Independents
Senators	80% Approves; 20% Disapproves the US President as the custodian of the implementation of the economics of the	72% Approves; 28% Disapproves the US President as the custodian of the implementation of the economics of the	50% Approves; 50% Disapproves the US President as the custodian of the implementation of the economics of the

	price of government. But don't trust a Democrat as the President.	price of government. But don't trust a Republican as the President.	price of government. But don't trust a Democrat or a Rublican as the President.
Representatives	94% Approves; 6% Disapproves the US President as the custodian of the implementation of the economics of the price of government. But don't trust a Democrat as the President.	80% Approves; 20% Disapproves the US President as the custodian of the implementation of the economics of the price of government. But don't trust a Republican as the President.	82% Approves; 18% Disapproves the US President as the custodian of the implementation of the economics of the price of government. But don't trust a Democrat or a Republican as the President.

Presidents	Republicans	Democrats
	94% Approves; 6% Disapproves the US President as the custodian of the implementation of the economics of the price of government. But don't trust a Majority Democrats in the Congress.	85% Approves; 15% Disapproves the US President as the custodian of the implementation of the economics of the price of government. But don't trust a Majority Republicans in the Congress.

Supreme Court Justices	Republicans	Democrats
	95% Approves; 5% Disapproves the US President as the custodian of	92% Approves; 8% Disapproves the US President as the custodian of

	the implementation of the economics of the price of government. But don't trust a Majority Democrats in the Congress.	the implementation of the economics of the price of government. But don't trust a Majority Republicans in the Congress.

Decision Rule:

1. From the open-ended note (decision) written by the 9 US Supreme Court Justices from the questionnaires obtained in accordance with H.R. 288, Separation of Powers Restoration Act of 2023, it critically indicates that the economics of the price of government based on the Judicial interpretation of the functions of the Quadrennial Commission can only be executed by the US President through the issuance of Executive Order. This is because the reduction of political emoluments and remuneration has never occurred, rather the increase of such in the history of all the cases submitted and reported by the quadrennial commission (as there is no such precedence); and because of nepotism boycotts that is antagonistic to the Congressional Rules.

2. The Republicans are most likely to implementing the economics of the price of government because of their socio-economic background and their fiscal ideology of less government as compared to their Democrats counterparts.

3. The Republicans are cynical for a Republic rather than Domocracy as compared to their Democrats counterparts.

3.4 Interpretations and Analysis of Secondary Data

The interpretation and analysis of secondary data for this analysis shall be done on the basis of the federal budget receipts and outlay presented in 3.2.1; and of the Postal Revenue and Federal Salary Act of 1967 as the thematic context of the implementation of the economics of the price of government of this research respectively, using the deconstructed method; the onion model of analysis, placing emphasis on originalism, non-orofinalism, textualism, and constructionism respectively.

3.4.1 The Federal Budget Receipts and Outlay Analysis

From the data obtained and presented in 3.2.1, the following table contains the analysis of the federal budget receipts outlay analysis in Simple Percentage Method Analysis (SPMA):

Table 3.4.1: The Federal Budget Receipt and Outlay Analysis.

Atomistic Budget Itemization	Budget Percentage (%)
Foreign Aid	1%
Debt Servicing (Domestic and Foreign)	17%
Unemployment Insurance, Student loans, Veterans' Benefits and Tax Credits for working families	20%
Education, Clean Energy, National Parks, Medical Research, Transportation, Food Safety and Health	12%
Medicaid, Medicare, and Social Security	20%
Political Emoluments and Public Renunciation	30%
Source: CBO, 2024	

Observation: Although, an economy could be face Tax Evation/Avoidance from the tax payers in one way or the other. But could this really be the empirical cause of fiscal/budget deficit in the 21st century economy?

It would be practically and theoretically ethical if Developed Economies prioritize and categorize their fiscal budget on the 'Recurrent and Capital Expenditure Basis', and not according to 'Item or Issue Basis'.

Although, the prioritizing of Fiscal Budget on the basis of 'Recurrent and Capital Expenditure' could have become conventional, outdated and obsolete in the modern fiscal scientific practices, but it still promises to facilitate and foster 'Fiscal Responsibility' in fiscal science (Osborn and Hutchinson, 2004).

It has been so ridiculous to maintain the ideology of the fact that the taxable revenue derived by the government from political elites before and after the payment of their emoluments and remuneration could ever be commensurable to the actual cut or slash in political emoluments and public remuneration in the 21st century political economic system.

The dichotomy behind the ideologies of the Left Wing and the Right Wing on Government Spending has become so cynical in all ramification especially when their paramount interest is to close 'fiscal-loopholes', that most often leads to a recurrent Government-Shutdown or fiscal recklessness as a result of the political intrigues in Washington, without considering the effect to which political emolument and public remuneration affects fiscal deficit and the economy at large.

The experiment and analysis of this research paper is to proffer scientific prospects and alternatives that could, should and must work for both the government and the governed (public and private economy development), and this would definitely in turn antagonize the political elites' materialistic interest on public funds, as long as there is strict legal framework, infrastructures and institutions put in place in line with the Rule of Law to checkmate Financial and Economic Crime, and Financial Regulations regarding the Price of

Government/ the Price of Political Campaigns for Political offices across all levels of government in the economy.

Does the price of government really affect economy development?

$ED = P^{o} + CL$

$ED = f(p, cl)$

Where: ED= Economy Development

P^{o}=The price of government

CL=Cost of living

$ED = P^{o} \geq {}^{20\%\ FB=FD}$

$\Delta^{Po=} \Delta^{T+} \Delta^{CP+} \Delta^{CL}$

FB= Fiscal Budget, FD=Fiscal Deficit, P^{o}=The price of government, T=Tax Code, CP=Cost of firms' production, CL=Cost of living

$\therefore CL=TC+TFC+TVC$*....economic cost model*

$CL=f(Q,T,PF,F)$*...cost function*

Where: TC=Total Costs, TFC=Total fixed cost, TVC=Total variable cost, Q=Firms' output, T= Technological input, PF=The price of the factors of production, F=Fixed factors*

$\therefore SP,CP,FP=C+Q+T+PF+F$

Where: SP,CP,FP= selling price, cost price, and fixed price.

This equation is economically illustrated using the graphs below:

Fig. 3.4.1 The role of the price of government on firms' production costs

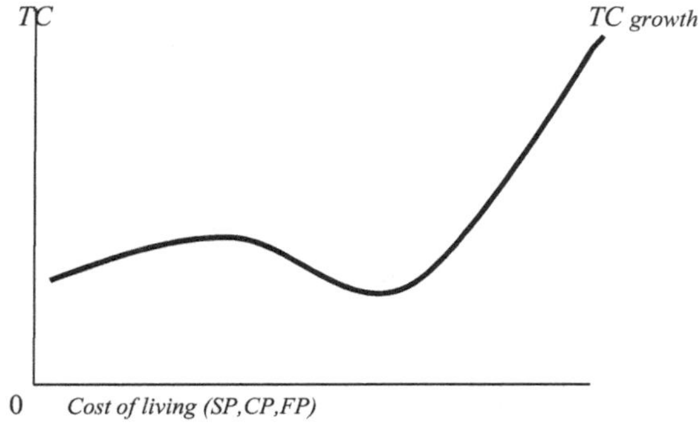

The fig. 4.1.1 depicts that the change in the Total Costs of firms will lead to the change and shift in the price of goods and services of firms. While, fig. 4.1.2 depicts that the shift in Corporate Taxes of firms, leads to a change in firms' Total Costs of production, thereby affecting the input, output, and the price of the firms' commodities in the market (Cost of Living in the Economy).

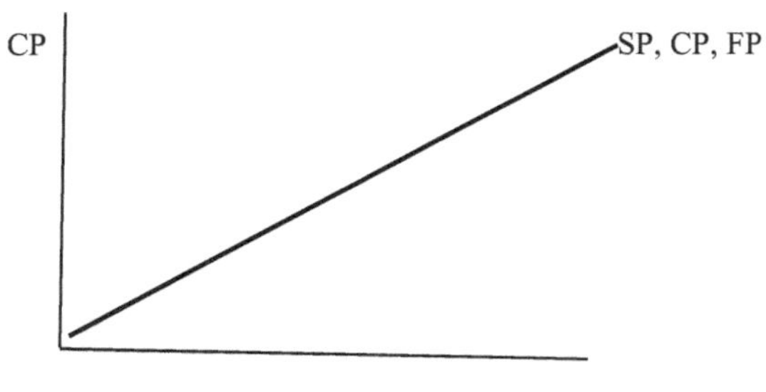

The increase in the cost living does not often lead to an increase in the standard of living. This is because the wholesaler most often has the monopoly of manipulating some commercial variables like fixed price, cost price, and selling price of the commodities, which is sometimes affected by the negotiating ability between the government and the manufacturer on the conditions surrounding the cost of transporting the commodities to the market in a regulatory economy.

But, in a non-Antitrust and a Deregulatory Economy, the prices of goods and services could be affected by a monopolistic market or corruption.

It is Economically and Politically understood that whenever a responsible government with the fiscal challenge of Budget Deficit, it tries to slash and cut the price of government in other aspect of the fiscal budget, but not in the area of political emoluments or public remuneration, or it looks for ways to increase her revenue through taxation, financial loans or other aspect of its revenue, which are either levied on firms and corporations or on private citizens as will be illustrated in fig. 4.1.3.

As a result, firms and corporations incur an additional cost in their production costs so as to maintain Economies of Scale, which in turn must affect the price of their commodities in the 'markets' for all the actors in the chain of commerce, thereby leading to a rise in the cost of living (price inflation).

At a dysfunctional level of the above explanation, firms and corporations can be forced to liquidate as a result of Diseconomy of Scale and Recession. While, the government might be to close her fiscal loopholes or don't, the economy begins to crumble, and the alternative or austerity measure of 'Economic Bailouts' become the order of the day, of which to a great extent return the fiscal budget to a deficit as will be illustrated in fig. 3.4.4.

Therefore, it takes a common sense Economics to strike a ballance between the ecomomic policy that works for the government and for the citizens at the same time, and this only be done by constitutionally a meaningful cut and slash in political emoluments and public remuneration as illustrated in the graphs below.

Fig. 3.4.1.3&4 Graphical illustration showing the effect the price of government on economy development.

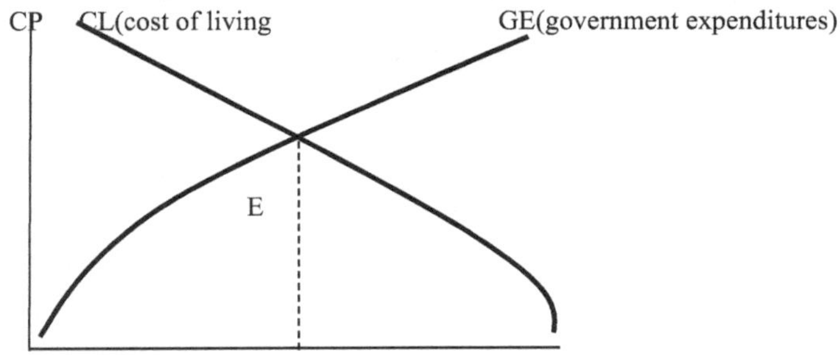

Fig. 3.4.4 Graphical illustration, showing the economic law of diminishing returns caused by the price of government as a demand a close on tax-loopholes in fiscal science.

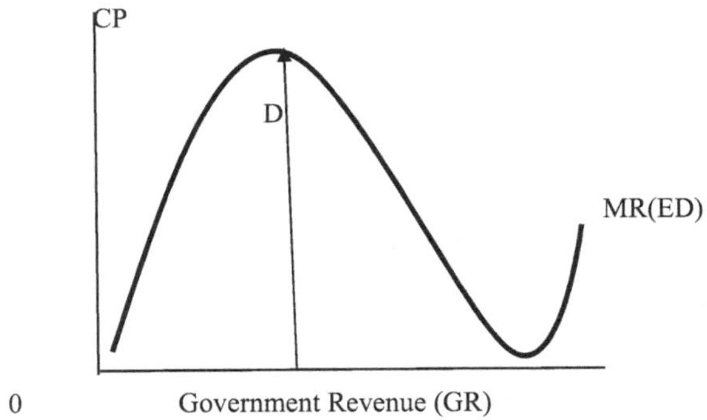

We should critically note that by 'Economy Development', we are giving meaning answers to the following political economic questions put forth by Dudley Seers, and Denis Goulet respectively.

Another important experiment and analysis in our first research question in this paper on the contending issue of Minimum-Wage as one of the important variables embedded in the economics of the price of government, and this experiment is as follows

$ED=P^o+MW$

$ED=f(P+MW)$

Where: ED=Economy Development

P^o=The price of government

MW=Minimum Wage

$\therefore$ if $X \geq Y=D$

Where: X=input

Y=output

D=diseconomy of scale as a result of a change(Δ) in corporate tax (T) of a firm,

$\therefore D=TVC+TFC+\nabla MW$

At any given time in an economy, if the price of government leads to a change in the input (Y) against the output (X) of a firm, as a result of the change or increase in corporate tax of a firm(T), there is certainly the tendency for firms to maintain Economies of Scales in a Perfect Competitive Market, thereby leading to an increase in Minimum-Wage of the workforce.

Therefore, it could be ironical if there is a legislative quest for an increase in minimum-wage when a government maintains and expensive recurrent expenditure. It is quite inevitable that a persisting diseconomy of scale of firms would lead to a change and increase in the price of goods and services (price inflation) in order to maintain some certain level of profit, but certainly not an increase in minimum-wage, which would negatively affect the purchasing power parity of the working class.

Fig.4.1.5 graphically illustrates the above scenario at a long and short run. Except, there is a reasonable slash or cut in both income and corporate taxes, which must also in turn affect government expenditures, until the price of government is considered a 'threat' to economy development.

Fig.3.4.5 Graphical illustration, showing the effect of the price of government on minimum-wage.

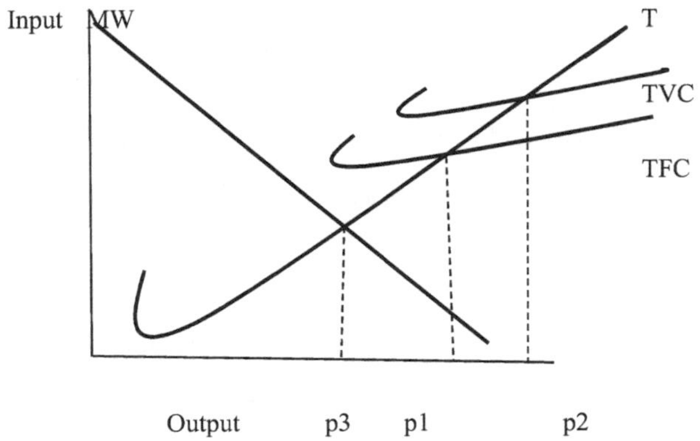

P1, P2, P3 show the point of interception between Corporate Tax (T); Total Variable Cost (TVC)]; Total Fixed Cost (TFC), and the decline in workers' minimum-wage as a result of the price of government when there is a persisting pressure for an increase on workers minimum-wage.

Though, the founding father of Regulatory Economics (Alfred E. Khan) asserted that trade regulation for a multi-dimensional economy could and can foster economic prosperity for her firms Nationally, and through Foreign Direct Investment(FDI) (Comparative Advantage or Reciprocal Demand), as suggested by David Ricardo and John Stuart Mill.

But, at the above analyzed economic scenario, considering the economics of the price of government, Khan's assumption would only lead to Trade Wars in the midst of Price Inflation and Fiscal Deficit for the Market Economy (Wall Street); Consumers (Main Street); and for the Government (Washington) respectively.

A critical close-up for Tax-loopholes can really work for this economic scenario if the tax derived or extracted from Multinational or Transnational Corporations override the taxable proceeds extracted or derived by the government in the host-nation or parent corporations.

Therefore, it could be politically and economically beneficial to the Domestic Economy, when such Corporations ship their profits (repatriation of profit) to the parent or domestic economy as an economic means of indirectly paying their fair-share of their taxes at home (economic patriotism).

It is politically and economically correct that Social and Economic Mobility has always been the yearning and quest of the 21st century Developed Economies, after the collapse of the Soviet Union. This quest is to create a political economy that encompasses the different class stratification, and to bridge the Social Inequality-gap. But, the most antagonistic or centrifugal forces to the actualization of the above economic quest in the 21st century is the 'price of government'.

There should be a proper understanding and clarification of the concepts of the 'Cost of lıvıng'; 'Standard of lıvıng'; and the 'Qualıty of living'. It can be quite enticing to the political class to raise the standard of living for the populace through strategic public policies at the expense of the cost of living and at the expense of the quality of living, which is likened to 'beauty that lies in the eyes of the beholder'.

Most times, there should be an objective question on what happens to the cost of living whenever there is a significant raise in workers' wages and corporate taxes at the expense at of the employees' tax cut in order to eliminate fiscal deficit as a result of actualising the 'economics of the middle class' or viz-verse, either by the Conservatives or Liberals (see fig 4.1.6).

The 'Economics of the political class' (the price of government) scientifically eliminates the cons of the Economics of the middle-class, underclass, and the upper class. This is because it would make more political economic sense, if the workforce of any firm can afford the goods and services where he or she works with from their earnable income. But, this can only be possible if the firms and their employees pay their fair-share of their tax returns (codes), even when the government can afford and maintain her fiscal surplus. Fig.3.4.6:

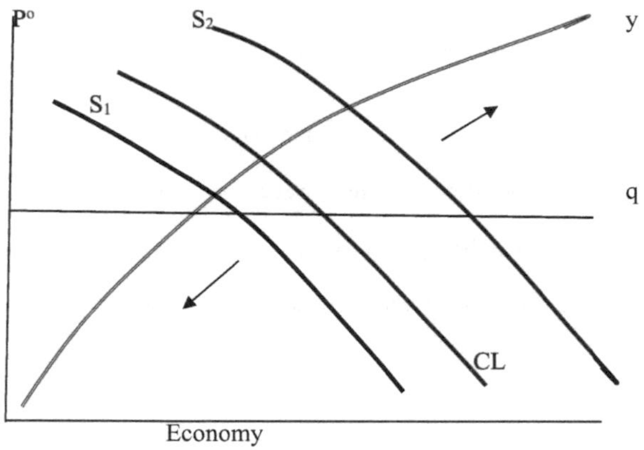

$CL = y + P^O + q$

$\therefore CL \leq S^2 = q$

$S^2 \leq C = q$

$C \leq S^1$

$C = y + p + q$

$\therefore C \geq S^2 = q$

$S^2 \geq C = q$

$C \leq S^1 = q$

Where: S^1 and S^2 = Standards of lıvıng;C = Cost of living; y = Workers' Income; q = Quality of living; P^o=the Price of goveernment.

$\Delta C = \Delta S^1$ *or* ΔS^2 (√)

but, $\Delta S^2 = \Delta C$ *or* Δq (×)

∴ ↑ S^2 *should economically and ideally lead to* ↑ q *and* ↓ C *at the slash in the price of government* (P^O).

The Economics of the Middle-Class or Common-Sence Economics assume that one of the viruses and cancer of Economic Development is the problem of Price Inflation in the midst of a High Standard of Lıving and a High Quality of Living in the Economy. Therefore, it means that a rise in the Standard of Living can not always lead to a rise in the Cost of Living (viz verse).

Economy Development in theory and in practice must be understood that it encimpasses two (2) major strans, which are 'Economic Growth' and 'Development'. By Economıc Growth, it emphasizes the Economics of GDP, GNP, and Statistical Employment Rates in a mere percentage values and illustration. But by Development, it emphasizes Marx's, Goulet's, and Seer's assumptions/

Therefore, the Liberals and the Conservatives must synthesize the political economic ballance af these approaches in their ideological arguments in matters concerning Economy Development. (see fig. 3.4.7 for further analysis).

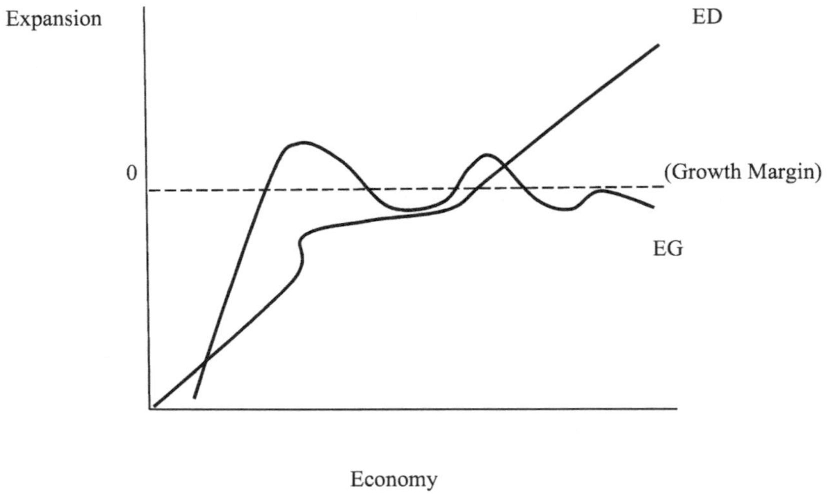

Though, Musgrave's Income Theory quiped that since Income Growth leads to Individual, Household, and Public Expenditure Growth, then Economic Growth should lead to Income Growth. But, his assumptions are practically weakened when the Cost of Raw Materials and Direct Costs remains static or increases as a result of the increase in Corporate Tax (progressive tax). Therefore, Musgrave's assumption can only be attainable during Government Fiscal Surplus.

The graphical illustration explains that Economic Growth(EG) is dependent on the Law of Deminishing Returns and on the Law of Elasticity that response to all factors of production when it reaches the Growth Margin, or if the Government is in Fiscal Deficit. But, Economy Development(ED) can maintain its progressive expansion if Government is in Fiscal Surplus, or if Government adopts the Keynessian Approach on Full Employment and on Fiscal Monetary Science at a short-run until Economic Growth(EG) gains its upward mobility above the Growth Margin and bounces back.

DECISION RULE:

$ED = P^O + CL$

Where: P^O *= slash in the price of government*

CL *= the fall in the cost of living*

$\therefore ED = f(P^O, C)$

$\dot{I}f\ P^O \geq 20\%\ FB = FD$

$\Delta P^O = \Delta T + \Delta CP + \Delta CL.$

The fiction between Economy Development and the Price Of Governement can never be overemphasized in the 21st century political economic system. If political and economic ideologies would be argued on political party lines, then economic facts, theories, and prcatices should often be considered objectively for dynamic solutions in our changing economic needs and changes.

Overtime, the fact and truth about politics and economics can be raped and aborted on the basis of Self and Group Interests. But, the physiological conception and the birth of such off-spring will always set the Economy at a disadvantaged recurrent implication and cycles.

Capitalism without failure and challenges is like Religion without Sin. But, just as sin could be avoided and controlled, so do challenges and failures in Capitalism can be put under control through 'The Economics of the price of govrernment'. This is because John Kynese and Milton Friedman opined that Fiscal Policies are the bedrock of Monetary Policies through thr instrument of government Capital Expenditures(whole), and not in Recurrent Expenditures: 'the price of government' (specific).

Political Economic leadership entailes leading and embarking on difficult but necessary task that must work for the well-being the greater number of the populace. There should be the denial of the pre-existing detrimental political economic ideologies for democracy processes to be innovative in the 21st century and beyound.

Empirical and Normative studies through this research have shown that theprice of government affects economy development, and that the concepts 'The price of government' and 'Economy Development' should be critically understood in their ideal perspectives, irrespective of political economic ideologies. If Politics has bankrupt human trust, Economics should restore such trust with dignity for the survival of democracy.

Are there possible Political Economic Alternatives to fostering Economy Development, while the issues of Inflation and Unemployment are Scientifically Managed and Controlled?

$ED = P^o + E + ES$

Where: ED = Economy Development

P^o *= The price of government*

E = Full Employment Alternative

ES = Economic Stability

$ED = f(p^o, e, es)$

$\therefore E = P^o + T + I + PC + A$

Where: E = Full Employment

P^o *= The Economics of the price of government*

T = Tax cut for businesses and workers

I = Availability of basic infrastructures for manufacturing and production for firms and industries

PC =Firms' production costs

A = Full Employment Alternatives.

Adam Smith and J. B. Clarks assumed (conservative capitalists) that the solution to 'Full Employment' is to maintain a 'Regressive Tax Code' in the Economy. This is because their economic ideas are premised on the fac that businesses, indusries, and firms are the engin-room for private sector employment in any economy.

However, their assumptions had pros and cons in solving the problem of Unemployment in the 21st crntury political economic system. On the contrary, John Keynese (liberal capitalist) assumed that the provision of Start-up Capital for Small and Medium-term Entreprises (SME) by the government would foster Full Employment in a economy .

The both perspecives however were to fster Full Employment in an economy, while the issue of Inflation maintain its lowest level, in accordance with the rrduction or elimination of Fiscal Deficit (if possible). As a result, Levison (1980), opined and proposed his 'Full Employment Alternative', anchored on the adoption of Robert Mundell's 'Supply-Side Economics' in Tax Policy of the State for firms, industries, and businesses that intend to create jobs for the middle-class, and raise the minimun-wage for the working class

Never-the-less, the Obama's Administtration adopted the above economicc principle alongside the 'Stimulus Package' as one of the blue-print of keynes' ideas on for the actualisation of 'Full Employment' (Economics of th midd-class).

But, the big quuestion is 'Did the pratical applicaion of Adam Smith's, J. B. Clarks', John Keynese, and Robert Mundell's political economic assumptions and philosophies solve the problem of Inflattion; Unemployment; and Fiscal Deficit atthe samee time n the 21st century political econommic system'?

The objective answers to the above question has continued to be a puzzle amongst the political class in their quest to solving the problems scientifically. Never-the-less, the following graphical iillustration and political economic analysis seeks to render experimental prospects to the above question and puzzle.

Fig. 3.4.1: The outcome of Adam Smith et al. on Full Employment in Economy

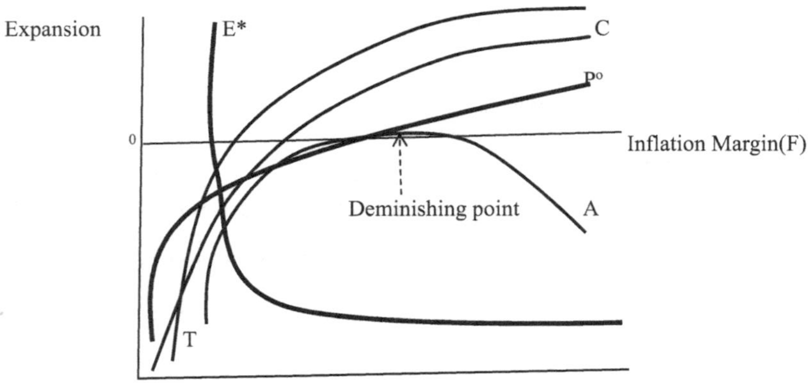

Therefore,

$A = E^{*} + C + I + P^{o} + G$

$\Delta P^{o} = \Delta C + \Delta I + \Delta T + \Delta G + \Delta PC$

Where: E =Government investment in all forms and levels of educatio*

C = Corporate tax

I =Income tax

P^{o}=The prrice of government

PC =Firms' production costs

G = Price of goods and services

If A= $\Delta (C,I,F,G,PC)$

$\Delta E^{*} = \nabla C + \nabla I + \nabla P^{o} + \nabla PC$

$\therefore A = D+BS$

Wher: D=Price and monetary deflation, BS = Budget surplus

Fig. 3.4.2: The Economics of the price of government for Econnomy Development

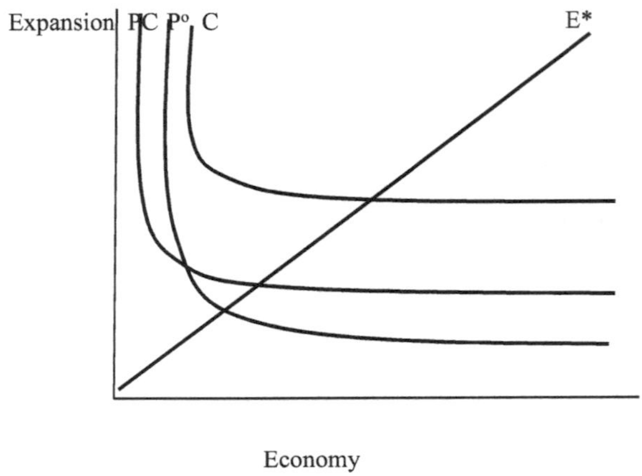

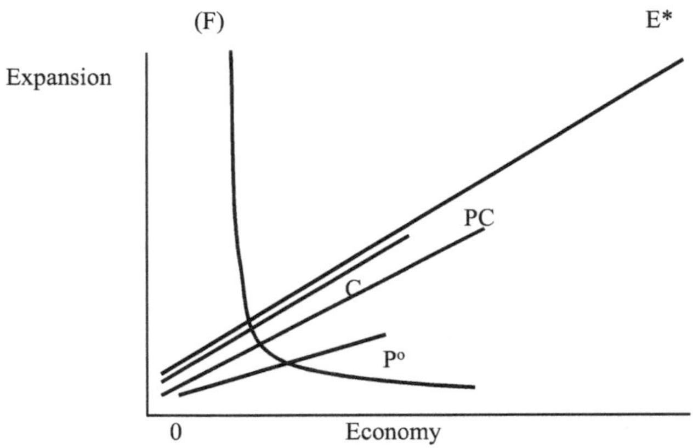

If Smith and his followers believed that High-Wages for the working Class would certainly ignite Economc Inflation in an economy, and if the Conservatives believe that Ttax Incentives for Big Businesses and Corporations/Regressiive Tax Code is an Economic Strategy in controlling Economic Inflation in the midst of Economic Growth, then we should really consider a Permanent Cut in the Price of government as a political economic strategy in reducing and eliminating Fiscal Deficits, maaging Economic Inflation, and permanently solving the puzzles put forth by Adam Smith , John Keynese, Miltton Friedman, J. B. Clarks , Robert Mundell, etc. on the issues of Inflation,Unemployment, Fiscal Deficit, and Financial Crisis.

Though Marx had opined that Social Injustice emanated as a result of socio-economic and socio-political marginalisation against the 'proleteriate' and the 'peasants' by the 'burgiosis', of which this factor could be embeded in Wheare's 'Centrifugal Forces'.

Never-the-less, Marx failed to be specific in stratifying and segmenting the components of his structures of the 'burgeoisis', and to what extent each of the components economically play their parts in the prevalence of social and economic injustice in the polity. Therefore, it is important to critically disect Marx's structure s of the society and the structure of the burgiosis so as to aid our nxt analysis in this research paper.

The structure of the society according to Karl Marx is made up of the Burgeisis, Petit-burgeoisis, Proletariate, Lumpen-proletariate, and the Peasants respectively. For te purpose of this research, it is important we understand that Marx's 'burgeoisis' is made up of four(4) sub-components namely the 'Political Elites, the Industrial Elites, the Petit-burgeiosis, and the Comprador-burgeosis' respectively in their percentage of inflence in the the structure and components as experimented and illustrated using the following pie-chats and equation.

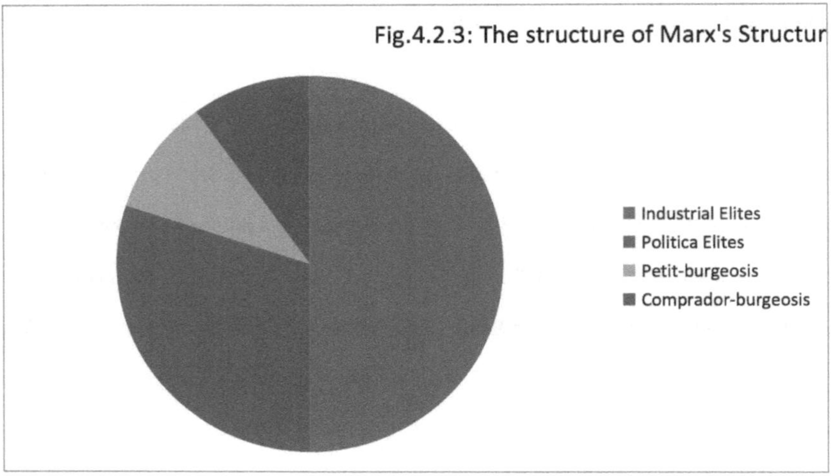
Fig.4.2.3: The structure of Marx's Structur
Industrial Elites
Politica Elites
Petit-burgeosis
Comprador-burgeosis

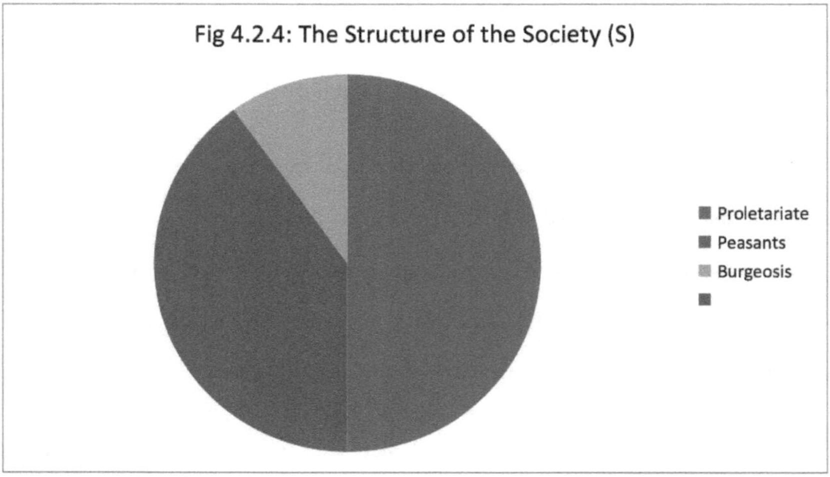
Fig 4.2.4: The Structure of the Society (S)
Proletariate
Peasants
Burgeosis

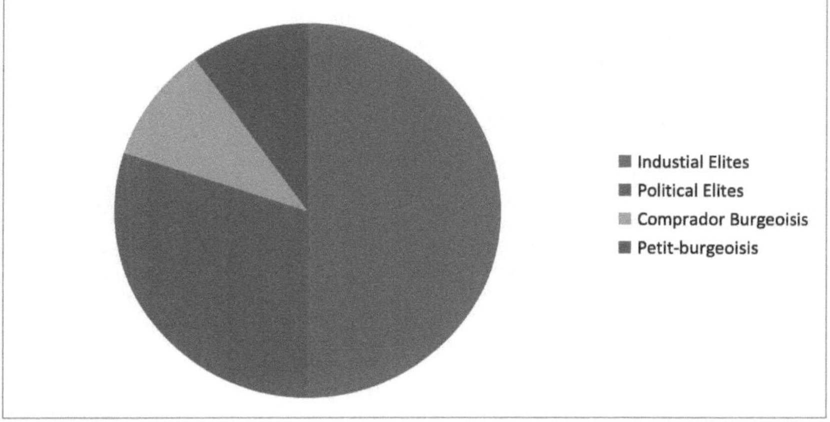

Fig.4.2.5: The structure of the Burgeoisis(B)

$\pi\ 100\% \sim 360^{o}$

$\therefore\ 30\% = G\ (100\%\ B)$

Where: $B = 10\%\ (100\%\ S)$

Since:

$d = 50\%\ (B)$

$b = 10\%(B)$

$c = 10\%(B)$

$G = 30\%(B)$

$$\therefore\ \frac{10\%(S)}{30\%(B)} = 0.333\%$$

Where:

$$det.\ ED = \left[0.333\%\ G\ \left(\frac{100\%\ B}{100\%\ S}\right)\right]$$

$0.333\%\ G = det.\ [P+ED]$

$\therefore P^{o} \Delta \leq 20\%\ (100\%\ FB) = PE.$

Where:

ED=Economy Development

P=Economics of the price of government

P^o*=The price of government*

S=Structure of the society

B=Structure of the burgeoisis

d=Industrial burgeoisis/Business elites

b=Petit-burgeoisis

c=Comprador burgeoisis

G=Political elites.

Though, the Industrial Elites make up the highest percent of the 'Burgeoisis Structure', but the allocated public remuneration allocated from the Public Treasury either makes or mar the Economy through the Distributive, Regulatory, and Extractive Policies formulated and implemented by the 'Political Elites' at the expense of other components of the Marx's 'structures', against the prosperity of the Economy at large.

Never-the-less, the aformentiond policies can be influenced by the other components of the 'Burgeoisis', but 'Political Interests' remain the paramoount determinant to such politcal economic influence at any given time during decision making process. (see, Noll and Owen, 1983).

In the 21st century political economic syystem, the 'Price of governmence' in general, and the 'Price of government' in particular have become two of the most important determinants of 'Who gets what, when, and how?; and the authoritative allocation of value for the entire society. As a result, the Political Elites in the 'Burgeoisis' stratum become the critical actors in the management of the economy. (see O'Connor, 1973)

Overtime, due to the advancement and complexity of the mordern Economic Employment Dynamics'(EED), the Political Class and Conventional Economists have abandoned the conceptual clarification of the conncept of 'Full Employment' by misguiding the populace on the difference between Full-Time Employment(FTE), Part-Time Employment(PTE), Unemployment, Under-Employmen, and Full-Employment(FE).

Though, Part-Time Employment(PTE) sometimes facilitates Labour-Mobility and Labour Diversification for skilled and unskilled workforce in subterrenean and mainstream economies. However, it most times leads to full-time employment and reduces unemployment rate in the labour market and in the economy.

On the contorary, Under-Employment to a great extent is more-or-less Unemployment when labour and income are under-bargained and under-prised, retirement benefits are gradually on the decline, and when trade-unionism is undermined.

One of the constraints and challenges of businesses in a Mixed-Economy is their ability to strictly adhere to legal and political legislative as its emanates from thier dilemma btween raising more capital and making more profit (input and output for production).

Developed and Developing Economies in the 20th and 21st centuries have adopted a binding legislation on the iddue of 'On the job and Off the job training and development' for their working class as a Statute that all business firms must strictly adhere to in the business environment and industries.

The implementation of this such Statute during the quest for a close in Fiscal-Loopholes of Corporate Tax by the government for public expenditures, therefore makes it a controversial but, binding legal and political obligation to businesses, firms, and industries. As a result, Guy Wrint (1966) and Ernest Frederick Schumacher (1973), suggested that the above economic scenerio is termed as 'Buddhist Economics' if it fails to work.

But how can this conomic controversy be adequaetly addressed in a bipartisan approach when one of the yardsticks for partisan and ideological argument is on 'ballanced budget and elimiination of fiscal deficitand loopholes'?

The belief that Immigration and Expertration of labour facilitates employment deficit in an economy, have to a greater extent not yielded objective debate that proffer pragmatic political economic solution that works for Washington, Wall-Street, and Main-Street compared to what the 'Economics of the price of government' could in a short and long term.

The Economics of the price of government can only makee sense if the political class will in genuine pleasure ignore Anti-Intellectualism and the objection of scientific political economics for the well being of Democratic Devellopment. Basic Economic Science , truth, and acts do not, but can only fade when they are abused and ignored overtime.

Michael Foucault (1966), once quipped that 'We have not yet chopped pff the kings head in political theory'. The same could be said by tracing the employble stratar of the 21st century to the 16th century protestant philosophical era that was divided on the basis of the 'Epicureans', the 'Stoic', and the 'Cynics' respectively.

The Employment Economists in their quest for Full-Employment Alternatives must take into consideration the scientific existence and prevalence of these aformentioned groups and stratar of the workforce in the mordern political economy.

As much as we should make no mistake in taking into considering the existence of these categories of the workforce in our labour market, these classes of the labour force should be synthesized into a productive relationship for economic development, through Redestibution of public policy.

DECISION RULE:

$ED = P^o + E + ES$

$ED = f(P^o, E, ES)$

$\therefore E = P^o + T + I + C + A.$

Adam Smith's, J. B. Clarks', John Keynese', and Andrew Levison's Full-Employment Alternatives has only profered Employment solutions that revolve around a recurrent decimal of ideological debates that have lingered between the liberals and the coonservatives.

Little have economists known or aggreed to the politcal economic factts that the 'price of governnment ' plays a crittical role in the attainmennt of Full-Employment and Price Stability in any econoomy. The 'theory and the Economics of the price of government' is a 'common-sense' ecnomics that fosters the prose and eliminate the cons of Full-Emloyment controversies in theory and in practice.

I research, right, and make the above assertions with the understanding of the fact that theories must be synthesized with practice, before any experiment or scientific investigation are put forth as a paradigm that must be globally acceptable and applicable to real life situation beyound reasoonable doubt.

The argument to the fact that education fosters full emploment alternatives has only necssitated a rational-deficit on economic science on the fact that the investment in public and private education in any economy is implemented through public policy from public revenue. However, such investment to a greater extent could indirectly be a burden to any economy that yearns for educational development, especially when the revenue to finance such basic economic need is derived from government loans that are product of fiscal deficit in the midst of expensive 'price of government' in her fiscal budget.

Therefore, the chronicle of educational investtment for potential employees can never be over-emphasized in the attainment of full-employment alternatives. But how can a state find such a necessiy alongside otherpolitical economic necessities without maintaining fiscal deficitt? The answer to the above answer is up to all of us.

The Income Theorists on the argument for a progressivre increase in public expenditurs opined that the increase in public nrrds and demands equals the increase in government spending, and that the increase in private sector business establishment and growth equals the increase in governmennt taxable revenue and further increase in governnment spending has become an outdated approch towards public financial management.

But, it is important to note that such assuptions lack empirical conclussion and global acceptability especially in the midst of a persisting increase in national and global population, while natural disaster is at the increase, and as a result of the abbovve phenomenon, Clarks', Keynese' ans Levisn's assumption on full-employment alternative must have been a practical disaster for the economy, if the economics of the price of government is not adopted to play a significant role in the tax economics of the economics of the price of government that will subsequently experimented in this research paper. However, let consider the following graphical illustration as a prospect against the Income Theory (fig. 3.4.5).

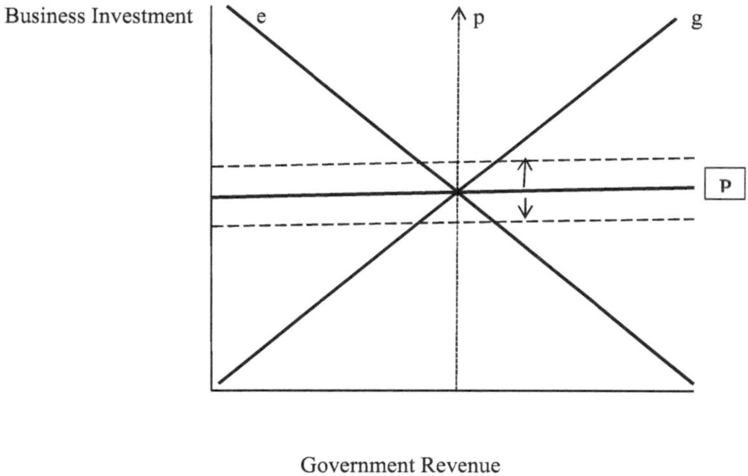

All other things being Equall (ceteris paribus), if there is an upward shift in p(population), is certainly be a downward slope in e(employment), and price of goods and services would be unstable. This is because there is bound to be a raise in Income-Tax and Corporate-Tax (Proportional Tax) that would likely increase firms' production costs and the cost of goods and services for working-class and for consumers.

As a result, it certainly would lead to the decline in employment rate , especially when the increase in population is constant, and vis verse. Economically, the 'Price of Government' is 'Fixed Cost' in the 'Recurrent Expenditure' in public finance. While, 'Government Investments' are 'Variabe Cost' that has the elements of 'Marginal Cost' that falls within the 'Capital Expenditure' of public finance.

This is because the Capital Expenditure of public finance facilitates the increase in new business investment that equal the increase government revenue and complements the increase in government spending for the persisting increase in human population and the unforseen circumstances that may arise from natural disaster.

It should be noted that though, the 'Price of government' is a 'Fixed Cost' only in 'Recurrent Expenditure' and in the 'Price of governance' of Public Expenditures. But , it should also be an 'Average Cost' that should be based on Economic, Psychological, Socioal, and Political variables pf Public Expenditures.

Technically, the engagement of individuals in different part-time jobs(dual or multiple jobs) placement for sustain able income most times necessitated by Under-employment or the availability of suitable employment vacuum for the suitable workforce. Therefore, it doesn't mean tha employment rate has really fallen in its percentage level.

Is the concept of 'Fiscal Responsiblity' limited to the cope of 'Capital Expenditure' in the management of fiscal deficit /debt of government?

$ED = \beta_1 + \beta_2 + \beta_3$

ED = Economy Development

β_1 *=Fiscal Responsibility*

β_2 *= Puritan Ethics*

β_3 *= The Price of Governmennt*

$ED = f(f,p,g)$

$F = \Delta r^e + \Delta c^e$

$F = \downarrow P^1 + \Delta P^2$

Where:

$Y \approx X$

F = *Fiscal Responsibility*

BS = *Budget Surplus*

PE = *Puritan Ethics*

P^o = *The Price of government*

P^g = *The Price of governance*

$P^1 + P^2$ = *Government Expenditures (r^e and c^e)*

T^* = *Governnment Investment*

D = *Debt Servicing*

The above economic equation and experiment is graphically illustrated below (fig. 4.3.1 & 2), using Zero-Sum Budgeting and Increamental Budgeting Principles to analysing Fiscal Responsibility on Puritan Ethics.

Fig. 3.4.1: Zero-Sum(Z) Budgeting for Fiscal Responsibility

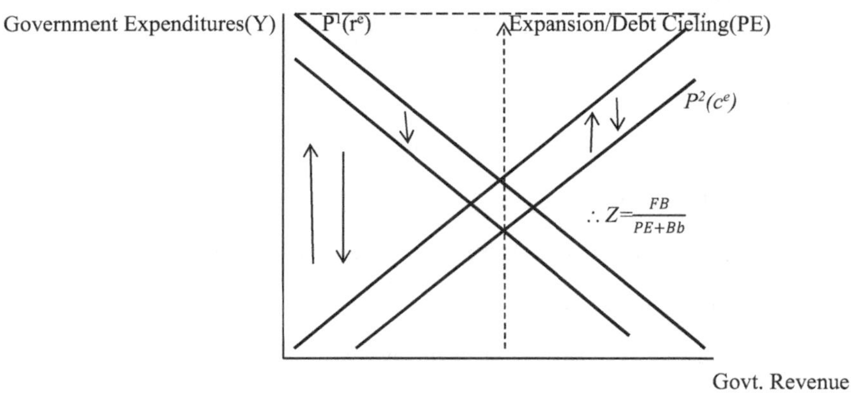

Fig. 3.4.2: Increamental (I) Budgeting for Fiscal Responsibility (Puritan Ethics).

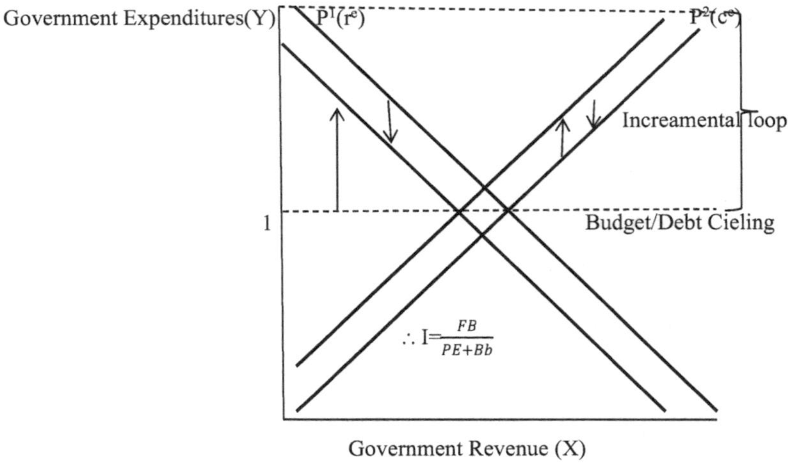

Where:

Z= Zero- Sum Budgeting

I= Increamental Budgeting

FB= Fiscal Budget

PE= Puritan Ethics

Bb=Ballanced Budget

Note: The Unconstitutional Legitimacy of the Political Debt Ceilig facilitates Fiscal Recklessness and Irresponsibility against the Puritan Ethics. The graphical illustration above depict that the 'Puritan Ethics' facilitate Fiscal Responsibility against the principle and politics of 'Debt Ceiling', either way of Increamental or Zero-Sum Budgeting Principles, as long as the 'Recurrent and Capital Expenditure' must maintain their Puritan effect of Basic Need and Policy Demand Approach (BNPDA) in line with the 'Pay-as-you-go' principles of public financial management (PAYGO).

The following Bar-Chart and Economic Experiment illustrates Fiscal Responsibility, using

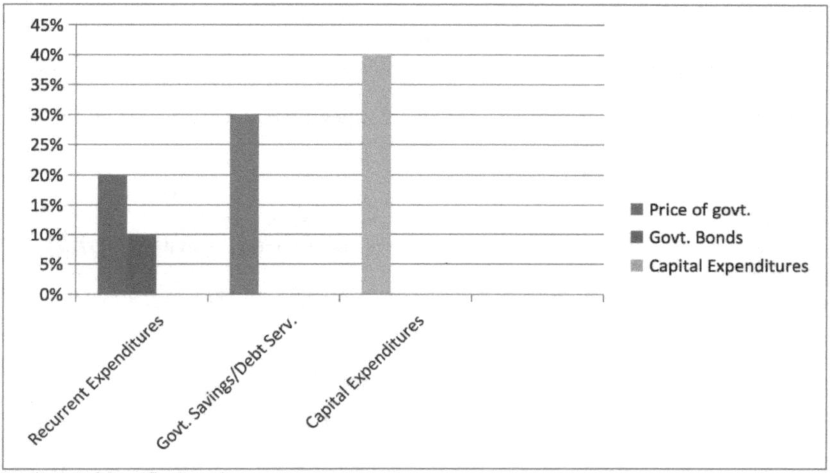

Puritan Ethics (fig.3.4.3).

$PE = P^o \frac{20\%Po}{100\%FB(Pg)}$

$= F = \frac{PE}{Bb}$

Therefore, $Bb = 100\%X - 80\%Y(r^e + c^e) = (30\%X) = S(t + d)$

$F = \downarrow I + \uparrow C$

$Q = \uparrow y + \uparrow e$

$\therefore ED = r^e + PE + Q$

İf, $F = PE$

$\therefore P^o = 20\% \ (20\% + 10\%: r^e)$

$= 30\% \ (t + d)$

= 30% (20% + 10%)+ 30% + 40%= 100%

$\therefore c^e$ = 50% (MDAs Fiscal Allocation based pn Basic Need and Basic Resource Approach : BNRA).

Joseph Schumpeter in his 'Creative Destruction' quipped that though Technological Change and Innovation cultivate the thorns on Fiscal Science and Economic Development, so does Government Budget and Expenditures when its prioritiews aren't appropriated in line with Fiscal Principles in Public Finance.

Though, fiscal innovation had aided fiscal changes in fiscal science, Schumpeter argued that the principles of fiscal science (Recurrent and Capital Principles shouln't be ignored in Fiscal Responsibility).

According to Schumpeter, Fiscal Responsibility is and should be the public financial adjustment that must affect the Recurrent and Capital Expenditures of Government Budget (see O'Connor, 1973 and Wanat, 1978). He (Schumpeter) in his 'Fiscal Science' concored to Walter Heller's 'Puritan Ethics', emphasizing on the common-sense fical adjustment in the midst of fiscal monetary crisis.

In the peak of Global Trade Wars, either Economies could give-in to Trade-Deficit or persisting Trade Wars. But the only long-run effect and advantage to the Economies that must win or intend to win, must be an Economy that totally eliminates their fiscal deficits or debt in a short-run.

Economic Growth and Economic Victory in the midst of Global Trade War promise never to be a long or outstanding victory. But, Economies that mentain Puritan Ethics does and would actualise the course of political economic freedom.

A smart and economic way to close tax-loopholes and end fiscal deficit in the 21st century public finance is to ballance her fiscal budget at the back of the 'back of the government'. Yes, this Public Sector Economics assumption and assertion calls for Scientific and Experimental Economic argument, but it can only be attainable when National Interest surpasses group, partisan and individual interests.

The Economics of the Middle-Class/the Economics of the Upper-Class begins and is totally dependenton the 'Economics of the price of government', as it must innovatively and radically facilitates Smith's, Marx's, Keynesean, Friedman's, Mundell's, Hume's, and Clarks' iscal and monetary economic assumptions.

We should make no mistake to think that the theory of the Price of government gives an open-cheque to fiscal recklesness in capital expenditur managaement of the expenditure framework of Basic Need and Basic Resource Approach (BNBRA) when and where public investment is of the essence on the principles of 'Pay as you go (PAYGO)' of public financial management.

The graphical illustration below depicts the 'Pay as you go(PAYGO)' principles of public financial management.

Fig. 3.4.4

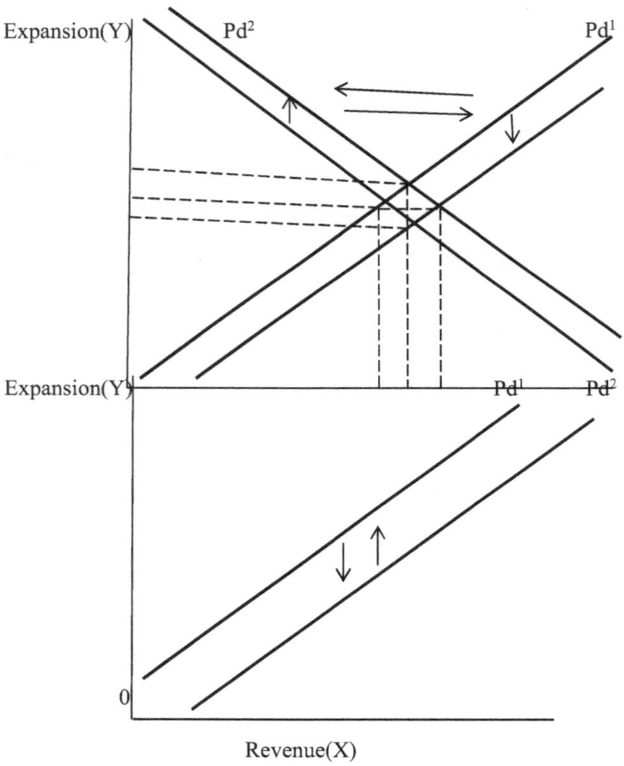

$\Delta Pd = \Delta Y$

Where, $Y + X = 1$ *(0%-100%FB):Bb*

$I = r^{e+} c^{e}$ *(Z/I)*

$\downarrow Pd^{1} = \uparrow Pd^{2}$

Or,

$\uparrow Pd^2 = \downarrow Pd^1$

$\therefore r^e = \leq 30\% + c^e = \leq 70\% \ (P^o \leq 2\%)$

$BS = 30\% \ (t + d)$

Economically, the Skeptists and the Sophists would want to raise progressive questions of the Conventional Economist on the economic conditions and situation levied at an increasing Economic Growth and increasing Government Revenue.

Bt, the scintific economic answer to the above question is that the price of government should at 1% at every 50% growth or increase of Budget Surplus. While, the Capital Expenditures increases on 'Basic Need and Policy Demand Approach' at every 50% growth or increase of Budget Surplus.

Though, the Liberals and the Conservatives may question the economics of the price of government, just like such criticisms were levied against Keynese' and Friedman's Monetary theories, assumption, and Recommendation. But, a critical and scientific study to this research work promises to facilitate objective theoretical and practical solutions to the research problems.

The presumptive 1% increase in the price of government at every 50% Budget Surplus increase or growth is facilitated by the theory of Public Fnance (Income Theory) put forth by Richard Musgrave. Therefore, an increase or growth in Budget Surplus at the afformentioned percent, should lead to a 1% increase in the price of government(P^o).

This Economics of the price of government frustrates 'Equastration', but facilitates 'Deveconomics', and enhances Fiscal Preventive Measures against the backdrop of Fiscal Austerity Measures(Fiscal Deficit).

The Economics of the price of governnment promises to be 'Tough Economics', but it also promises to be the right, ideal, and realistic Economics for the attainment of fiscal responsibility in the 21st century political economy. Therefore, this Economic Science is an antidote fo the fiscal principle of 'Debt-Ceiling' and it controversies of the ideological divide.

Never-the-less, the Economics of the price of government is not to pose Economic Warefare between the market economy or the government economy. But to enhance and facilitate a common-sense economic mathematics.

It is always popular to promise the moon in politics, and ignore facts and truth at the detriment of economic science. Towards the payment of debt, there must be revenue. But to have revenue, there must be taxable and non-taxable revenues, and non of these can be devices which are not more-or-less inconvinient or unpleasant . This is because dealing with debt is always a choice of difficulties.

However, public officer in the ideal sense are not elected to do what is easy and politically advantageous. But, to put the economy first before political parties along the line of arguable ideologies, and to do what is politically and economically right for the future, by eliminating the fiscal cancer of the price of government and governance.

The ext important issue of analysis in this discussion is to economically present and experimental relationship between Public Debt , Uemployment, and the Price of government , showing its effect on fiscal responsibility (Puritan Ethics).

$FD = P^{o} + S + M + U$

Where,

FD=Fiscsl Deficit

P^o=The Price of government

S=Social Security

M=Medicaid and Medicare(Affordable Care Act)

Graphically Illustrated as follows(Fig. 3.4.5):

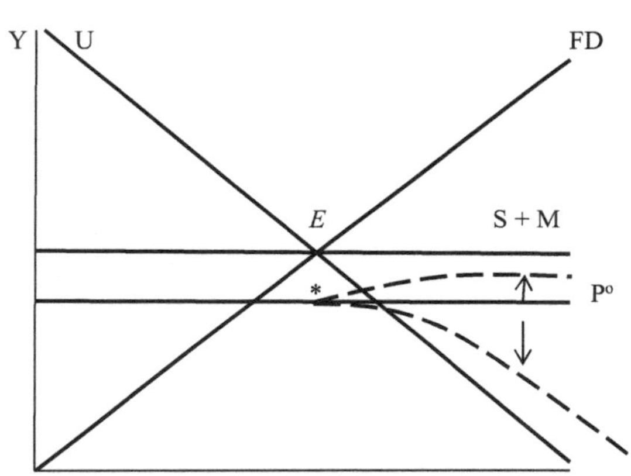

if, $FD=P^o+S+M+U$

$\therefore \Delta FD= \nabla P^o + \Delta S + \Delta M + \nabla U$

Where,

$ED=\uparrow R\,(S+M)$

İf, $S+M=42\%FB$

$\therefore \downarrow P^o=BS\,(\uparrow S+\uparrow M)$

if, $U=\downarrow T\,(R)$

when, $S+M=(K)$

$\therefore P^o =\geq 20\%\ FB$

But if, $\uparrow U=\uparrow T\,(R)$

When, $S + M = (K)$

therefore, $P^{o} = \uparrow 1\% = (\uparrow 50\% BS)$.

Where:

FD *= Fiscal Deficit*

P^{o} *= The Price of government*

S *= Social Security*

M *= Medicare and Medicaid (Affordable Care Act)*

R *= Revenue*

B *= Budget Surplus*

T *= Tax*

(K) *= Constant*

ED *= Economy Development*

U *= Unemployment*

Since, Social Security, Medicared, Medicaid increase due to increase of Population, of which can also lead to lead to the increase in Nation Debt (Fiscal Deficit). The political economic remedy tthat is bipartisan can only be the parmanent cut in the price of government , so as to tackle the economic problem of Unemployment, and facilitate the increase in Public Revenue throuh Progressive and Regressive Tax Code. While Tax-friendly policies and Basic Infrastructurs are ehanced foe Small and Medium-Term Entreprises(SME), and Big Businesses at a short and long-ru, so as to boost Public Revenue for other Capital Expenditures that are necessities.

The essence of applying the Economics of the price of governmnt as the remmedy for Public Debt or Fiscal Deficit against the cut in other aspects and classifications of Government

Expenditures like Social Security, Medicaid, and Medicare because the latters are basic necessities in the development of the 21st ccentury political economy.

We should make no mistake to think that Mechanization of Financial Tools and Instruments by the Cental Bank, Commercial Banks, and other Financial Institutiions can totally eliminate Public Debt/Fiscal Deficit, or solve the fiscal problems of the 21st century political economics.

The justification to the above assertion cpould be empirically provened when we consider the economic fact that the injectionn of addition Bailout fund an Stimulus-packages in the midst of persisting fiscal det, crisis annd deficit without the applicatipon of the Economics of the pricce of government would lead to a recurrennt and worse Recession , Inflation, Depression that be likeed to olitical economic cancer and suicide that can affect economies as an overdosed substance injected into the heart of the economy.

The following graphical illustration explains this prospects in line with the Economics of he price of governnment (fig. 3.4.6).

Fig. 3.4.6

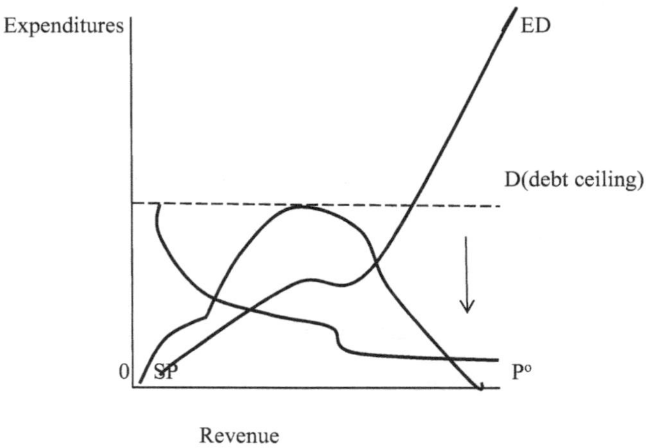

$F = \downarrow P^{o} + \uparrow ED + \downarrow SP$

$\therefore \Delta ED = \Delta SP + \Delta P^{o}$

Where,

ED = Economy Development

SP= Stimulus Package

D= Debt Ceiling.

The graphical illustration abone depicts that at the debt ceiling, becomes a 'Bubble' tha must 'Burst' due to Economic Growwth , Inflation, Fiscal Deficit, and the increase in Population that lead to increase in government spending. The only solution(preventive mearsure) to curbing the next presumtive 'Burst' can never be and would never be the injection of another Stimulus Package (Bailout), but the application of the Economics of the price of government.

The government has, and can only save the Banks and thr Firms from the Global Financial Crisis. But who can or would save the government when the next presumptive financial crisis occures?

The essence of this question is to be to our intellectual deficit that the 'Stimulus or Bailout' will not always solve the problem of the global financial crisis during an era of a high acumulated government debt/deficit.

The scientific and experimental political economic solution to the paramount global financial crisis can only be dependet on the Economics of the price of government, and these principles and theory should be embraced as a matter of urgency. Time is ticking too fast, and there is limited time for partisan politics because the 'Special Drawing Right: Leading Rescue Currency (SDR)' of the IMF to reliquify the Wold's Economy would be a detrimental 'Austerity Measure' to such presumptive Global Debt and Financil Crisis.

The different Debt Management Strategies like Debt Embargo, Debt Swap, and Debt Rescchedule has never solved the problem of Public Debt in the 21st Century growing population and rapid technological change that havve become competitive in the modern economy. The question is how can the different Debt Management Strategies in practical application help in solving the Global Debt Crisis at a high and sophisticated 'price of government'?

However, different economists have argued on National Debt (Government's, Firms', and Consumer's Debt respectively); GDP; GNP; and Trade Deficits as the Conventional Economic Apprach in search for an accurate experimental economic analysis.

The new and common realitty is that the conventional debt management strategies has never and would never solve the issues of National Debt(especial government debt) to its minimmal point. This is because the reduction or elimination of government debt plays a significant role in other spectrum of national debt . Therefor, let us consider a radical and pragmatiic approach (the Economics of the price of government) in solving the global fiscal and financial crisis as follows (see fig. 3.4.7).

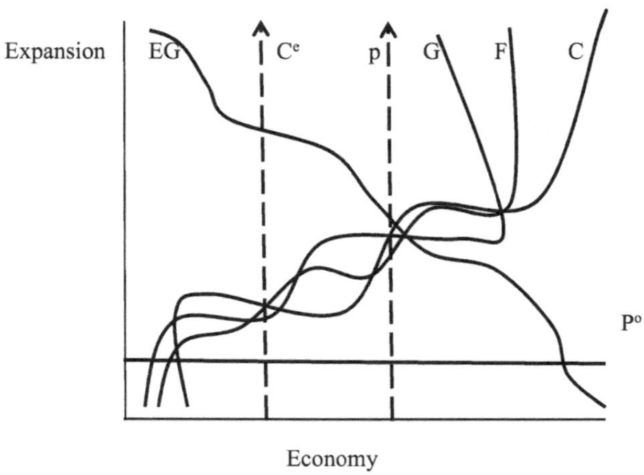

R= ND

When,

ND= G +F+C

$\Delta G = \Delta F + \Delta C$

$\therefore \uparrow G = \uparrow F + \downarrow C$

But,

$\downarrow c = \downarrow F + \downarrow G$

$\therefore ND = \sum P^{\circ} - P$

$\sum ND = D$

When,

$\sum_{D^{\circ}}^{D*} = ND$

$P^{o} = ND - R + \downarrow ND$

$P^{o} = D^{o}$

When,

$\downarrow P^{o} = \downarrow G + \downarrow F + \downarrow C$

$\Delta G = \Delta F + \Delta c$

$\therefore EG = GDP + GNI$

$GNP = GDP + D1$

Where:

GNP= Gross National Product

GNP= Gross National Product

GNI= Gross National Income

D1= Direct Taxes

R=Recession

ND= National Debt

G= Government Debt

F= Corporate Debt

C= Individual/ Household Debt

EG= Economic Growth

C^e=Capital Expenditures

P^o= The Price of government

P= Population

D= Deflation*

DS= Debt Serving(government)

BS= Budget Ceiling

D^o= Economic Depression

Ceteris Paribus, the experiment/equation above depicts National Debt during Economic Recession and Depression. The Economics of the price of government depicts the following graphical illustration and experiment in the midst of global debt.

The increase or decrease in interest rate on government loan would only lead financial senselessness that places National Debt in a detrimental cycle.

Fig. 3.4.8

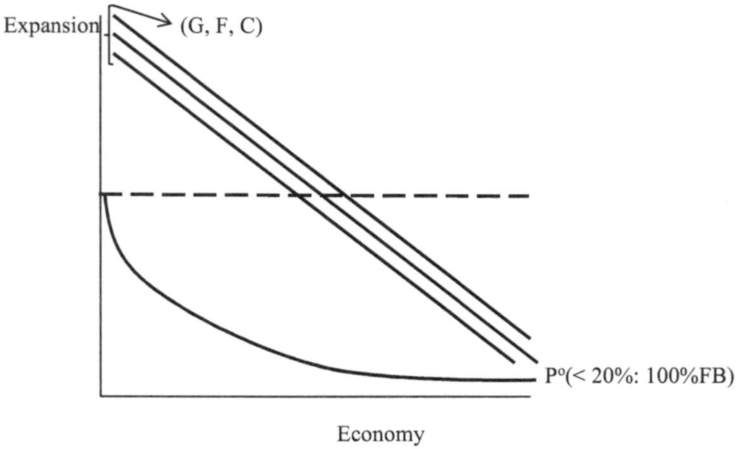

The political economic assumption of GDP and GNP as the determinant to measuring National Debt can only lead to a normative anaysis , traditionally to facilitate economic analysis without proferring a radical solution to the problem of National Debt.

The increase and persisting growth in Fuul-Employment; increasing Workers' Income; Standard of Living aren't the thorns on the flesh of Economy Development , but the increasing and persisting National Debt and the Price of of government are. The absence of the Economics of the price of government in the management of Economic Growth promises to lead to a 'Boom' that is latently and manifestly embeded with a 'Burst'.

It should be technicall noted that the increase in Human Population doesn't always lead to the increase in GDP. But except' there are critical investment in foral and informal Education; and in Job Training /Development for an employable workforce.

However, the above factual explanation leads us to next phase of the Economics of the price of government in relations to Social Security, Medicare, and Medicaid in fiscal science.

If,

$M + S = 42\% \ (100\% FB)$

$R^e = 30\% \ (100\%)$

$\therefore \ 30\% = R^e \ (100\% FB)$

$42\% = R^e \ (100\% FB)$

$\sum_{P*}^{M+S} = 72\% \ R°(100\% FB)$

$70\% \ R^e - 30\% \ C^e = F(Fiscal \ Irrsponsibility).$

But,

If, $M + S = R^e$

$P^o = R^e$

$M + S = <20\% \ (100\%FB)$

$P^o = <20\% \ (100\%FB)$

$C^e = <60\% \ (100\%FB)$

$P^g = 80\% + 20\% \ (t+d)$

$= 100\%$ *(Puritan Ethics)*

The empirical solution to Government or National Debt is not to scrap the Federal Reserve System as the advocacy for such revolution has increased over decades due to Global Debt. But, the Economics of the price og government promises to be the answer to the problems at this juncture.

TheVirtual Monetary Conspiracy(VMC) of the Federal Reserve as a major problem that leads to National Debt or Global Debt Crisis have never solved the looming Debt Crisis neither. The Global Central Banking System (World Bank and IMF) arev not the major problem to Global Debt, but, the ignorance of the Economics of the price of government is.

From our previous equation and experiment, it certainly means that as much as the price of government falls within the tenent of government recurrent expenditures in fiscal budget, so should Social Security, Medicare, and Medicaid.

A recurring item in the fiscal budget over two decades irrespective of its increase or decrease in accruable monetary value, becomes scientifically a part of the reccurn expenditures of government budget.(see O'Connor, 1973).

The above discussion brings us to a very important aspect of the Economics of the price of government. Many mainstream economists believed that the FED a major role to play in every 'Economic Boom and Burst' at all times. It is best believed by the Liberals and Conservatives that the 2008 global financial crisis was as a result of the FED's moetary policies on Interest rates, prior to the crisis, and this ideology has become mainstream accross the both aisle.

Never-the-less, it would be imperative that we integrate the role of the FED in the Economics of the price of government for a ballanced apporoach in our prospects and analysis. Though, John Keynese in his 'theory of employment' suggested that the issuance of bank loans and incentives for business at a low interest rate towards the creation of job and employment in the midst of economic recession , inflation, and depression would facilitate economic growth.

The FED and different economists endorsed such recovery policies put forth by Keynese. But, the outcome of such policies worsened the financial crisis in 2007 through 2009, while economic growth was at a slow pace, even through 2018.

This outcome wasn't and isn't because John Keynese or the FED were dysfunctional in their intellectual property of Economics. But, because the Economics of the price of government was and is still outof place to complement such monetary policies, as it relevance can be experimented and analysed below.

$ED\downarrow P^o + \downarrow M,S + L = ED$

Where,

$L + \downarrow R = \uparrow E\ (\uparrow R^I + D: r^I + d)$

$\therefore ED = \downarrow P^{o} + L\ (\downarrow D)$

R^{e1}=*Part of Recurrent Expenditures*

R= Interest Rates

R^{1}=*Fiscal Revenue*

F= Full Employment

D(d) = Government Debt

L= Bank Loans

H(h)= Price of Housing/ Mortgage

C= Price of goods/services

Fig. 3.4.9

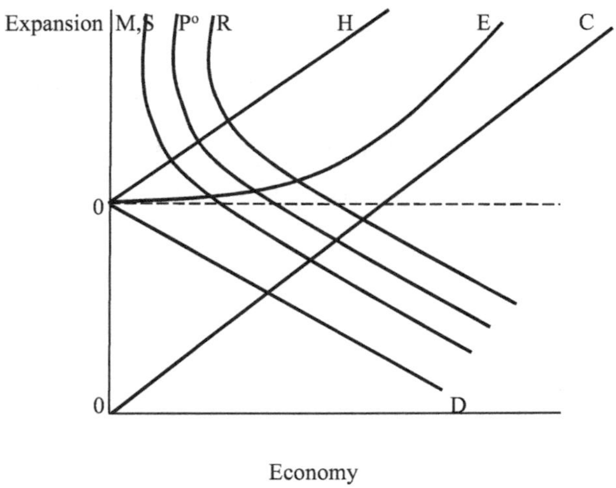

$\uparrow H = \uparrow R$

$\therefore \uparrow C = \uparrow R$

When, $P^o + M + S = < 30\%(R^{e1})$

The Monetary Economists on the assumption of 'Money' as the major cause of Inflatin or Deflation cannot be over-emphasized since it could be empirically provened, most especially when the the price of government is measured in monetary value. This fact leads us to the relationship between 'Monetarism' and the 'Economics of the price of government' in our next analysis.

$\uparrow P^s + \downarrow P^o = \downarrow C$

But if,

$\uparrow P^o + P^s = \uparrow C$

$\therefore P^o + P^s = C$

$\Delta P^o = \Delta P^s = \downarrow MC$

Where,

$\downarrow MC = \downarrow PC + \uparrow Y$

$\therefore MC + \downarrow PC = \downarrow C$

P^s*=Money Supply*

C= Price of goods and servives

M= Marginal Costs of firms' production

PC= Production Costs

Y= Workers' Income

I= The Third Industrial Revolution

Fig. 4.3.10

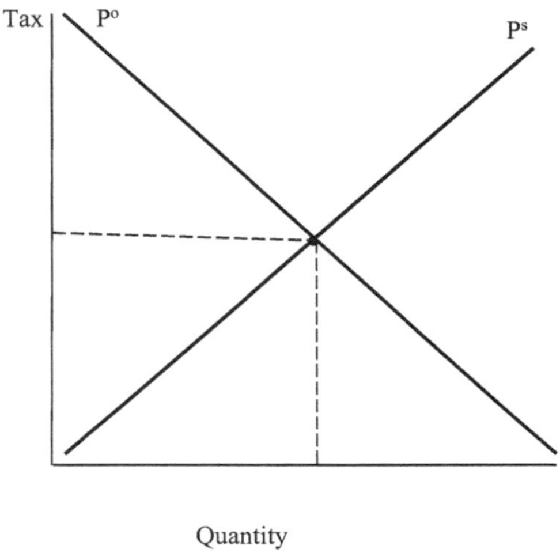

Newton's Physics had and has given birth to modern days Economics because there was a quest for 'Economic Science'. Newton asserted that 'for every action, there is an equal and opposite reaction'. However, Adam Smith adopted Newton's metaphor in his 'Demand and Supply' theory, thereby, stating that 'for every action on the Supply side, there is an equal action on the Demand side'

But, Economists have failed to understand that Newton's physics had little or nothing to do with Economics, beacause Economics is dynamic beyund human limited immadination and bounded rationality.

The vission of the 'Third Industrial Revolution' promises to facilitate Global Economic Boom. But, Economists and Governments have failed to care about what would happen to National, Regional or Global Debt that 'Must' emanate from the increasing price of governance to financing the 'Better Machines, Better Workforce, and Better Aggregate

Efficiency(New Infrastructures), while the the quest for fiscal reas[onssibility is of the essence in public financial management in the 21st century and beyound.

The quest for 'Green Political Economy' as a rsult of Climate Change and Global Warming has necessitated the quest for 'Zero Marginal Costs(0MC)' for firms' and industries that must sphere-head Green Global Political Economy(GGPE) for the Third Industrial Revolution.

The Green Political Economics for the Third Industrial Revolution requires a Zero-Sum Marginal Cost for production , and this can never be possible without the Economics of the price of government, else, a Global Debt Crisis would be inevitable.

Therefore, the analysis and experiment below depicts the prospects for a Global Debt free Third Industrial Revolution.

$GP = \downarrow P^o + PC$

$I = N + W + AG$

$\therefore I = PC + \downarrow N$

$GP = I = MC < 1\% \ (AG = C^e)$

Where,

$\downarrow P^o = \uparrow t \ (C^e) + \downarrow PC$

$\downarrow CL = \uparrow SL \ (\Delta Q) = I$

SL= Standard of living

t= Government Investment

I= Third Industrial Revolution

Q=Quality of living

N=Better Machines

W=Better Workforce

AG= Aggregate Efficiency

D= Government Debt

GP= Green Politics

CL= Cost of living

Fig. 3.4.11

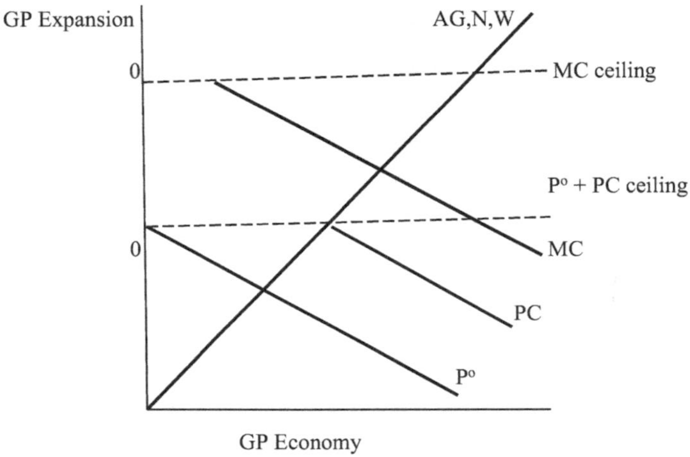

The issue of Climate Change has become a paramount and contending discussion in Green Politics, and as a result, several Green Political Economists have advocated for for Government Regulations on Industries and Firms, while others have advocated for Extractive Policies(Tax Policies) on the firms and industries that faulter on environmental statute.

The aformentioned standpoints are fostered on the bedrock of the efficacy of global warming, government revenue, and the dilemma of economic growth and development. Though, the issue of Climate Change over dacades has become one of the major political economic that foster 'External Costs', and the global effort to tackle such issue seeks to foster 'External Benefits' even to the slight disadvantage to the cost of governance.

The Economics of the price of government would make no objective sense when it can't give give tangible and scientific solutions to conventional economic problems on how it tend to solve and facilitate the payment of government debts that has emanated from reckless goveernment expenditures.

We should keep in mind that the Economics of the price of government does not only seek to solve the problems of the price of governance, but to proportionately facilitate 'Economy Development and Economic Growth(for government and for the populace)' in it applicability.

Therefore, the following model and experiment shows the prospects on Tax-code for Fiscal Responsibility and Puritan Ethics.

$$TC = \uparrow P^t + \downarrow R^t + \downarrow S^t \left(\frac{U>M}{Bb>S^o}\right)$$

$$\therefore \Delta P^t = \Delta R^t + \Delta S^t \left(\frac{PD:BNA}{FY}\right)$$

$$PE = R^e < 30\%(P^o + M + S) + C^e < 40\% \, (PD/BNA) \rightarrow 30\%$$

$$=(t + s + d: PAYGO):100\%FB \, (PG)$$

Where,

PE= Puritan Ethics

R^t= Regressive Tax

P^t= Progressive Tax

t= Government Investment

FS=Fiscal Surplus

d= Debt Ceiling

PAYGO=Pay as you go principle(public finance)

FB=Fiscal Budget

P^o=the price of government

FY= Fiscal Year

r^e= Recurrent Expenditures

PG= the price of governance

M= Medicare and Medicaid

S= Social Security

C^e=Capital Expenditures

PD=Policy Demand

BNA= Basic Need Approach

S^t= Students Loans/Tax

U= the Upper-class(elites)

M= the Middle—class

B^b = Big Businesses

S^o= Small Businesses

Fig.3.4.12: Graph showing Tax-code analysis for the Economics of the price of government

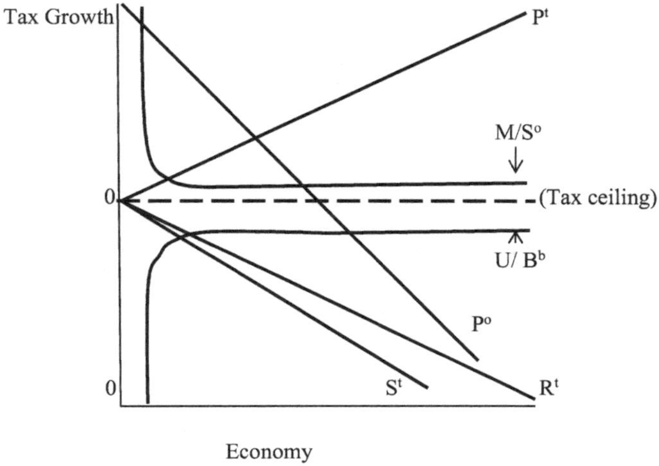

$$TC = \uparrow P^t + \downarrow R^t + \downarrow S^t\left(\frac{U>M}{B^o>S^o}\right)$$

$$\therefore \Delta P^t = \Delta R^t + \Delta S^t\left(\frac{PD/BNA}{FY}\right)$$

Fig 3.4.13: Graph showing Fiscal Responsibility (Puritan Ethics) analysis of the Economics of the price of government.

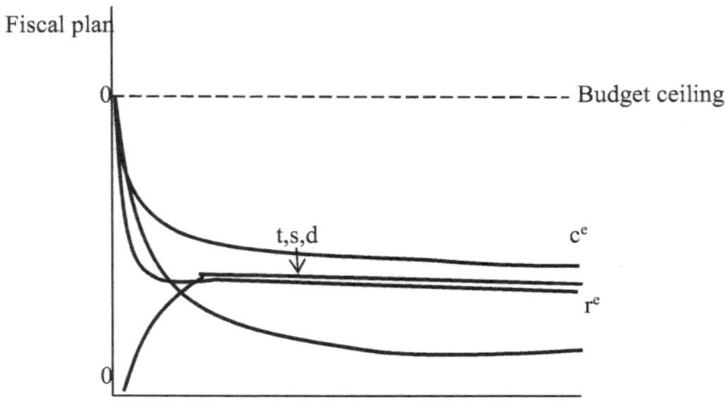

$PE = r^e < 30\%(P^o + M + S) + C^e = 40\%(PD/BNA)$

$\rightarrow 30\%\ (t + s + d{:}PAYGO){:}100\%FB(PG).$

The above Tax-code analysis/prospects and the fiscal responsibility analysis are dependent and must be empirically applicable in line with the forms and system of government or tax system.

The Top-Bottom Tax Economics or the Bottom-Top Tax Economics debates had and has only led to recurrent debates, revolving around regressive cycle. The empirical solution for Taxation and Fiscal Science that can work for the government, the market, and the populace is the 'Bottom-Top-Top-Bottom-Horizontal Tax Economics(BTTBHTE)'. This Tax-code simply means 'a permanent cut on the price of government; a mandatory cut on the middle class and small business' tax; but a progressive and regressive tax cut on the upper class and big businesses on policy emand and basic need approach basis(PDBNAB) per fiscal year.

The PDBNAB Tax Economics is so important because it eliminates Social Inequality, fosters Job creation, improves Employment rate, reduces Government Deficit in short and long run, and facilitates Puritan Ethics(fiscal responsibility) in public financial management for the government and for businesses.

Do the Taxable Revenue and other sources of Government Revenue contribute to Inflation and Unemployment rate in the Economy?

$ED = P^o = TC + PE + PC + E + CL$

$ED = f(P^o, tc, pe, pc, e, cl)$

Where,

ED= Economy Development

P^o=The Price of government

TC= Governmnt Tax Code

PE= Puritan Ethics

PC= Firms' Production Costs

E= Full Employment

Therefore,

$ED = P^o + TC + PE + PC$

Where,

$TC = \uparrow P^t + \downarrow R^t + \downarrow S^t\left(\frac{U>M}{B^o>S^o}\right)$

$P = r^e < 30\% \ (P^o + M + S) + c^e = 40\% \ (PD/BNA)$

$$\rightarrow\left(\frac{30\%\left(t^{\circ}+s+d{:}PAYGO\right)100\%FB\ (PG)}{\Delta P\tau=\Delta R\tau+\Delta S\tau\left(\frac{PD/BNA}{FY}\right)}\right)$$

$$P^{o}=\frac{<20\%FB}{r^{\circ}=<30\%\left(P^{\circ}+M+S\right)+C^{\circ}40\%\left(PD/BNA\right)\rightarrow 30\%\left(t+s+d{:}PAYGO\right){:}100\%\ FG\ (PG)}$$

$$CL = TC + TFC + TVC$$

$$E = P^{o} + t^{x} + I + PC + a$$

$$PC = \frac{C+I+P^{\circ}+t+g}{d+BS}$$

Where:

E=Full Employment

P^{o}=A cut in the price og government

t^{x}= A tax cut for small and big businesses, and for working class

I= Availability of Infrastructures

PC= Firms' Production Costs

a= Full Employment Alternatives

C= the price of goods and services

t= A cut in firms' production costs

d= price/monetary deflation(fall in price of C)

BS= Budget Surplus

T= Taxable Revenue

Fig.3.4.14: Graphical illustration for the above experiment (prospects).

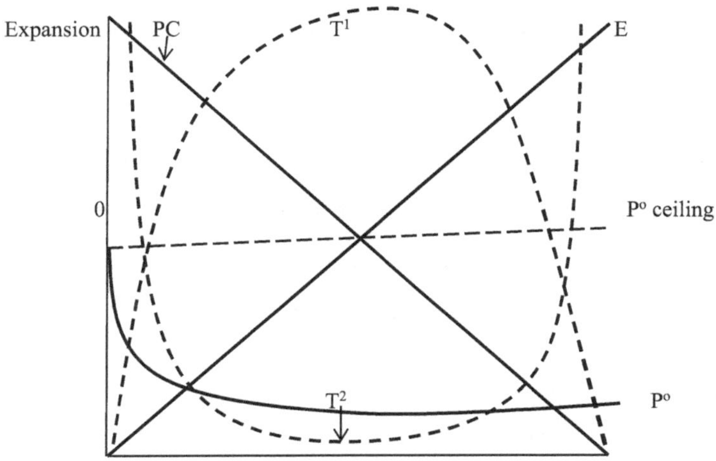

↓ Po = ↑ TC + PE + ↓ PC + ↑ E + ↓ CL →(Deflation)

But if,

↑ Po = ↓ TC + ↓ PE + ↑ PC ~ ↓ E + ↑ CL →(Inflation)

∴ Po = ↑ E + ↓ CL →(Deflation)

Po= ↓ CL + ↑ E →(Full-Employment)

Where'

T ~ ↓ Po + ↓ PC

T ~ ↑ E + ↓ CL

∴ ED = T (E = CL.

The Economics of Taxation and Extractive Policy (Taxonomics) could be controversial because it is always entangled with one of the contending issue in the definition of 'Politis' and 'Interest'.

As a result, every strata of the economy seeks to protet their different interest , just as the government's interest could also be paramount in making sur she(the government) maintains a ballanced approach in her fiscal plans, and reduce or eliminate fiscal deficit in her annual budget. However, the following analysis further explains these facts.

$$PE = \begin{bmatrix} P^{\circ} =< 20\%(100\%FB) \\ r^{\circ} =< 30\%(100\%FB) \\ PG =< 60\%(100\%FB) \\ t, s, d => 30\%(100\%FB) \end{bmatrix} \sim T = [\ FB = TR + OR$$

Where: $TR + OR = PG$

$\therefore GR = FB$

$FB = r^{e} + c^{e} + t + s + d$

If, $TR + OR < FB = BD$

$TR + OR > FB\ (BS)$

$P = \frac{GR}{FB} = GP > PG$

Where: $GR = P^{o} + r^{e} + c^{e} + t + s + d\frac{(PG)}{TR+OR} = 100\%FB$

The political economy of Taxation (Taxonomics) ideally should foster Social Equality and Economic Justice, irrespective of group interests in its intruiging ang manipulating ideologies on the backdrop of the Liberals or the Conservatives, especially if the above experiment and model become the paramount essence of any Extractive Public Policy in any economy (see Anderson, 1975 & 1986: Dye, 1972).

The Top-Bottom Tax Economics or the Bottom-Top Tax Economics debates had and has only led to recurrent debates, revolving around regressive cycle. The empirical solution for Taxation and Fiscal Science that can work for the government, the market, and the populace is the 'Bottom-Top-Top-Bottom-Horizontal Tax Economics(BTTBHTE)'. This Tax-code simply means 'a permanent cut on the price of government; a mandatory cut on the middle class and small business' tax; but a progressive and regressive tax cut on the upper class and big businesses on Extractive Policy Demand and Basic Need Approach Basis(PDBNAB) per fiscal year.

The PDBNAB Tax Economics is so important because it eliminates Social Inequality, fosters Job creation, improves Employment rate, reduces Government Deficit in short and long run, and facilitates Puritan Ethics(fiscal responsibility) in public financial management for the government and for businesses.

This New Tax Economics is illustrated as follows in Fig. 3.4.2-4 respectively

Fig. 3.4.15

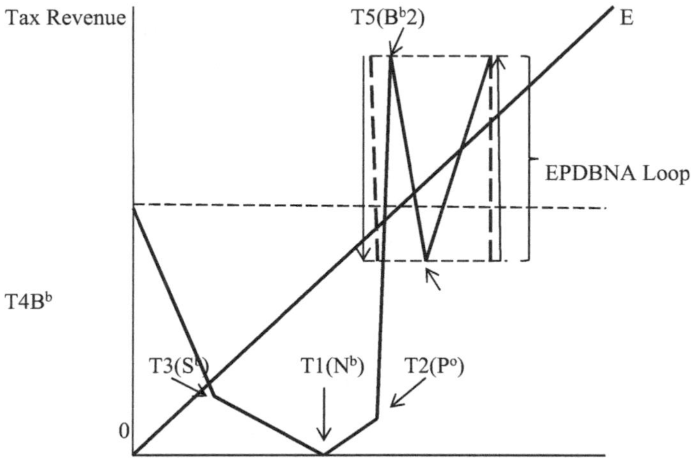

Fig. 3.4.16

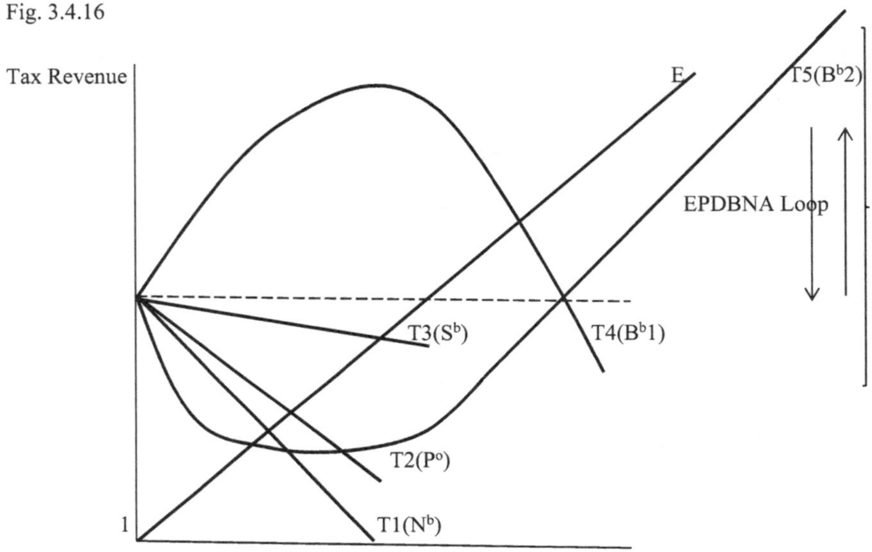

Fig. 3.4.17

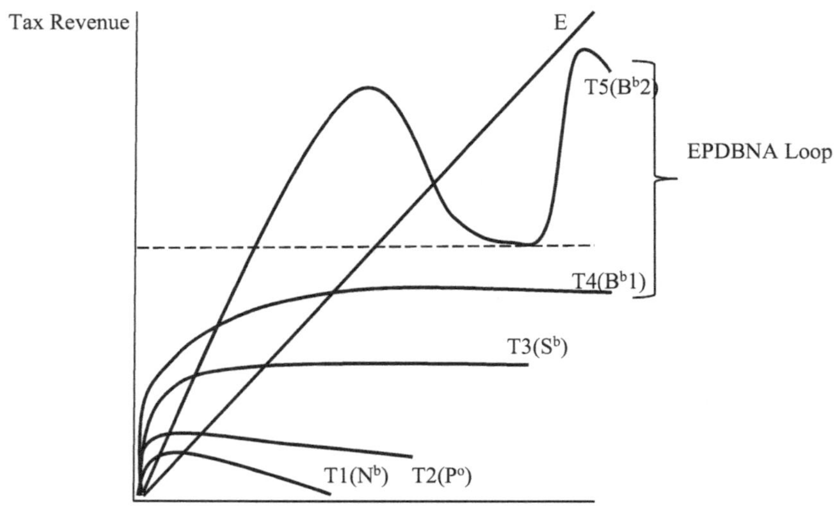

$\uparrow E = \downarrow I + \uparrow PC + \downarrow TR$

$\downarrow E = \uparrow I + \uparrow PC + \uparrow TR$

But,

$\uparrow P^{o} = \uparrow I + \downarrow PC + \downarrow TR$

$= BS\ (ED)$

$\therefore\ \Delta E = \Delta I + \Delta PC + \Delta TR$

$\Delta P^{o} = \Delta FB$

$\Delta E = \Delta I + \Delta PC + \Delta CL.$

The BTTBHTE (Tax-Code) envisage a dynamic bipartisan ideology that enhances growth and development for the economy at large, if it is adopted and pragmatically/judiciously applied to reducing or eliminating fiscal deficit and national debt.

The above graphical illustrations depict the same Tax-Codes and Principles known as BTTBHTE. The conventional equation or Economic Model (FB = GDP + GNP + T) had and has only facilitated the conventional economics questions of 'what' and 'when', but negates the 'how' question and solution to solving the fiscal deficit syndrom.

We should make no mistake to think that the above conventional economic equation fo fiscal budget should be completely neglected . This is because it facilitates the preliminart stages or experiment in understanding fiscal science, while we venture and embark on the metaphysical approch, model or experimental economic equation of the Economics of the price of government on fiscal science which is :

$$PE = \frac{GR}{FB} = GR > \frac{PG}{TR+OR} = 100\% FB\ (PG)$$

Therefore, a synthesis of economic equation for fiscal science is thus:

$$FS=\frac{FB=GDP+GNP+T}{PE=\frac{GR}{FB}=\frac{GR>PG}{TR+OR}}=100\%FB\ (PG).$$

The Economics of Taxation in its ideal sense is to combat Social Inequality and Economic Injustice, while the economy maintains growth and development, plus fiscal surplus in all ramification.

Adam Smith and J. B. Clark opinion on Full-Employment demphasized and militate against the existence of Labour Unionism and the raise in workers' Income(Austrian Economics). This is because they assumed that such factors would facilitate Inflation in concordance with the Monetariests ideology on Inflation.

However, John Keynese in his Alternatives on Full-Employment opined that 'Government Bailout and Stimulus Package' facilitate Full-Employment ad Economic Growth/Development.

Andrew Levison in his book 'The Full Employment Alternative' quiped that Tax incentives for new businesses, small business, and big businesses can facilitate Full-Employment, Economic Growth and Economic Development. It is important to note that Levisonn assumptions and recommendations could be workable, but to an extent could also have ripple effect on the price of governance (fiscal budget). As a result, governments seek for other alternatives that can work for the market and for the government.

But, ll to no avail have government ascertained such alternatives. Never-the-less, National Debt and Fiscal Deficits are are on the progressive increase per annum. In the same vein, David Ricardo and John Stuart Mill theories on Foreign Trade promises to facilitate reciprocal or absolute revenue for either economies in trade deals . Scientifically, such reciprocal or absolute benefits have eithere led to Trade Wars or Increases National Debt nd fiscal deficits.

John Stuart Mill, David Ricardo, David Hume, Adam Smith,. And Jeremy Benthan have opined that the theories and cannons of Taxation emphasizes the ability to pay taxes by the tax payers; the cst of services rendered by the by the government from the tax proceeds; and the benefits derived from government investment from the tax procedes are paramount in the political economics of eliminating social inequality and economic inballance through taxation.

Therefore, the above cannons should and must be the DNA and the blueprint of any economy's tax codes of BTTBHEA of the Economics of the price of government.

The concept 'Inflation' has its major strans that are divided into Price Inflation; Currency Inflation; and Monetary Inflation. By 'Price Inflation', it simply meaans 'the rise in the general price of goods and services in the econoy. By 'Currency Inflation' , it means 'the rise in the value of any currency in the foreign exchange or money market. By 'Monetary Inflation', it simply means the rise or increase in the value of money in ant domestic economy.

Critically, it is economically factual that not all Price Inflation leads to Monetary Inflation or Currency Inflation. But all Monetary Inflation leads to Price Inflation. Currency Inflation is determined by Economy's Bllance of Payment and Ballance of Trade, plus GDP, GNP, and Perchasing Power Parity (PPP) in an economy. Economically, such currency inflation is depicted as a zig-zag polygon alongside monetary and currency inflation as illustrated beloew, using the following equation, experiment and graph that should be considered as a common sense prospect in the Economics of the price of government.

Fig. 3.4.18

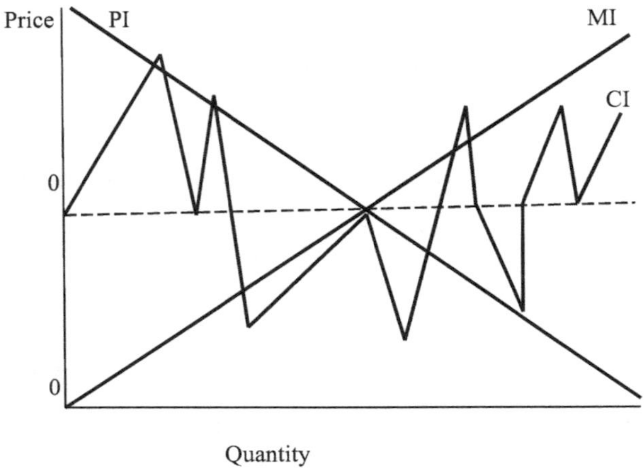

$\Delta PI \neq \Delta CI + MI$

But, $\Delta MI = \Delta PI$

$CI = \frac{BOP+BOT+GDP+GNP}{PPP}$

$\therefore \sum_{CI+MI}^{PI} + PPP = CL$

Where,

$CL = \frac{P^{\circ}+PC+PG}{GR}$

CI= Currency Inflation

MI=Monetary Inflation

PI= Price Inflation

Since, $CL = \frac{P^{\circ}+PC+PG}{GR}$, therefore the ideology of gender equality in workers Income as a partisan issue related to the Liberals in a Capital or Mixed Economy can only be implemented by business firms and industruies of such ideology is at the organisational and managerial economic advantages.

The above economic equation and graphical illustration mostly depicts the Economis of the price of government in an Indegenous Economy that has 90% National Products of her goods and services (GDP and GNP), especially in the midst and era of International Political Economic Sanctions that can hurt any Dependent or Inter-Dependent Economy.

If J. B. Clarks and Adam Smith quiped the cut in Workers' Income and the elimination of Trade Unionism as the recipes for Full-Employment that negates Inflation. John Keynese assumed that 'Government Bailout and Stmilus' facilitate Full-Employment without taking into consideration the problem of Inflation.

If, Andrew Levison quipped that 'Tax incentives for corporations would solve Unemployment issues, in respect to curbing economic inflationn in the economy. Then, we should critically apply some common-sense Economics in evaluating tthe above assumptions on Employment.

However, it can be considered that the above assumptions have failed to address the problem of Unemployment, especially when the fail to consider how their assumptions should work for the government and for the populace (for Washington, Wall Street, and Main-Street).

One important factor to be considered in political economic assumptions is to creat a ballanced approach in synthesizing prospects that must serve as a pragmatic paradigm and recipe for real life situations.

Never-the-less, the graphical illustration shows the relationship between the importance of the Economiccs of the price of government, Inflation, and Full-Employment in the midst of economy development.

Fig.3.4.19

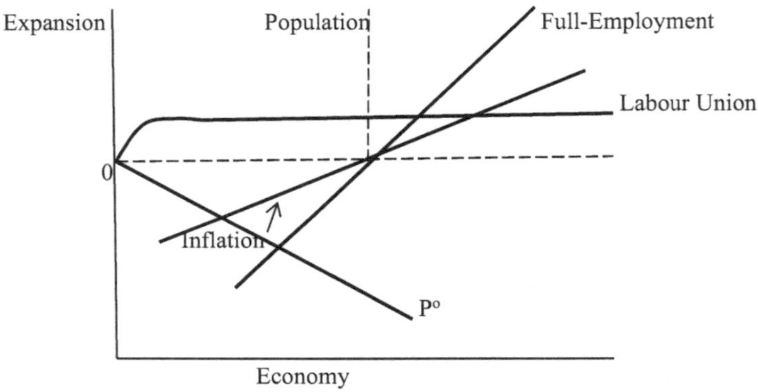

The above graphical illustration depicts that though Levison's assumption on Full-Employment Alternative affects (negatively) the price of governmence (fiscal deficit) at a short and long run, while Economic Inflation is inevitable, and Employment rate maintains a slower pace upward.

The Pº in the graph depicts that a permanent cut in the price of government would certainly strike apolitical economic ballance in solving the problem of Inflationn and Unemployment in a progressive pace (ceteris paribus).

Therefore, any assumption on Full-Employment Alternative that seeks to foster Economic Growth and Economy Development, must not neglect the essence of its effect on the inevitable and persisting growth in human population.

The effect of the price of government on Full-Employment Alternative can never be completely discussed or analysed if we fail to bring to bare the concept of the 'Blue-Colar and White colar Employment' dichotomy for some political economic reasons, and as a result, we tend to ignore the appropriateness of Labouur Demand on the basis of Specialisation and Professionalism.

Rather, measuring Employment rates are virtually based on creating jobs that facilitate 'Purchasing Power Parity' against the strata of an economy's labour-force demand and labour demography in respect to an objective and bipartisan Immigration Policy and it relevance in the labour force.

As a result of this dysfunctionality in the Labour Market and in Labour Economics, a Policy Labour Demand (PLDA) and Basic Labour Approach (BLA) should be adopted after a comprehensive survey on the economy for the appropriateness of Full-Employment Alternative.

The advancement of Vocational Education and Expertees, and Technological advancement in the Labour Market really affected the workforce positively and negatively. Therefore, these facts have to be considered in quest for Full-Employment Alternatives, where 'On-the-Job and Off- the-Job Training and Development' have become the cooperate responsibilities of the private and public sectors, most importantly on the innovative reinvestment in States' formal and informal Educational System by the government.

The above function of the government has become the matrix and manifest function of the State to meet up her challenges so as to contain K. C. Wheare's 'Centrifugal Forces' that tends to militate against Economic Growth.

Another important issueand concept to be taken into consideration in this researcch analysis is the issue of 'Economic Patriotism' on Full-Employment Alternative in line with Citizens' Diplomacy, and the International dimention of Monetary and Financial Management through 'Capital Jet and Transfer Pricing' that are paramount and sensitive in the area of the Economics of the price of government.

Hovever, Alfred E. Khan's Economics of Regulations is to a great extent advantageous and disadvantageous . But its advantages could be ideally harnessed if the Economics of the pricce of government is intertwined with the Economics of Regulations and Antitrust, when the essence of such regulations must benefit the economy (for the interest of the middle-class and under-class). See the graphical illustration and experiment for further analysis.

$$R = \sum_{MSM}^{CRM} + \frac{\Delta P^{\circ}}{\Delta PG}$$

$$\therefore E = R + \frac{\sum_{MSM}^{CRM}}{\Delta P^{\circ} + \Delta PG}$$

Fig. 3.4.20

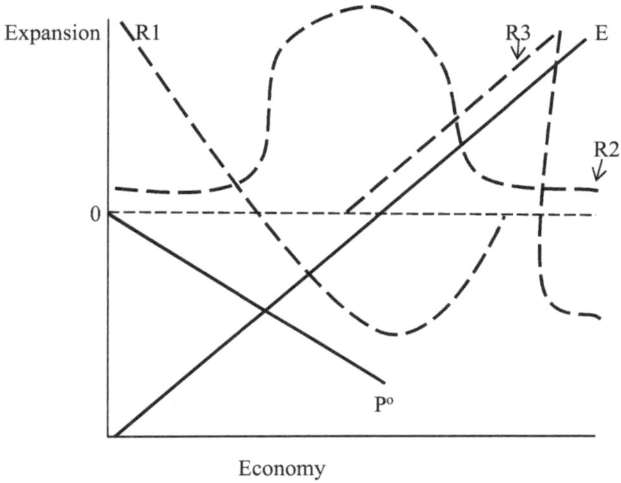

Where CRM=Comprehensive Rational Model

MSM= Mixed Scanning Model

P°= The price og government

PG= The price of governance

E= Employment (Full-Employment Alternative)

R1, R2, and *R3 + ED and P°* depict the economic prospect that the Economics of the price of government and the Economics of Regulation/Antitrust should be guided by a 'Comprehensive Rational and a Mixed Scanning Public Policy Models' prpounded by Sydney Weber and Amitai Etzioni respectively, at the beginig of every fiscal year in respect to the ethics of fiscal policy.

The essence of the 'Economics of Regulation/Antitrust' in this analysis is that we need to return to the political economic debates that are essential and that are against the economic theory and ideology of partisanship that have weakened the economy over decades in the aspect Regulation and Antitrust, since it plays a vital role in fostering job employment in the economy.

Therefore, the Economics of the price of government takes the opposite alternative against every partisan views. This is not because we tend to raise another ideological standpoint, but because it is essential know our history,while we try something new, especiallly when scientific prospects are of the essence.

However, the above equation and analysis would raise some fundamental criticism on the basis of giving a scientific prospect on the rate of Employment and Unemployment to which the Economics of Regulation and Antitrust should be applied. As a result, i empirically assert that the Economics of government negates 'Employment and Unemployment Rating' in percentage value, and as the yardstick or benchmark for embarking on Economic Rgulations.

Rather, the operational definition of the term 'Economy' in the literature review of this paper, should serve as the yardstick or benchmark to determining the application of the Economics of the price of government, and the Economics of Regulation/Antitrust or Deregulation in the economy.

It could be appropriate for Economists to set the rate of Employment/Unemployment or the rate of Economic Growth as the tools for determining the relevance or irrelevance the Economics of Regulations. But, it is politically and economically inappropriate because history can attest to this fact, and we should refuse to be traped by the urgly political economic equation of the past.

Therefore, empirically and experimentally, the following equation and analysis should serve as the benchmark and the yardstick for the determinant of the Economics of Regulation, nd the Economics of the price of government.

$$ED = \left[P^{\circ} + \sum \frac{W^{\circ}, E, SE}{F, ES, SR} = (ED)\right]$$

Since: $\frac{P^{\circ} = <20\%}{PG = <60\%} + FB = 100\%$

$$FB = \left(\frac{P^{\circ} = <20\%; r^{\circ} = <30\%; c^{\circ} = <60\%; s,d,t = >30\%}{100\% FB}\right) \rightarrow PE$$

$$\frac{FB = 100\%}{ED = 100\%}$$

$\therefore$ *det.* $ED = [P^{\circ} + FB + (ED)\%]$

det. $R = [P^{\circ} + FB\ (PE) + (ED)\%]$

Where,

E= Economics of Regulation/Antitrust

SE = Social Equality

E= Full Employment

W°= Wealth (individual, gruop, national)

ES=Economic Sustainability

SR= Self Reliance

F= Political Economics of Freedom

The experimental rationale behind the adoption of Sydney Weber's and Amitai Etzioni's for the Economics of Regulation and Antitrust emphasizes the necessity opined and quiped by Charles Lindblum and Herbert Simon (Theory of Bounded Rationaliy) that could lead to the recklessness and excessiveness of the 'markets', as antagonised through Marx's Social Thoughts.

Therefore, the Economics of Regulation and Antitrust had and would become a recipe for to curb the 'Bounded Rationality' and recklessnes in 'Washington', 'Wallstreet', and in 'Mainstreet'.

The issue and delinma of job creation, and the pproduction of goods and services of any economy has become a necessity in the 21st centuury states' poer and might. However, this issue have left economies (mostly Developing Economies) with the dilemma of 'Economy Diversification'.

Researchers and scholars are likely to question the adoption of the issue of 'Economy Diversification' in this research paper and analysis, especially when the focus of the '**Research Question 4**' is on the concepts of 'Employment, Economic Inflation, and the Economics of the price of gernmeent'.

But, it is so important to address the conceppt or issue of 'Economy Diversification' because the managers of any economy or the Economists have ignored this major Macro-Economic problem for far too long in the global economy.

No doubt that the creation of jobs and employment opportunities in the 21st century political economic system is harnessed by the private sector, but must through 'Responsive Public Policy formulation and implementation', based on 'Basic Resource and Basic Need Approaches' of Development Administration in striking a political economic ballance between the availability of jobs, and the availability to the provision of the needs and wants (goods and services) of the people in the domestic and global markets by the private sector and the government respectively where necessary, while the government maintain ' Puritan Ethics' in her fiscal and monetary policies.

This is because Public Expenditures that foster Economy Diversification are determined by the Extractive; Distributive; Redistributive; and Responsive Policies of the government , and as a result, the price of government and the price of governance play a vital role in the quest for government to embark on the political economic reality of diversifying an economy; providing jobs; and ensuring the availability of goods and services for her markets, and for development purposes in the 21st century.

However, the economic experiment and equation simplifies the above discusion, and give an empirical prospects on the aformentioned political economic issues.

$D = PE + \downarrow CT + \downarrow P^{\circ} + \uparrow EX(F, I, V) + \uparrow C + \frac{50\% NII}{50\% FDI}$

Where:

$D = \uparrow E + \uparrow GS\ (BRBNA)$

PE(r^e= <20%, c^e=<60%, t,s,d =>30%: 100%FB)

$$\therefore D = \frac{\Delta TR + \Delta NTR + \Delta P^{\circ} + \Delta FB(FY)}{PE}$$

$D = \uparrow E + \uparrow GS(BRBNA) + \uparrow EX + \downarrow I$

Where:

TR= Taxable Revenue

C= Investment in Basic Infrastructures

EX= Investment in all forms and levels of Education

CT= Corporate Tax

NII= National /Indegenous Investment and Businesses

E= Full-Employment

BRBNA= Basic Resources and Basic Need Approach of Government Inveatment

GS= Availability of goods and services in the economy and markets

D= Economy Diversification

FDI= Foreign Direct Investments

F,I,V= Investment in formal, informal, and vocational education and training.

The equation above draws and depicst a dichotomy between Developing Economies(mono-economies), and Developed Economies, while it gives a relative equation that fosters the prospects for economy diversification in the both economies.

A comprehensive and empirical approach to the knowing the basic need of any economy(BRBNA) can only determined through a coprehensive sampling techniques of public survey on the remarkable question of 'How can the government serve you?' and of which should serve as a determinant of fiscal and monetary policies of such economy per annum (fiscal year).

The Basic Resource(BR) Public Policy Approach can be determined through a comprehensive acknowledgment of the political economic 'Resources' of the economy , while the political economics of 'National Interest' are applied in harnessing or exploring such resources for a short or log term, especially in the midst of the growing human population of the Millenials in the economy.

Belowis the equation for the above discussion and sprospects:

$$D = \sum_{det.\,BRA=}^{det.\,BNA=} \left[\frac{\frac{PS}{FS}(FB)}{\frac{SAED}{FY} FB} \right] + PE\,(P)$$

Where:

BNA= Basic Need Approach

BRA= Basic Resource Approach

PS= Public/Government Saving

FS= Fiscal Year

SAED= The System Approach of Development Administration/Economy Diversification

PE= Puritan Ethics

P= The Economics of the Price of government.

The analysis of Economy Diversification brings us to the relationship between Economy Diversification; Economics of Regulation/Deregulation; Trade; and Job Creation in the 21st century political economy.

One of the most contending issues that are embedded in Economy Diversification is the issue of Economic Regulation and Deregulation. This has become a paramount factor because the quest for job creation and economic development have led the managers of economies into the initiation and the adoption of Foreign Direct Investment(FDI) as the last resort for job creation at the expense of 'National Interest', thereby leading to political economic dependency against the backdrop of 'Interdependency' as supposed, using the instruments of Economic Regulation.

The trend and metamorphosis of Public – Private Partnership (PPP) has become inevitably important in New-Public Administration/Management (NPAM); and in Development Administration in the quest for job creation in the 21st century.

But we should make no mistake to over-emphasize the role of Public- Private Partnership in Economic Growth in the current dispensation of the new age of political economics. However, the Economics of Public-Private partnership could be detrimental to the economy when the

'Private interest' suppasses 'National interest' (the host economy), especially when it is related t Foreign Direct Investment (FDI).

Therefore, the application of the Economics of Regulation and Antitrust must be on a sensitive dimension, when the Economics of the price of government is of the essence.

It is of no doubt that causes of National Debt or Economic Inflation are not necessarily Employment or Unemployment rates, but technically because of the psychological changes in human political and economic in proportion to the rising cost of technological and luxerious goods and services that are directly or indirectly manufactured or produced from the procedes of the government financial baiout just to maintain economic growth. As a result, Economic Inflation becomes inevitable in all spectrum of the economy.

The experiment below shows this political economic reality.

$$ND = \frac{S+L+PC}{GD+BD+HD+CD}$$

$$\therefore ND = \frac{\uparrow S + \uparrow L + PC}{\uparrow GD + BD + HD + CD}$$

$$But, \downarrow S = \downarrow det. ND$$

$$Since, det. ND = \left[\frac{S+L+PC}{GD+BD+HD+CD}\right]$$

$$\therefore P \propto ED + ES$$

Where:

ND= National Debt

S= Stimulu (government bailout)

L= government and private loans

PC= Firms production costs

GD= Government debt

BD= Business Debt

HD= Household Debt

CD= Consumer Debt

P= economics of the price of governmen

ED= Economy Development

ES= Economic Stability

Fig. 4.4.21

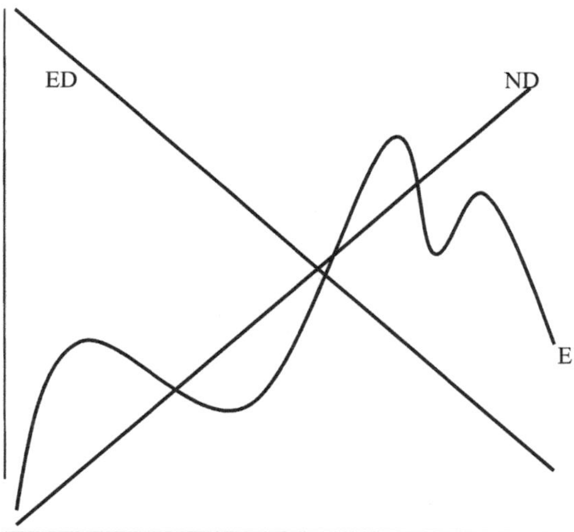

The concept of 'Fiscal Equithy' goes beyound government tax-code, and its scientific actualisaton or implementation lies within the caprisis ot the Economics of the price of goverment and the price of governance (if only it could be adopted and implemented).

One of the most important aspect of this research emphasizes the need to solving the yearnings and the quest for the equity in the raise of Income for government employees, and for private sector employees (the political economics of minimum-wage) in the midst of economic growth or in the midst of economic inflation/recession.

Many have argued that the Income disparity/ dichotomy has created controversies in the Labour Economics, therebye, creating an intellectual vacuum for an objective, but scientific solution to such controversy in the nearest future.

As a result, it is importantt that such economic experiment should be bipartisan, so as to avoid partisan atrgument or bias. To this effect, the following equation and experiment seeks to contribute to the economic problem of income disparity or dichotomy (minimum wage).

$Y = YU + YR$

Since,

$YU = P^{o} (PO + PS)$

$$\therefore \Delta PO \sim \Delta PS$$

$$\downarrow PO = \uparrow PS$$

$$det.YU = \left[\frac{50\%PO}{50\%PO}(100\%P^{\circ})\right]$$

Where,

$$\uparrow YU = det.\left[\uparrow BS \neq \uparrow GDP/GNP\left(50\%BS \sim \uparrow 50\%PS + 1\%PO\right)\right]$$

$YR = (T \sim P)$

When,

$YR = \downarrow P^{\circ} \sim \uparrow PC + YR$

$$\therefore det.YR = [BG]$$

$det.\ YR = [T + P]$

$det.\ M = [L \sim P + B] \sim MS + MP$

$det.\ MS = [P]$

$det.\ MP = [PC\ (BG)]$

BG= Business Growth

BS= Budget Surplus

T= Tax code for P

P= The Economics of the price of government

YU= Public sector income

YR= Private sector income

PO=Political officers' emoluments

PS= Public/civil servants' emoluments

MS= Public sector's minimum-wage

MP= Private sector's minimum-wage

M= Minimum wage

Y= Income

L= Government legislation on M and Y

Fig. 3.4.22 Public Income Analysis

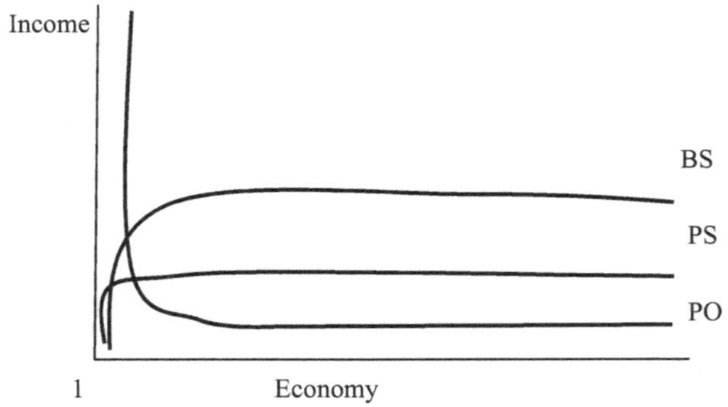

The essence of Minimum-wage and its determinant for a raise or for a cut in an economy would be innovatively attainable when we completely ignore its value on the basis of 'percentage (%)', and when we to a greater extent adopt or lean on the growth of 'government budget surplus', against the conventional GDP and GNP approaches for it raise or cut in the public sector .

In the private sector, the level of firms' production costs and business growth (GDP and GNP), should be a determinant to the raise or cut on minimum-wage. The following graphical illustration depicts the analysis and prospects for the Economics of minimum-wage (M).

Fig. 3.4.23 Minimum-wage analysis

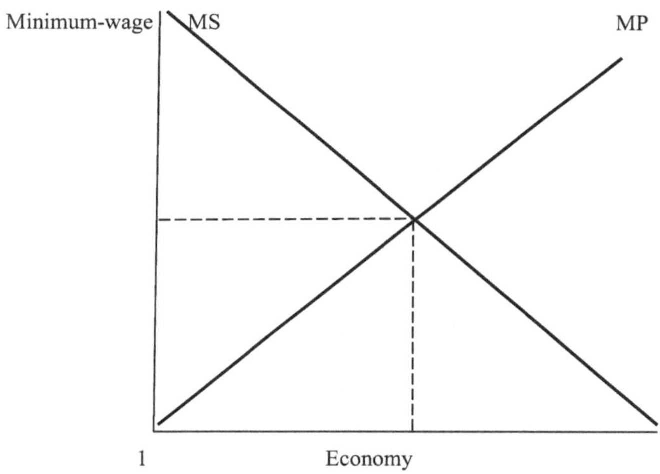

The graphical illustration for Minimum-wage (M = MS + MP) simply takes the basic 'demand-supply' like curves, depicting the dichotomy/ disparity in public and private minimum-wages (MS and MP).

In addition, the Economics of the price of government on the controversy surrounding the aise in the income of public/ civil servants' emoluments (PS), to a great extent presents us with a ddetrimental decision making choices (experimental economic choices) between the emoluments for political office holders, and the emoluments for public/ civil servants (government employees), if the quest for the raise on the latter becomes or posses a revolutionary threat to politics or to the economy.

Therefore, the following experiment and analysis serves as the scientific alternatives for the raise on government's employees' income.

$$P^{\circ} = PO + PS$$

But if,

$$\uparrow PO = \downarrow PS$$

$$\therefore \downarrow PO \sim \uparrow PS$$

Since:

$$P^{\circ} = < 20\% \, (100\% FB)$$

When,

$$P^{\circ} = (100\% \, PO + PS \, (P^{\circ}))$$

$$\therefore If, PO \sim \uparrow 60\% \left(P^{\circ}20\%\right)$$

$$PS \sim \downarrow 40\% \left(P^{\circ} < 20\%\right)$$

$$\therefore YU = \left(\frac{60\% PO}{40\% PS} \, (100\% P^{\circ})\right)$$

Or

$$PO \sim \downarrow 40\% \, (P^{\circ} < 20\%)$$

$$PS \sim \uparrow 60\% \, (P^{\circ} < 20\%)$$

$$YU = \left(\frac{40\% PO}{40\% PS} \, (100\% P^{\circ})\right)$$

Fig. 3.4.24 Graphical alternative for government's employees' income (minimum wage)

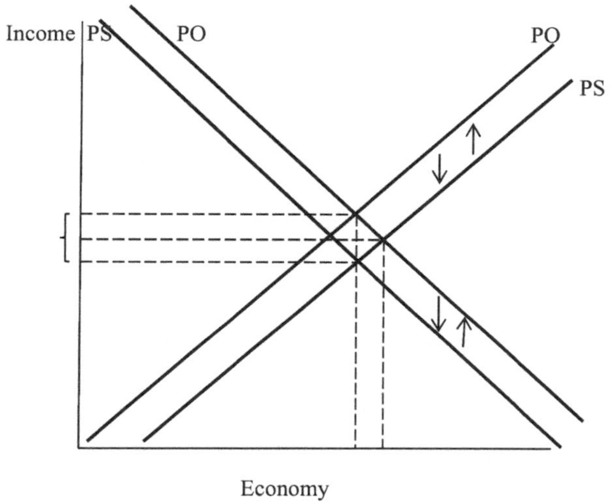

Though, Richard Musgrave (Income Theorist) assumed that the above analysis on the private sector would foster economic and social inequality. But J. B. Clarks, Adam Smith, Milton Friedman, and John Keynese quipped that the above prospect and analysis on Income and Minimum-Wage could lead to price and monetary inflation at the detriment of economic growth.

But, the disparity/ dichotomy of the above prospect and analysis and prospecton the private sector and the public sector income disparity definitely strikes a ballance in labour economics , while it eliminates Clark's and his contemporaries' assumptions without any resistance or shortfalls of Musgrave's assumption in a bipartisan model/ approach.

Conclusive, this analysis on the Econoics of the price of government or the 'Theories of the price of government' is a revolutionary economic experiment embarked upon to eliminate public financial waste and fiscal irresponsibility, while economic growth and economy development is attained, using pragmatic models.

Just as there are theories for 'everything' or laws that governs 'everything' in the universe, it certainly means that should be a theory for 'the price of government' to solving the problem of government fiscal irresponsibility in public financial management and in the economy in general.

This research would has and would certainly raise sophisticated and sceptical questions and arguments in the specialties of Decision Sciences towards a more perfect engineering of the economy that can be properly and ideally managed by the government for the entire benefit of the society.

A blinded and lopsided political economic assumption without concrete and empirical research and experiment leads to a vague contribution to the body of scientific knowledge for recurrent debate and provocative arguments that can escalate further problems , rather than proffer scientific solutions to the problems facing mankind.

However, this memoir, through it topic emphasizes the relevance of the research 'analysis and prospects' that is deducted from the research problems, rather than fostering negative criticisms voide of scientific solutions to the outstanding issues.

The content of this paper encompasses an experimntal economic analysis and prospects that promises to be solution- oriented, using economic models/ equation, and the basic tool of economic analysis if judiciously applied to real life situations.

The price of government has over decades and centuries been understood as one of the major determinant of economic development , and also as the major factor militating against fiscal surplus and fiscal responsibility in the process of managing the economy for man-kind and his inhabitants.

The most interesting aspect of this paper is to enhanvce a bipartisal political economic ideology is objective in solving the problem of the economy in a new and dynamic dimension that seeks to foster a revolutionary knowledge, ideology, and interest in poltical science and economics science.

The Economics and the theories of of the price of government is likened to the 'theories of everything' on the surface of this universe. This is because David Easton in his definition of 'Politics' quipped that 'politics is he authoritative allocation of values for the entire society'. By 'values', it simply means that 'everything' in the society tends to be valuable to every member of the society. Therefore, 'the price of government and governance' determines the 'price of everything'.

Never- the- less, researchers and scholars to a great extent might criticize this research paper on the basis of its model in the shift from the conventional/ traditional research approaches. But, it is arguably factual that any academic or scientific research are categorized into descriptive, normative, prescriptive, and experimental methods. As a result, the researcher through this paper adopts the Experimental (qualitative and quantitative) Method that seeks to proffer scientific and technical solutions to the research problem in its field of study and profession.

However, at the begining of the chapter four(4) of this paper (4.1), a recent and an empirical case study is presented and analysed, and this case-study serves as the scientific embodiment of the research prospect.

The beauty of any academic or scientific research begins when there could be an introduction of a new and fresh ideas adopted, and embarked u[pon by researchers, scientists or scholars in solving human problems pragmatically through the aplication of the research recommendations and prospects to real life situation.

As much as this paper ventures to experimentally analyse and give prospect to its research problem, it also correlates political economic variables in seeking for practical political economic solutions, by analysing and experimenting how the pric of government affects virtually 'everything' in the economy.

This research after it findings and experiment adaopt Walter Heller's 'Puritan Ethics' as an instrument or aparatuse to solving the problem of government fiscal irresponsibilty, of which would surely hurt the ruling – class and their interest in a short and long run, but benefits the greatest number of the people (Utiliterianism).

The bedrock to this research analysis and experiment is faclitated by the four(4) research questions formulated and validated by the researcher, tested using economic models and economic functions, with different graphical illustration and equation, depicting the enhancement of various economic theories and political theories put forward by several thinkers and writters as the living paradigm in Decision Sciences.

There is no doubt that this research would raise diufferent intellectual eyebrows in the field of political science and economics, because the revolutionary and progressive nature of this paper tends to question the status-quo in the history of polical economics research.

But what other scientific research could be more demanding and of necessity in this dawn of global financial crisis and economic recession than this experimental economic masterpies that addresses the root and solutions to the societal political economic problem our time?

This masterpiece is just about the pro nor anti Socialism/ Cpitalism, but it about what can necessitate the practical solutions to human problems through through the application of academic intellectual properties / scientific findings that must stand the test of time in theory and in practice irrespective of ideological argument that only seek to foster political or electoral agenda.

I have made the above assertion because it seems to an extent senseless to argue for, or against 'Socialism' or 'Capitalism', when the paramount goal of state/ government is to grow and develop the polity in all shere of human and natural lives.

Bipartisan politics makes politics interesting and dynamic. But, what makes the society grow and develop are objective are innovative human solution-oriented ideas that can change and imorove the state, its democratic processes, and the lives of the people overtime.

I have endeavoured to avoid and neglect emotion, sentiments, and bias in presenting the experiment and analysis of this paper, because it is of the ethical essence that pushing blames on personalities or groups in any academic masterpiece would never facilitate any Political Correctness(PC), and maintain professionalism in academic research. Therefor, this paper is experimentally for intellectual and critical minds to decifer the tools and processes to which the memoir is experimented upon.

It is of importance that we truly understand that the analysis and prospect of this paper can be applicable to all forms, systems, and organs of government as long as public financial and resource management is of necessity at any level of the economy.

One important fact about Economics is that it is dynamic, but not static in nature. As a result, it aids open – ended solutions to human problems at any givrn time and era, as long as long as its principle and living paradigm can be thought through, and applicable in solving human problems, irrespective of the fact that such economic decisions could be detrimental at a short – run .

Although, Karl Marx and his contemporaries for a revolutionary political economic change through 'Socialism', even though their approches were radical in nature. But the aftermath of their 'Manifestoes' brought the need for Capitalist – Socialist synthesis in the 20th and 21st century, that has changed the nature of political economics today.

This research manifesto (The Economics of the price of government), through absolute research ethics and civility in the spirit of its words, literatures, analysis, and experiment seek to foster a new intellectual orientation on how political economic ideas can never wax old, but that a cosistent intelleectual brainstorm can enancethe progress of man – kind's socio – economic and socio – political wellbeing when all hope seems to have been lost.

The researcher have adopted the concept 'Economy Development', instead of the concept 'Economic Development' as his Dependent Variable. This is because, the essence of the research is to cover a more comprehensive and broader spectrum of the human polity (the economy), rather than 'Economic Development', that ia 'part of the whole'.

This clarification has become necessary because there is always a neccessity in maintaing the 'rule of concord' in any researchable topic , so as to avoid 'sentence fragmentation' in lexical structure.

It is empirically unavoidable that 'politics' and 'protection (Secrete Service)' are inseperable , and are both likened to 'oil and water', of which they must be perfectly blended closer to 'perfection'. As a result, a permanent cut in the price of government and governance can never be over – emphasized in the development of the economy, so as to facilitate an appropriate fscal allocation to the issue of state security.

The Economics and the theory of the price of government can be likened to 'the mission of salvation and repentance from sin', of which its avoidance would definitely lead to political economic 'hell', just like the avoidance of Climate Change can lead to unsafe plan plannet for the nexxt generation.

I may not be a partaker in the management and administration in 'Washington' , but 'I must have thoroughly understudied the scientific activities on the the desk and blocks of the government objectively 'in theory and practice', and also in-line with their ideological differences, assumptions, principles, practices, formulation and implementation of political economic dynamics from Plato to Walter Heller et al., just like Karl Marx and Benneth Omalu did to change the phase of Global Political Economy, and Neorology respectively, as these intellectual revolution led to the foundation and laboratories of 'Socialism/ Communism, and Chronic Traumatic Encephalopathy (CTE).

The notion 'Money answereth all things, while it is the root of all evil' has become an arguable/ debateable statement that could hamper on the practical implementation of this research recommendations, especially to the cynics.

But one inevitable force in human history has been the spirit of unity towards the surrendering of personal/ group interest for 'National Interest', and this is why the greatness of the United States would forever remain unbreakable in generation to come.

We should make no mistake ti think that the Economics of the price of government can be effectively implemented without Constitutional Reforms that must take into pragmatic effect the degree to what aspect of the Economys' Constitution is always refered on matters of Political and Public Emoluments/ Remuneratins.

Never – the – less, It should be noted that the Theory or the Economics of the price of government seeks to enhance the reforms for the **'Graham – Rudman- Hollings Ballanceed Budget and Emergency Deficit Control Act of 1985'** that is void of any Constitutional debable clauses of the Act.

One of the major thornson flesh of Global Economiv Strategies has been 'Economic / Financial Austerity Measures', at the detriment of its 'Preventive Measures' that could have been the most prefered alternative in salvaging Global Political Economic Issues.

This paper ventures into further experimental analysis of the embedded issues and concepts that tend to be controversial in each of the research questions. As a result, these expanded analysis widens the intellectual horizon and scope of the research work, thereby, addressing many fundamental political economic issues.

The necessity for th choice and for the mothod of analysis in this paper is as a result of the need to scientifically innovate the the persisting normative methodology of contemporary postgraduate research in Decision Sciences that have only seek to discuss and manipulate data of already laid down events and failed policies of the govenment.

Previous research have only focused on 'how it is, and how it has been done', rather than focusing on 'how it can be done in a scientific and more better ways through pragmatic experment and analysis/ prospect'.

The research analysis of 'how things are done or were done' has led to research burdom in recent years of academic and intellectual bacnkruptcy. In my expereriences and quest to contributing to some basic scientific solution in solving the socio- economic and socio-political problem that have befall humanity, i have yearned to know what has really happened to researchable intellectual properties in the field f humanites, social, and managerial sciences in the recent past. Therefore, such intellectual curiosity has facilitated this academic masterpiece at this time of urgent global necesity.

Who could have ever thought that ' Football' would result to 'CTE' syndrom; Whocould have ever thought that the revolutionary work of Marx et al 'Socialism/ Communism' would trigger a global shift in polical economy; Who could have ever imagined that the seperation of 'Siammese Twin' could be possible through the intellectual application of the conventional knowledge in Neorology and Cardiology to transforming the Medical Sciences by Dr. Ben Carson?

These questions should trigger and ignite the left and the right hemispheres of our brain in understanding that the analysis, experiment, and recommendations in this research need an urgent attention so as to solve the recurrent economic epidemic and pandamic facing our economy today against further and future political economic catastrophy.

Economy Developent in the 21st century should not be 'ONLY' determined by GDP and GNP, or through 'Ballance of Trade/ Ballance of Payment', but also through 'Puritan Ethics

(The Economics of the price of government)', and by applying the political economics of 'Forward Thinking' against 'Backward Thinking'.

We should make no mistake to think that a 'Developed Economy' is void of a strong Military might. The Economics of the price of government takes into an esteem consideration the necessity for a comprehensive rational Military spending for National Interest per fiscal year.

The 'Positivists approach' to the study of political economy was adopted for this research paper , against the 'Conventional approach'. This is because the researcher needed to creat a dynamic and more liberal model for the experiment and analysis of this work.

Although, the 'Conventional Approach' is was not completely ignored as it aided it aided the different experimental equations. For example, we rather did not concentrateon the fact that 'when public investment excceds public savings , it equals exports.' Rather, we concentrated on 'how public investment and public savings are derived and how it affects fiscal deficit'.

One of the essence and beauty of 'Democracy' is to maintain financial accountability in public financial management, and this essence would not get better if the same essence is defeated and suffocated to 'death', through fiscal deficit and fiscal irresponsibility/ recklessness that emanate from 'Individualism and pluralism' at the detriment of 'Nationalism'.

This academic masterpiece is embedded with different symbolic abbreviations and interpretations at the end of every equation and experiment for simple understanding of the applieed economic models.

Therefore, the 'Economics or Theory of the price of government' is experimentally thus:

$$\boldsymbol{P = PE + ED + EG}$$

Where,

$$PE = \frac{P^{\circ} = <20\% + r^{\circ} = <30\% + c^{\circ} = 60\% + s,t,d = >30\%(100\% FB)}{FY}$$

$$PE \equiv \sum \left[\frac{W^{\circ}, E, S^{\circ}}{F, S^{\circ\circ}, S^{\circ\circ\circ}}\right] + EG = \frac{rGDP\tau + rGDP\tau - 1}{rGDP\tau} +$$

$$PE = \frac{P^{\circ} = <20\% + r^{\circ} = <30\% + c^{\circ} = 60\% + s,t,d = >30\%(100\% FB)}{FY}$$

Finally, 'The Economics of the price of government' can also be refered to as 'The theory of the price of government' as its comprehensive perspective of this academic expose, as it also recommends empirical solutions to the research problems.

3.4.2 The Postal Revenue and Federal Salary Act of 1967 Analysis

Summary of Action on HR 7977 (Postal Revenue and Federal Salary Act of 1967):

HR 7977 – Reported by House Post Office and Civil Service Committee (H Rept 722) Sept. 28, 1967.

HR 7977 – Passed, amended, by a 319–89 roll-call vote of the House Oct. 11. (For voting, see p. 72-H.)

HR 7977 – Reported, amended, by Senate Post Office and Civil Service Committee (S Rept 801) Nov. 21.

HR 7977 – Passed, amended, by an 85–2 roll-call vote of the Senate Nov. 29. (For voting, see p. 62-S, 63-S.)

HR 7977 – Conference report (H Rept 1013) agreed to by a 327–63 roll-call vote of the House Dec. 11 and by a 72–0 roll-call vote of the Senate. Dec. 12. (For voting, see p. 100-H, 66-S.)

PL 90-206 – Signed into law Dec. 16.

On Dec. 12 1967, the US Congress cleared the Bill for the President's mark: a bill (HR 7977) expanding postage on all classes of mail, raising compensations of government non military personnel representatives and laying out a changed disaster protection program for them. Last activity came when the Senate Dec. 12 acknowledged the meeting form of the bill (H Rept 1013). The President marked the bill into regulation (PL 90-206) Dec. 16.

The last variant of HR 7977 joined three measures - the Organization upheld Postal Income Demonstration of 1967 (HR 7977), a government cover bill (initially HR 8261) and a bureaucratic worker life coverage plan which was connected to HR 7977 in the Senate. The government take care of bill was put on the truly necessary income bill after President Johnson took steps to reject pay raises costing more than the planned sum. Pay expansions in HR 7977 surpassed his planned expenses by $63 million in monetary 1968. At the point when completely successful, the compensation arrangements were supposed to cost $2.6 billion every year.

The disaster protection plan was assessed to cost $35.4 million a year more than the current arrangement. In August, President Johnson had rejected a government protection charge (HR 11089) that would have cost $61 million a bigger number of than the current arrangement. The Organization's unique proposition had required an arrangement that would have cost $13 million a bigger number of than under existing regulation, yet in his rejection message, the President demonstrated that he would acknowledge an arrangement costing $30 million.

In a significant arrangement, HR 7977 laid out a commission to suggest compensations of judges. Individuals from Congress and top officials of the Presidential Branch at regular intervals. Future increments for other government representatives (aside from two programmed increments gave in HR 7977) would need to be authorized by Congress.

Postal Rates. HR 7977 expanded the expense of mailing a top of the line letter to 6 pennies from the current 5 pennies. It expanded the rate for airmail letters to a dime from the current 8 pennies. Both were compelling Jan. 7, 1968.

HR 7977 raised postage on all classes of mail to deliver from $885.9 to $914.6 million in new incomes when completely powerful, or a limit of about $90 million a larger number of than mentioned by the President. Nonetheless, the Mailing station Division assessed that it had lost impressive income in monetary 1968 because of Congress' postpone in establishing the bill. The Organization had suggested that specific rate increments produce results July 1, 1967. (For new rates, see diagram on p. 590.)

Significant discussion based on ordinary second rate class mass rate increments (primarily publicizing matter frequently alluded to as garbage mail). As cleared, HR 7977 expanded normal mass rates to 3.6 pennies least per piece from Jan. 7, 1968, until June 30, 1969. On July 1, 1969, the rate under HR 7977 was to go to 3.8 pennies least per piece for the initial 250,000 pieces sent, and to 4 pennies least for every piece for all pieces more than 250,000.

The House had set a solitary rate - 3.8 pennies, the Organization demand - powerful Jan. 7, 1968. The Senate had expanded the rate to 3.6 pennies Jan. 7, 1968, and to 4 pennies Jan. 1, 1969. The half year defer in the 4-penny rate was consented to in gathering. (For second rate class mail entryway action, see box p. 606.)

The incomes from the new rates, when completely compelling, were supposed to cover 72% to 75 percent of the expenses of dealing with the standard second rate class mass mail. Existing rates covered around 61% of the expenses.

Government Salary increases. Compensations for government regular citizen workers (counting authoritative and legal branch representatives) were helped 4.5 percent, retroactive to Oct. 1, 1967, as mentioned by the Organization. Mailmen, notwithstanding, were conceded an underlying 6-percent pay increment (likewise retroactive to Oct. 1), which was gone against by the Organization as being too exorbitant and unfair President Johnson had asked that all representatives get a 4.5-percent raise.

In a significant takeoff, the bill gave programmed future boosts in salary that wouldn't need Legislative activity. On July 1, 1968, mailmen were to get a 5-percent pay increment and nonpostal representatives were to get a portion of the distinction between their compensation levels and tantamount confidential endeavor pay levels (in light of the June 1967 Department of Work Measurements pay overview), however at the very least 3%. A third-stage change was to be made July 1, 1969, to close the "likeness hole" between pay rates of private representatives and Government laborers, including both postal and ordered workers. This was to adjust with Legislative strategy, laid out in a 1962 take care of bill yet not yet followed, that Administration representatives be paid a compensation equivalent to that which they would get in a practically identical confidential industry work. (1962 Chronological registry p. 355)

Pay Commission - *Another, and more questionable, part of HR 7977 was the foundation of a "quadrennial commission" to suggest paces of pay for judges, Organization leaders and Individuals from Congress. The commission was to incorporate three individuals designated by the President, two by the Leader of the Senate, two by the Speaker of the House, and two by the Central Equity of the US. Starting in financial 1969, the commission was to present its proposals to the President, who was to suggest in his Spending plan the specific paces of pay "he considers prudent" for government leaders, judges and Individuals from Congress. His proposals" could be either higher or lower than those of the commission, or he could suggest that compensations not be changed. The proposals: would produce results in no less than 30 days except if Congress either disliked all or part of them or sanctioned a different take care of bill. (Past compensation commissions have needed to present their proposition in bill structure, requiring positive activity by Congress.)*

Arrangements laying out the commission, emphatically moved by the House and apparently supported by the Organization, let Individuals free from Congress of the politically awkward assignment of raising their own compensations.

Nepotism Boycott - *Likewise remembered for HR 7977 was a boycott against nepotism which restricted public authorities (counting Individuals from Congress) from delegating or impacting the arrangement or advancement of family members in the office where the authorities serve. The boycott covered all authorities, including the President, yet didn't cover family members previously utilized. Be that as it may, the language of the arrangement* *didn't forestall an authority in one organization or place of Congress from trying to get work for a general in another office or house.*

The boycott had been put on the tab on the House floor when barely any Delegates were available. Rep. Neal Smith (D Iowa), creator of the arrangement, said his correction was pointed for the most part at conditions in more modest mail centers where "numerous postmasters... won't take a long-lasting representative except if their better half is on the qualified rundown." (The Related Press Feb. 20 expressed that somewhere around 42 Individuals from the 90th Congress as of now utilized family members on their Washington or home region staffs, every one of them paid with public assets.)

Arrangements

Title II - Government Pay. Expanded government regular citizen pay as follows:

Changed the current 20-level postal field administration pay timetable to a 21-level timetable and high level workers one compensation level (a 6-percent salary increase), retroactive to the main payroll interval in October 1967.

Truly 4.5-percent pay increments to workers subject to the General Timetable (grouped), Unfamiliar Help Official and Staff Timetables, Veterans Organization clinical and careful compensation ranges, Horticultural Adjustment and Protection province board pay plan, and Legal and Regulative Branch pay rates, powerful the main payroll interval in October 1967.

Given second-gradually work expansions in July 1968 - a 5-percent raise for postal representatives and a raise for different workers equivalent to one-a portion of the contrast between their compensation levels and practically identical confidential endeavor pay levels (in view of the June 1967 Department of Work Measurements pay overview), however at the very least 3%. (The vital changes for these different representatives were to be made by the President minus any additional official activity.)

Required a last, third-work change in July 1969 to bring all government regular citizen representatives' pay rates satisfactory with private undertaking, not set in stone by the June 1968 BLS review. (This likewise was not set in stone by the President minus any additional regulative activity.)

Expanded pay rates for leader levels III, IV and V from $28,500, $27,000 and $26,000 to $29,500, $28,750 and $28,000.

Laid out a supposed "quadrennial commission" to decide legitimate levels for Leader, Regulative and Legal pay rates once like clockwork, starting in financial 1969. The Commission was to present its suggestions to the President, and he was to suggest in his Financial plan the specific paces of pay for government chiefs, judges and Individuals from Congress. The proposals would produce results in the span of 30 days except if Congress sanctioned a different cover bill or rejected all or part of the President's arrangement inside that period.

Given that a previous Part (assuming that Congress who resigns and is thusly selected to a situation in the Presidential Branch might choose to get a common help retirement annuity dependent either upon his last essential compensation as an Individual from Congress or the last fundamental compensation of the named position. (The main individual impacted by the revision was previous Rep. Paul J. Kilday (D Texas, 1939-61), as of now an Adjudicator of the U.S. Court of Military Requests, under the Protection Division. Under HR 7977, he would get 80% of $33,000, or $26,400; any other way, he would get 80% of his last compensation as an Individual from Congress ($22,500), or $18,000.)

Denied any government or Region of Columbia official or worker (counting the President and Individuals from Congress) from selecting or suggesting for arrangement or advancement a comparative with serve in a similar office or division as the public authority. (The preclusion did exclude circumstances where the individual was an inclination qualified, like a veteran, and his being ignored would bring about the choice of a nonpreference qualified.)

Expanded the greatest measure of office cost reserves accessible for installment of staff individuals from previous Presidents from $65,000 per year to $80,000 with a restriction that no worker could get more than chief level II compensation.

Reached out to wage board workers the option to interest the Common Assistance Commission when their positions are renamed by their organization.

Approved government representatives, including wage load up and mailmen, to include time spent in genuine travel outside customary long stretches of work for extra time, Sunday or occasion pay purposes. Such travel was to be by the most speedy means practicable and to adjust to the obligations of the worker in question.

Title III - Pandering Notices. Approved the Postmaster General, upon demand by the recipient, to arrange the source of a "pandering notice" which the recipient considers "sensually stirring or physically provocative" to cease mailings to the complainant.

***Government PAY.** Likewise in his April 5 message to Congress, President Johnson expressed his "restored conviction" that the hole among Government and industry pay scales should be shut and proposed an arrangement intended to accomplish full equivalence in three stages. The President's suggestions incorporated an overall 4.5-percent pay increment for regular* *citizen workers compelling Oct. 1, 1967, with the excess similarity hole to be taken out in two stages by Oct. 1, 1969. The initial step was to produce results in October 1968 and the second a year after the fact. To close the hole in one year would require a typical boost in salary of 7.2 percent and would be financially unwise, the President said.*

For more than 100 years the guideline of likeness was applied to workers having their compensations fixed by wage sheets. Continuously a fundamental consider the assurance of other compensation scales, the rule was not authoritatively taken on by Congress until order of the Government Pay Change Demonstration of 1962 (PL 87-793). (Congress and the Country p. 1471; 1962 Chronicle p. 355)

The fundamental information for laying out equivalence among government and non-bureaucratic pay rates was gathered every year by the Department of Work Measurements (BLS) - a program started in 1960. To determine equivalence calculates the BLS got compensation information for obligations in industry which might measure up to explicit compensation grades in the general timetable (GS) utilized for government workers.

Archive Reference

"Postal Rates, Government Take care of Expanded in Single Bill." In CQ Chronicle 1967, 23rd ed., 08-589-08-609. Washington, DC: Legislative Quarterly, 1968. http://library.cqpress.com/cqalmanac/cqal67-1314834.

Archive ID: cqal67-1314834

Archive URL: http://library.cqpress.com/cqalmanac/cqal67-1314834

3.5 Experimental Analysis

The Experimental Analysis of this research shall be carried out using the experimental formular in Research Methodology 1.6 to testing the outcome of the results obtained from the distributed questionnaires, as analyzed in 3.3 of this research.

$$\Psi = \quad det.\left[\frac{\text{ꭗ} = \sum \text{ꭗʊ̊} \ (\text{ꟻ}) + \sum \text{ʊ̊ʊ̆} \ (\text{ɔ}) + \sum \text{ʊ̊ʊ̆} \ (\text{Ł})}{\dfrac{\Phi 1 + \Phi 2}{\text{Ƀ} = \sum \dfrac{}{1 + \ 2 \ \amalg \ 3 + \ 4 \sim (\text{Ŧ})}}}\right]$$

Where Ψ denotes US fiscal decisions for the economics of the price of government (fiscal decision). P is the Economics of the Price of Government - [PE(x): puritan ethics, ED(y): economic development, and EG(z): economic growth]. R denotes Rationality in decision making process. Φ1 dipicts personality, Φ2 depicts political behavior, φ 1 denotes Public Choice, φ 2 is Rational Choice, and φ 3 depicts Rational Action, 4 represents prospect theory of behavioural finance, and (Ŧ) dipicts the legal framework, Act, or Constitutional Framework for the Economics of the Price of Government. Adding up, gives a mathematical expression for this dissertation. Hence, the ∑P and ∑R (independent variables) are the determinants of Ψ (dependent variable) in the fiscal principles of decision sciences.

In an integrated level of equational model, this doctoral research work shall adopt the Experimental research design, explanatory and prescriptive analysis, deconstruction techniques, construtionists theory, and Experimental method in interpreting all the secondary qualitative and quantitative data (the United States' Constitution, and all Congressional Acts pertaining fiscal matters) that shall be adopted for this research presentation, analysis, and discussion. The other synthetic methods shall be the Reform-

Oriented method; Doctrine legal & non-doctrine legal method; Process-tracing method; and Comparative method cooperatively. The Onion Model of Conflict as propounded by Edgar Schein shall also be applied to the analysis of this paper.

Thus, the integrational experimental equation formulated and adopted in this paper is as follows:

Ψ = det. [ᛯ= ∑ᛯʊ̈̆ (ɹ)+ ∑ʊ̈̆ʊ̈̆(ɔ)+ ∑ʊ̈̆ʊ̈̆ (Ⱡ)

Ƀ= ∑ Φ1 + Φ2

Φ1 + Φ2 1 + 2 [[3 + 4 ~ (Ŧ)]

R = Φ1 + Φ2

[1 + 2 [[3 + 4 ~ (Ŧ)]

Ψ = f (Ŧ + R)

Where Ŧ (Ψ)...............k

Ψ = Ω π LEJ (πE)
= πE (Ω = QUADRENNIAL COMMISSION DECISIONS)
= PRFSA(1967) ΔP πEO
= P=ꝺ L J
πJ (Ω): PRFSA (1967)
= EO: QCD
= P= πLEJ = Δ(πE)
QCD(PRFSA1967)EO
= ΔP
Where: National Economic Interest ~ Personal and Private Interests
NEI ~ PPI

$\Delta NE = \Delta PPI$
$f(\Omega)$: PRFSA (1967) QCD
$= f(E) = \Delta P$

As: EO= Executive orders; P= The Price of Government; LEJ= Legislature, Executive, and Judiciary; QCD= Quadrennial Commission decisions; PRFSA= Postal Revenue and Federal Salary Act of 1967; NEI= National Economic Interest; PPI= Personal and Private Interest; Ω= Constitutional provisions for US. Fiscal Budgets.

Where Ψ denotes US fiscal Decisions for the economics of the price of government (fiscal decision). P is the Economics of the Price of Government - [PE(x): puritan ethics, ED(y): economic development, and EG(z): economic growth]. R denotes Rationality in decision making process. Φ1 dipicts personality, Φ2 depicts political behavior, φ 1 denotes Public Choice, φ 2 is Rational Choice, and φ 3 depicts Rational Action, 4 represents prospect theory of behavioural finance, and (Ť) dipicts the legal framework, Act, or Constitutional Framework for the Economics of the Price of Government. Adding up, gives a mathematical expression for this dissertation. Hence, the ∑P and ∑R (independent variables) are the determinants of Ψ (dependent variable) in the fiscal principles of decision sciences.

R denotes Rationality in decision making process. Φ1 dipicts personality, Φ2 depicts political behavior, φ 1 denotes Public Choice, φ 2 is Rational Choice, and φ 3 depicts Rational Action, 4 represents prospect theory of behavioural finance, and (Ť) dipicts the legal framework, Act, or Constitutional Framework for the Economics of the Price of Government. Adding up, gives a mathematical expression for this dissertation.

3.6 Discussion of Finding

Without any sentimental arguments, void of research unprofessionalism, our discussion of findings must be anchored on professional research precedent, as a result, we carefully chose the opinions of Daniel Kahneman as a foremost authority in the research area of fiscal decisions. You could call Daniel Kahneman the rare gem of fiscal matters in the 21st century. As a clinician, he impacted individuals who scrutinized the homo fiscal issues, the hypothetical thought that our monetary choices are in every case entirely sane, rather showing how individuals really decide. His experiences always changed the field, preparing for what's currently called social financial aspects. To get it and shape the framework, Kahneman claims that we want to comprehend the people who act within it first. Long-term friend Amos Tversky and Kahneman devoted their scholastic lives to the mental peculiarities around judgment and direction, laying out a better approach for contemplating human blunders in light of heuristics and predispositions.

Kahneman is recorded as perhaps of the main fiscal analyst alive today, despite the fact that he passionately denies this to be valid. While discussing in light of decisions, he utilizes a crucial word: clamor. "Judgment is considerably less steady and a lot noisier than the vast majority think," he says. "I call commotion an undetectable issue. Instinct feels simply the equivalent when it's off-base and when the issue lies when it's right."

Moreover, Kahneman alludes to as manufacturing plants of choices and decisions, it is vital to diminish commotion. "In the event that you have various individuals who will arrive at a choice together, the sound decrease strategy is to have all of them record their response before the conversation," he says. "Since in any case the primary individual who talks has an excessive amount of impact."

There's one more regular safety buffer concerning judgment and dynamic in associations, which Kahneman alludes to as inborn inclinations. Individuals who ascend in an association are probably going to be positive thinkers. He adds that these individuals are typically more ready to face challenges too. "They're individuals who finish things," he says. "A couple of choices are effective, and they advance you further."

To comprehend independent direction, individuals need to all the more likely figure out their own reasoning first. Kahneman's exploration on what he'd later call the two frameworks, began with an a surprise in a research center, and oddly, with an eye.

"It's the absolute best proportion of mental exertion," he says. Kahneman demands it's superior to pulse, circulatory strain or skin conductance, alluding to the recognition of a guinea pig's understudy as the "most rich discoveries" he at any point ran over. At the point when she was posed an inquiry, her understudy expanded and contracted. In any case, unintentionally, he saw that when she was essentially conversing with someone sitting in the lab, nothing occurred. "Having a discussion is more straightforward than recalling your telephone number," he says. "I turned out to be extremely keen on exertion from that sort of perception. What is demanding, what is easy."

Kahneman later fostered the two frameworks to portray our psychological life. Framework one characterizes the easy, instinctive piece of our reasoning while framework two makes sense of the sort of focus that includes exertion. "My #1 model is making a left transform into traffic," he says with energy. "You'll stop the discussion. While you're investing energy into a certain something, you can't do different things simultaneously. Framework one doesn't have that limit." On the grounds that throughout everyday life, we advance naturally and apply it.

While simply deciding, we have the decision between those frameworks. "You could run or you could walk," Kahneman says. "Our psychological life is like strolling gradually. Mental life is simple, generally. We can focus, yet generally we could do without to, we stay away from it." "Shrewd individuals who can take care of numerous issues easily can pull off being more languid," he adds.

Kahneman shares some counsel on the best way to go with significant choices. "You ought to dial back and get guidance from a specific sort of individual. Someone who likes you yet couldn't care less about your sentiments. That individual is bound to offer you great guidance."

As a clinician, Kahneman explores where our convictions come from. Particularly while perusing the news, being defied with strict clash and separation and the emotional results of political decisions, his contemplations wander back to the brain research of single inquiries. Abstractly, it seems like you trust in something since you have the contentions for it," he says. "Yet, it works the opposite way around. You put stock in the end, and afterward you make supporting contentions. That is central.

For what reason truly do individuals have faith in these ends? Halfway on the grounds that individuals we love and trust put stock in a similar end. Kahneman refers to this being as "genuinely sound." It's mentally cognizant, however not as in it gives strong proof. According to casting a ballot, he, is sincerely determined and one of the most impressive feelings is outrage. It drives individuals to search out a common foe.

Kahneman shares an account of his young life in Paris, where he grew up Jewish in The Second Great War. "I'd gone out to play with a companion and I had my sweater with my star on it," he says. He'd turned it back to front, so nobody would see it. "I saw a German warrior in a dark uniform, and I realize that those were totally the most exceedingly terrible," he proceeds. "We strolled towards one another and afterward he called me. I was worried about the possibility that that he would see the star inside the sweater, yet he didn't. He embraced me and showed me photos of a young man. Also, he really gave me some cash."

Both headed out in a different direction, however the meaning of the collaboration stays with him right up to the present day. "It showed the intricacy of individuals. He would have killed me effectively, however in that specific situation, he was only a dad of a young man." Indeed, even in our current society, Kahneman realizes that society has no authentic memory. All sides utilize strong profound triggers, they address individuals' apprehension and direct their resentment towards the unexplored world.

At any point, we might reach a point where the errors of the past can be stayed away from in future? Kahneman says that he's a timeless worrier and not ready to take care of such issues. However, as he says, this isn't his work. "I'm just a clinician," he says. He puts on his dark coat once more, opens his umbrella and steps out into the deluge. In this unique circumstance, it's certainly not a sluggish choice.

From our findings, the implementation of the economics of the price of government requires the strict adherence to the US constitution via the different Constitutional provisions stated in the 3.2.2 and 3.2.3 of this research. This is because the United States is a Constitutional democracy and practices Constitutionalism in words and deeds, except for the technicality of courts' decisions that might be politically motivated sometimes. However, the several Constitutional amendments and several Acts of 1960s through 19870s in regards to the implementation of the economics of the price of government by objective legislative and judiciary interpretations empowers the the US President for it's implementation by Executive Order or through the Quadrennial Commission.

CHAPER 4

CONCLUSION AND RECOMMENDATION

4.1 Conclusion

The implementation of the theory of the Price of Government is beyond the enhancement of fiscal justice like the adherence to the concept of justice can be interpreted by the district courts. Just like the duty of the Appellate courts and the Supreme Court is to interprete legal statutes according to judicial philosophies of the Judges and Justices, so is fiscal decisions are to be made in line with constitutional provisions. Just the Medical doctors and Justices spend time on researching on living paradigms to profer medical solutions and Legal decisions to everyone challenges before them, in the same manner should fiscal decision makers spend judicious time in knowing what the Construction says in regards to the theory of the price of government.

The Postal Revenue and Federal Salary Act of 1967 through the establishment of the Quadrennial Commission give the Federal Executive in the person of the President of the United States to invoke executive order in cutting the cost of public emoluments and remuneration without the concent of the Congress. Therefore, it means that the 14th Amendment (Section 4) is not the only Constitutional provisions that gives the President an exclusive right of fiscal matters.

It is to be critically reviewed that all the fiscal Acts and Constitutional amendment of 1970's reflected most of fiscal responsibilities of the Congress delegated to the Executives, thereby undermining the efficacy of a Republic for Democracy (a paradigm shift from the founding fathers' intentions due to fiscal dynamics. We should make no mistake to misunderstanding the price of government (Political Emoluments and Remuneration) to the Price of Governance (fiscal or budget appropriate), as the former is at the mercy of the Executive through the Quadrennial Commission of four fiscal year review (one Presidential term and administration as stipulated by the US Constitution). While the latter is at the mercy of the Congress and the Executive concurrently.

Nevertheless, the actualisation of the Economics of the Price of Government is not for the scoring of political points from the two sides of the political isles, but embracing the objective fiscal facts that works for fiscal democracy, as I believe that America loves to always be the first to set a democratic standards for other democracies to follow suit.

The implementation of the price of government despite the dictates of the US constitution, and the strict adherence to Constitutionalism seems bounded to political parties' ideologies -oriented, as the findings from our studies have shown ND indicated that the Republican Party (GOP), and the Arms of the federal government teal towards the implementation of the purpose and recommendations of this research. While their Democratic counterparts find it difficult to comply with the fiscal demands of the 21st century and beyond.

Therefore, this research outcome shows that if this research is published, it can shapen the electorates' choice in general elections (if the citizens and electorate are fiscally responsibility prone); as the suggestion further Postdoctoral research topic shall be entitled *The Theory of the Price of Government and Public Choice (An Experimental Analysis of the Electorates in the United States of America* in order to investigate the outcome of this research from the electorates' perspectives; as it is also a major determinant to the purpose of this research if we can recall and understand the principles or doctrine of Plato's Leviathan vs. Dragons.

4.2 Recommendations

According to Hans Morgenthau, political Economic Resources are globally scarce in Internation Politics. So is government financial resources, therefore, it is wise to advocate for for fiscasl responsibility or 'Puritan Ethics' in the 21st century political economics.

The recomendationsof this research is derived derived from the four (4) research question as its bedrock to addressing the prospects in line with research problems.

This is because 'The price of government' as a constitutional issue in some economies, and as a 'genesis' of the legal and administrative problem embeded in public sector economics. But, for the economies that have exclusively made the provision of political and public emolument/ remuneration a constitutional framework, they are of greater advantage of implementing the 'Economics of the price of government'.

The 'price of government' recommended for Economy Development should be less than tenty percent of he fical bdget, per year (<20%:100%FB/ FY). 'The price of government' MUST and should be embeded in the Constitution of the State. Its increase should be at a 1% pace per 50% increase of Budget Surplus, while the Capital Expenditures increases on the basis of 'Fiscal Demeand and Basic Need Approach (FDBNA) per 50% increase on fiscal surplus.

The concept 'The price of government' should be theoretically and practically differentiated from ' The price of governance', while, the totality of the entire fiscal budget should denote the dichotomy between 'Recurrent Expenditures' and 'Capital Expenditures' in their priorities respectively.

The concept 'Puritan Ethics' as propounded by Walter Heller denotes the ideal applicability of 'Fiscal Responsibilty' in Public Financial Management on the basis of 'Zero – Sum – Budgeting Principles' that foster Economy Development.

The experimental recommendation for the Economics of the price of government on 'Government Investment; Government Savings and Debt Servicing (t, s, d)' of the fiscal budget should maintain the 'PAYGO(pay as you go principl of public financial doctrine) in order to in other to strike a fiscal ballance in the afformentioned issues of government expenditures during fiscal budget surplus.

The fiscal recklessness , irresponsibilty, and harlotary in application and adoption of 'Supplentary Budget' doctrin by government is a detrimental fiscal practice that could ever be thought of and adopted in fiscal science and practices. Therefore, it is highly prohibited in all ramification, if the actualisation of Economy Development is a necessity, nay in the Economics of the price of government.

The fiscal policy of 'Debt Ceiling' in the management of 'Fiscal Government Debt' has only endangered the actualisation of 'Budget Surplus', as much as such fiscal politics lacks a constitutional framework , but enhances a persisting partisan politics of government – shutdown.

Therefore a Constitutional Framework on the backdrop of 'Puritan Ethics' would facilitate 'Fiscal Responsibility'. This is because the Economics of the price of government to a greatest extent the urgent need for 'Zero – Sum Budgeting Principles'.

David Osborne and Ted Gaebler in their book 'Reinventing Government' emphasized that one of the tools for efficiency and effectiveness in the management of both human and financial resources in private and public organisations is the avoidance or eliminiation of unnecessary portfolios and personnels in administrative and management processes .

It is necessary that we understand the fact that creating and establishing new and unnecessary portfolios in public administration is 'NOT' the most dynamic way to to creating publlic sector jobs. Rather, it saps public fund and revenue its micro and macro processes, and has a critical and crucial effect in public financial management .

We should make no mistake to contradicting the process of hiring the intellectual properties for advisory and assisting roles in governance versus congesting the public sector with unnecessary personnels as public sector job creation alternative. Rather, the Economics of the price of government should be highly considered in the aformentioned processes. This is because every wasteful public financial resources stop the chain and flow of Economy Development.

As a matter of 'Political Correctness' , it is important that we understand that 'he who fails to plan, plans to fail' , and this assertion is politically and economically correct and factual. The causes of National Debt is not necessarily because of Unemployment, and the causes of Unemployment is not because of the increase in workers' minimum – wage (Austriaan Economics). But it is technically it technically because there is a psychological change in human political behaviour and consumer behaviour in proportion to the rising cost of technological and luxerious goods and services that are mostly manufactured from the proceeds derived from government bailout to keep businesses affloat. As, a result, Economic Inflation and Debt hit all spectrum of the economy.

Therefore, it generally acceptable and generally proven that government bailout is only an 'Austerity Measure' that leads to Economic Reccession and Depression. But, 'Preventive Measures' against 'Austerity Measure' is the 'Economics of the price of government.

Strategic Trade Wars can enhance the strategic interest of Nations and their Economic Growth(latent and manifest). But it definitely does not eliminate Fiscal Deficits/ National Debts for Economy Development.

The political Economics of Taxation has over decades has been on the arguable disagreement on the 'Top – Bottom' or 'Bottom – Top' approaches or ideologies that only enhance ideological norms of partisan divide. But, it (the Economics of Taxation) can be ideally or objectively engineered if it takes the 'Centrer – Circle – Approach (CCA), where the fiscal cuts begins with the 'government', before a considerable cut accross other parts of government expenditures.

It is of neceessity that this research would trigger some sort of criticism on the issue of an increase in the income of civil/ public servants as a result of Musgrave's Income Theory and Adolf Wagner's Publiv Finance Theory. But, at the same time we should make acritical consideration of Jackwiseman's and Alan Peacock's 'Displacement Theory' quipping that government has the obligatory responsibility on Adolf Wagner's propositions and assumptions, but that the major focus should be on the 'Sources' of government revenue in proportion to such government responsibilities, of which should guide government expenditures.

Therefore, the raise in public servants'/ civil servants' income should maintain the Economics of the price of government as experimented in this research paper rather than basing such incrase proportionate to GDP and GNP growth. This is because the GDP and

GNP add little or nothing to government revenue most times, especially when Economic Growth is proportionate increase in National Debt.

But, the raise in the private sector workers' income in the midst of Economic Growh is 'Politically and Economically Correct' and appropriate. Lete's make no mistake to hope that the elimination of 'Carried Interest Loopholes' in fiscal science can or will totally solve the political economic intrigue of Taxation or Fiscal Loopholes/ Deficits.

This is because the issue of 'Public Pension' for ex – political ioffice holders or administrators has become a contending in fiscal science and in public financial management. Therefore, we must take into consideration the concept ' Public Pension' in its recommendation by asserting that 'public pension' is not excluded in government 'Recurrent Expenditures' as illustrated in this memoir.

The researchrer has adopted a 'percentage (%)' value against a fixed or assmed monetary value in the experiment of this paper because he hopes that this paper can be helpful to other economies apart from the U.S Economy , of which such Economies maintain different monetary values in their fiscal plans.

The following are the scientific recommendations of this research dissertation:

1. To foster a national fiscal articulation, aggregation, and orientation of all nationals in the United States (from Junior High School through to the University levels) in order to inculcate the necessity to maintain fiscal responsibilities at home and in public affairs.

2. A paradigm shift in the reorientation of political party ideologies from mere sociopolitical and socioeconomic sphere to the specifics (fiscal sphere) for a better and a dynamic fiscal engineering in the United States of America.

3. A national campaign, education, and reorientation of the grave effect of the national debt to the electorates', nationals, and the populace in America in order to foster a paradigm shift in their electoral preference during general elections.

4. A proper reorientation for the political class on the difference between the fiscal economics of *Nature vs. Nuture* as elaborated by Plato in his Republic of Stoicism, Epicureanism, and Cynicism.

Ironically, the US Dollar bank notes is engraved with a sacred word *In God We Trust* , as this bank notes are the symbol of America's fiscal revenue and expenditures. What ever went wrong that she (America) departed from the aforementioned sacred watchword?

The United States of America is known to be a nation guided by laws, and these laws are written in the constitution by the founding fathers, anended by the government that came thereafter, concurrently with the original framework as the DNA to which can be amendable by *We the People,* having its origin from the Holy Scriptures, and as the Holy Scriptures records as follows:

Joshua 1:8 (KJV):

Joshua 1:8 This book of the law shall not depart out of thy mouth; but thou shalt meditate therein day and night, that thou mayest observe to do according to all that is written therein: for then thou shalt make thy way prosperous, and then thou shalt have good success.

Exodus 15:23-26 (KJV):

Exodus 15:23 And when they came to Marah, they could not drink of the waters of Marah, for they were bitter: therefore the name of it was called Marah. 15:24 And the people murmured against Moses, saying, What shall we drink? 15:25 And he cried unto the LORD; and the LORD shewed him a tree, which when he had cast into the waters, the waters were made sweet: there he made for them a statute and an ordinance, and there he proved them, 15:26 And said, If thou wilt diligently hearken to the voice of the LORD thy God, and wilt do that which is right in his sight, and wilt give ear to his commandments, and keep all his statutes, I will put none of these diseases upon thee, which I have brought upon the Egyptians: for I am the LORD that healeth thee.

Deuteronomy 28:1-14:

Deuteronomy 28:1 And it shall come to pass, if thou shalt hearken diligently unto the voice of the LORD thy God, to observe and to do all his commandments which I command thee this day, that the LORD thy God will set thee on high above all nations of the earth: 28:2 And all these blessings shall come on thee, and overtake thee, if thou shalt hearken unto the voice of the LORD thy God. 28:3 Blessed shalt thou be in the city, and blessed shalt thou be in the field. 28:4 Blessed shall be the fruit of thy body, and the fruit of thy ground, and the fruit of thy cattle, the increase of thy kine, and the flocks of thy sheep. 28:5 Blessed shall be thy basket and thy store. 28:6 Blessed shalt thou be when thou comest in, and blessed shalt thou be when thou goest out. 28:7 The LORD shall cause thine enemies that rise up against thee to be smitten before thy face: they shall come out against thee one way, and flee before thee seven ways. 28:8 The LORD shall command the blessing upon thee in thy storehouses, and in all that thou settest thine hand unto; and he shall bless thee in the land which the LORD thy God giveth thee. 28:9 The LORD shall establish thee an holy people unto himself, as he hath sworn unto thee, if thou shalt keep the commandments of the LORD thy God, and walk in his ways. 28:10 And all people of the earth shall see that thou art called by the name of the LORD; and they shall be afraid of thee. 28:11 And the LORD shall make thee plenteous in goods, in the fruit of thy body, and in the fruit of thy cattle, and in the fruit of thy ground, in the land which the LORD sware unto thy fathers to give thee. 28:12 The LORD shall open unto thee his good treasure, the heaven to give the rain unto thy land in his season, and to bless all the work of thine hand: and thou shalt lend unto many nations, and thou shalt not borrow. 28:13 And the LORD shall make thee the head, and not the tail; and thou shalt be above only, and thou shalt not be beneath; if that thou hearken unto the commandments of the LORD thy God, which I command thee this day, to observe and to do them: 28:14 And thou shalt not go aside from any of the words which I command thee this day, to the right hand, or to the left, to go after other gods to serve them.

The conclusion of the matter is, if the foundation be destroyed, what can the righteous do? The United States of America should fear the Lord her God, and keep His Commandments forever in order to enjoy fiscal prosperity and success.

RELEVANT BIBLIOGRAPHIES

Acemoglu, Daron and Robinson, James A. (2013). Why Nations Fail: The Origins of Power, Prosperity, and Poverty. London: Profile Books Ltd.

Abels, Michael L. (2018). Policy Making in the Public Interest: A Text and Workbook for Local Government. New York: Routledge.

Adda, Jerome, & Cooper, Russell (2003). Dynamic Economics: Quantitative Methods and Applications. Massachusetts: The MIT press.

Adelman, Clem, (1984). The Politics of Ethics and Evaluation. New York: St. Martins Press.

Allis, Janine (2016). The Accidental Entrepreneur: The Juicy Bits. Australia: John Wiley and Sons.

Allen, Tom (2013). Dangerous Convictions: What's Really Wrong with the US Congress. New York: Oxford University Press.

Almarzoqi, Raja M., Mansour, Walid, & Krichene, Noureddine (2018). Islamic Macroeconomics: A Model for Efficient Government, Stability and Full Employment. New York: Routledge.

Anderson, D. (2015). It's Not Rocket Science: 4 Simple Strategies for Mastering the Art of Execution. New Jersey: John Wiley & Sons.

Anderson, R. L., and Bancroft, T. A. (1952). Statistical Theory in Research. New Yok: McGraw- Hill Book Co., Inc.

Aronson, Elliot; Ellsworth, Phoebe C.; Carlsmith, J. Merril; & Gonzales, Marti Hope (1990). Methods of Research in Social Psychology. New York: Mcgraw-Hill Publishing Company.

Ashton, Michael (2016). What's Wrong with Money? New Jersey: John Wiley and Sons, Inc.

Audretsch, David B. (2015). Everything in its Place: Entrepreneurship and the Strategic Management of Cities, Regions, and States. New+ York: Oxford University Press.

Auerswald, Philip E. (2017). The Code Economy: A Forty-Thousand Year History. New York: Oxford University Press.

Awofeso, Olu, (2005). Element of Public Administration. Lagos: Mcgrave Academic Resource Publications.

Axelrod, Robert (2015). Structures of Decision: The Cognitive Maps of Political Elites. New Jersey: Princeton University Press.

Axilrod, Stephen H. (2013). The Federal Reserve: What Everyone Needs to Know. New York: Oxford University Press.

Baert, Patrick (2015). The Existentialist Moment: The Rise of Sartre As A Public Intellectual. Massachusetts: Polity Press.

Baker, Eric (2017). Barking Up the Wrong Tree. New York: Harper Collins Publishers.

Ball, Alan R. (1988). Modern Politics and Government. New York: Springer

Bambra, Clare (2011). Work, Worklessness, and the Political Economy of Health. New York: Oxford University Press.

Bartels, M. Larry, (2008). Unequal Democracy: The Political Economy of the New Gilded Age. New Jersey: Princeton University Press.

Bauman, Zygmunt, & Obirek, Stanislaw. (2015). On the World and Ourselves. Massachusetts: Polity Press.

Bauman, Z., Bauman, I., Kociatkiewicz, J., & Kostera, M. (2015). Management in a Liquid Modern World. Massachusetts: John Wiley & Sons.

Baumol, William J. (1961). Economic Theory and Operations Analysis. New Jersey: Prentice- Hall, Inc.

Beardshaw, John, & Palfreman, Davıd (1990). The Organisation in its Environment. London: Pitman Publishing.

Berger, Peter L, and Luckman, Thomas (1966). The Social Construct of Reality: A Treatise in the Sociology of Knowledge. New York: Doubleday and Company Inc.

Bernanke, B. (2013). The Federal Reserve and the Financial Crisis. New Jersey: Princeton University Press.

Bernanke, Ben S. (2015). The Courage to Act: A Memoir of a Crisis and its Aftermath. New York: WW Norton & Company.

Berzin, Stephanie, & Camarena, Humberto (2018). Innovation from Within: Redefining How Nonprofits Solve Problems. New York: Oxford University Press.

Best, John W., and Kahn, James V. , (2003). Research in Education. Boston: Pearson Education Company.

Bharat-Ram, Vinay (2017). Evolution of Economic Idea: Smith to Sen and Beyond. New Delhi: Oxford University Press.

Bindseil, Ulrich (2014). Monetary Policy Operations and the Financial System. New York: Oxford University Press.

Birdthistle, William A. (2016). Empire of the Fund: The Way We Save Now. New York: Oxford University Press.

Birkland, T. A. (2015). An Introduction to the Policy Process: Theories, Concepts, and Models of Public Policy Making. New York: Routledge.

Bishop, Patrick, et al. (2008). Building Trust Through Civic Engagement. New York: United Nations.

Blanchard, O., Akerlof, G. A., Romer, D., & Stiglitz, J. E. (Eds.). (2014). What Have We Learned? Macroeconomic Policy After the Crisis. London: MIT Press.

Blank, Leland, and Tarquin, Anthony (2014). Basics of Engineering Economy. New York: McGraw-Hill Company.

Bolman, L. G., & Deal, T. E. (1995). Leading with Soul: An Uncommon Journey of Spirit. San Francisco: Jossey-Bass Inc., Publishers.

Bookstaber, Richard, (2017). The End of Theory: Financial Crises, The Failure of Economics, and The Sweep of Human Interaction. New Jersey: Princeton University Press.

Boulton, Jean G., Allen, Peter M., & Bowman, Cliff (2015). Embracing Complexity: Strategic Perspectives for an Age of Turbulence. Oxford: Oxford University Press.

Bradley, Harriet (2015). Fractured Identities: Changing Patterns of Inequality. Massachusetts: Polity Press.

Bray, Daniel, and Slaughter, Steven (2015). Global Democratic Theory: A Critical Introduction. Cambridge: Polity Press.

Bridge, Rachel (2016). Ambition: Why It's Good to Want More. Sussex: John Wiley and Sons.

Britt, Thomas W., & Jex, Steve M. (2015). Thriving Under Stress: Harnessing Demands in the Workplace. New York: Oxford University Press.

Brodie, James, (2002). Critical Concepts: An Introduction to Politics. Ontario: Prentic Hall Publications.

Brooks, A. (2017). The End of Development: A Global History of Poverty and Prosperity. London: Zed Books Ltd.

Brown, C. V., and Jackson, P. M. (1996). Public Sector Economics. Cambridge: Blackwel Publishers.

Bruce, Duncan D., & Crook, Geoff (2015). The Dream Cafe: Lessons in the Art of Radical Innovation. Sussex: John Wiley & Sons.

Buchanan, Patrick J., (2004). Where the Right Went Wrong. New York: Thomas Dunne Books/ St. Martin's Press.

Buchholz, Todd G., (1995). From Here to Economy: A Shortcut to Economic Literacy. New York: Penguim Group.

Bunting, Michael (2016). The Mindful Leader: 7 Practices for Transforming Your Leadership, Your Organisation and Your Life. Australia: John Wiley & Sons.

Burke, Kenneth (1984). Permanence and Change: An Anatomy of Purpose. London: University of California Press.

Burkeman, Oliver (2016). Real Ambition. Sussex: John Wiley and Sons.

Burt, Everett J. (1972). Social Perspective in the History of Economic Theory. New York: St. Martin's Press.

Butler-Bowdon, Tom (2012). The Republic: The Influential Classic. Sussex: John Wiley & Sons Ltd.

Cair, S. H. (1945). The Responsible Citizen. London: Thomas Nelson and Sons Ltd.

Cairney, Paul (2012). Understanding Public Policy: Theories and Issues. New York: Palgrave Macmillan.

Callahan, William A. (2013). China Dreams: 20 Visions of the Future. Oxford: Oxford University Press.

Calloway, Joe (2013). Be The Best at What Matters Most: The Only Strategy You Will Ever Need. New Jersey: John Wiley and Sons.

Camerer, Colin F. (2003). Behavioral Game Theory, Experiments in Strategic Interaction. New York: Russell Sage.

Campbell, John L., & Pedersen, Ove K. (2001). The Rise of Neoliberalism and Institutional Analysis. Princeton University Press.

Campos, Jose Edgardo, & Root, Hilton, L. (1996). Root. The Key to the Asian Miracle: Making Shared Growth Credible. Washington D.C.: The Brooking Institution.

Cannan, Edwin, (1923). Wealth. New York: Staples Press Limited

Card, David, & Krueger, Alan B. (2017). Wages, School Quality, and Employment Demand. New York: Oxford University Press.

Chamblis, Daniel F., and Schutt, Russell K., (2010). Making Sense of the Social World Methods of Investigation. California: Pinc Forge Press.

Champney, Leonard (1995). Introduction to Quantitative Political Science. HarperCollins College Publishers.

Chang, Ha-Joon (2014). Economics: The User's Guide. London: Penguin Books

Chomsky, Noam (1997). World Orders, Old and New. London: Pluto Press.

Chowdhury, Arjun (2018). The Myth of International Order: why weak States Persist and Alternatives to The State Fade Away. New York: Opxford University Press.

Clayton, Blake C. (2015). Market Madness: A Century of Oil Panics, Crises, and Crashes. New York: Oxford University Press.

Colby, Ira C.; Dulmus, Catherine N.; and Sower, Karen M. (2013). Social Work and Social Policy: Advancing the Principles of Economics and Social Justice. New Jersey: John Wiley and Sons.

Colby, Ira C.; Dulmus, Catherine N.; and Sower, Karen M. (2013). Connecting Social Welfare Policy to Fields of Practice. New Jersey: John Wiley and Sons.

Coleman, J. (2015). Unfinished Work: The Struggle to Build an Aging American Workforce. New York: Oxford University Press.

Collier, P. A., Cooke, T. E., & Glynn, J. J. (1988). Financial and Treasury management. Oxford: Butterworth-Heinemann Ltd.

Collin, Nigel (2016). The Game of Inches: Why Small Change Wins Big Results. Australia: John Wiley and Sons.

Connolly, S., & Munro, A. (1999). The Economics of the Public Sector. Prentice Hall.

Conley, C. (2017). PEAK: How Great Companies Get Their Mojo from Maslow Revised and Updated. New Jersey: John Wiley & Sons.

Conte, R., Andrighetto, G., & Campennl, M. (Eds.). (2014). Minding Norms: Mechanisms and Dynamics of Social Order in Agent Societies. New York: Oxford University Press.

Cook, Tımothy E. (2005). Governing with the News: The News Media as a Political Institution. Chicago: University of Chicago Press.

Cooney, Nick (2015). How to Be Great at Doing Good: Why Results Are What Count and How Smart Charity Can Change the World. New Jersey: John Wiley and Sons.

Cooper, Colin (2019). Psychological Testing: Theory and Practice. Oxon: Routledge.

Covey, S. R., Merrill, A. R., & Merrill, R. R. (1995). First Things First. New York: Simon and Schuster.

Coyle, Diane. (2014). GDP.: A Brief but Affectionate History. New Jersey: Princeton University Press.

Coyle, Diane. (2014). The Ups and Downs of GDP. Organisation for Economic Cooperation and Development. The OECD Observer, 20.

Cramp, Andy, and McDougall, Julian (2019). Doing Theory on Education: Using Popular Culture to Explore Key Debates. Oxon: Routledge

Crouch, Colin (2016). The Knowledge Corrupters: Hidden Consequences of the Financial Takeover of Public Life. Massachusetts: Polity Press.

Cummins, Robert (1989). Meaning and Mental Representation. Massachusetts: MIT Press.

Cunningham, Kathleen Gallagher (2014). Inside the Politics of Self – Determination. New York: Oxford University Press.

Currall, Steven C.; Frauenheim, Ed; Perry, Sara Jansen; & Hunter, Emily M. (2014). Organized Innovation: A Blueprint for Renewing America's Prosperity. New York: Oxford University Press.

Czinkota, Michael R. ; RonKainen, Ilkka A. and Moffet, H. Michael, (2004). Fundamentals of International Business. Ohio: Thomson South – West Publications.

Kahneman, Daniel (2011). Thinking, Fast and Slow. London: Penguin Books.

Danner, John, & Coopersmith, Mark (2015). The Other" F" Word: How Smart Leaders, Teams, and Entrepreneurs Put Failure to Work. New Jersey: John Wiley & Sons.

Daniels, Joseph P., & Van Hoose, David D. (2018). Global Economic Issues and Policies. New York: Routledge.

Davies, Howard (2015). Can Financial Markets Be Controlled? Massachusetts: Polity Press.

Davies, Anna. R., Fahy, Frances, & Rau, Henrike (2016). Challenging Consumption: Pathways to a More Sustainable Future. London: Routledge.

Demertzis, Nicolas (Ed.). (2013). Emotions in Politics: The Affect Dimension in Political Tension. Hampshire: Palgrave Macmillan.

Dernburg, Thomas F. (1985). Macroeconomics: Concepts, Theories, and Policies. New York: McGraw-Hill Book Company.

De Vries, Michiel S. (2010). The Importance of Neglect in Policy-Making. Hampshire: Palgrave Macmillan.

Dewey, John (1957). Human Nature and Conduct. New York: The Modern Liberia.

Dobel, J. Patrick (1999). Public Integrity. Baltimore: The John Hopkins University Press.

Dowling, Simon (2016). Work with Me: How to Get People to Buy into Your Idea. Australia: John Wiley and Sons.

Draai, Enaleen; Van Rooyen, Enslin J., and Raga, Kishore (2017). A Practical Introduction to Public Management. Cape Town: Oxford University Press Southern Africa.

Drezner, D. W. (2014). The System Worked: How The World Stopped Another Great Depression. Oxford: Oxford University Press.

Drezner, Daniel W. (2014). The System Worked: How the World Stopped another Great Depression. Oxford: Oxford University Press.

Drucker, Peter (2012). Managing the Non-Profit Organization. London: Routledge.

Drucker, Peter (2015). Five Most Important Questions: Enduring Wisdom for Today's Leaders. New Jersey: John Wiley and Sons.

Dunnett, Andrew, (1987). Understanding the Market. New York: Longman Inc.

Dutta, Prajit K., (1999). Strategies and Games: Theory and Practice. Massachusetts and London: MIT press.

Dwivedi, O. P. (2011). Publıc Administration in Global Context: IASIA at 50. Canada: Bruylant Bruxelles.

Dyck, Rand, (2006). Studying Politics: An Introduction to Political Science. Toronto: Thomson and Nelson Press.

Edwards, Ward (1954). The theory of decision making. Psychological bulletin, 51(4), 380.

Edwards, W. (1961). Behavioral decision theory. Annual review of psychology, 12(1),473-498.

Edwards, W., & Tversky, A. (Eds.). (1967). Decision making: selected readings (Vol. 8). Penguin Books.

Ekpe, Aniekan E., and Okereke, Okechukwu O., (2002). Development and Underdevelopment: Politics of the North – South Divide. Enugu: John Jacob's Classic Publishers.

Ellis, Charles D., Munnell, Alicia H., & Eschtruth, Andrew D. (2014). Falling Short: The Coming Retirement Crisis and What to do About It. New York: Oxford University Press.

Eysenck, Michael W., & Brysbaert, Marc (2018). Fundamentals of Cognition. London: Routledge.

Farrell, Chris, (2004). Inflation: What Happens When Prises Fall. New York: Harper Collins Publishers Inc.

Fenton, Natalie (2016). Digital Political, Radical. Massachusetts: Polity Press.

Finer, S. E. (1950). A Primer of Public Administration: Man and Society. London: Frederick Taylor Ltd.

Fishman, Ray, and Golden, Miriam A. (2017). Corruption: What Everyone Needs to Know. New York: Oxford University Press.

Flinders, Matthew (2013). Defending Politics. Oxford: Oxford University Press.

Folks, R. William Jr., and Aggarwal, Raj, (1988). International Dimensions of Financial Management. Boston: PWS – KENT Publishing Company.

Forbes, William. (2009). Behavioral Finance. Sussex: John Wiley & Sons.

Foresman, G. A., Fosl, P. S., & Watson, J. C. (2017). The Critical Thinking Toolkit. Sussex: John Wiley & Sons.

Foroohar, R. (2016). Makers and Takers: How Wall Street Destroyed Main Street. New York: Crown Business.

Fox, Jason (2016). How to Lead a Quest: A Handbook for Pioneering Executives. Auatralia: John Wiley and Sons.

Fox, J. J. (2010). How to be a fierce competitor: What Winning Companies and Great Managers do in Tough Times. California: John Wiley & Sons.

Frazer, William J. Jr., (1973). Crisis in Economic Theory: A Study of Monetary Policy, Analysis and Economic Goals. Gamsville: University of Florida Press.

Freedman, Lawrence (2015). Strategy: A history. New York: Oxford University Press.

Frey, Bruno S., & Gallus, Jana (2017). Honours versus Money: The Economics of Awards. New York: Oxford University Press.

Frieden, A. Jeffry and Lake, A. David, (1987). International Political Economy: Perspectives on Global Power and Wealth. New York: St. Martin's Press, Inc.

Friedman, Milton (1953). Essays in Positive Economics. Chicago: University of Chicago press.

Friedman, Milton, and Heller, Walter Wolfgang (1969). Monetary Vs. Fiscal Policy. New York: Norton.

Froman, A. Lewis Jr., (1967). The Congressional Process: Strategies, Rules and Procedures. Boston: Brown and Company United.

Gamble, Sarah, (2001). The Routledge Companion to Feminism and Postfeminism. New York: Routledge Publications.

Gartner, Manfred (2003). Macroeconomics. Essex: Pearson Education Limited.

George, Susan, (1988). A fate Worse Than Debt. Middlesex: Penguin Books.

Gerver, Richard (2016). Simple Thinking: How to Remove Complexity from Life and Work. Sussex: John Wiley and Sons.

Ghosh, B. N. (2002). Contemporary Issues in Macroeconomic Management. Leeds: Wisdom House Publications Ltd.

Givens, David, (2008). Crime Signals. New York: St. Martin's Press.

Goch, Desmond (1971). Finance and Accounts for Managers. London: Pan Books Ltd.

Gold, Jacob (2016). Money Mindset. New Jersey: Jon Wiley and Sons, Inc.

Goldfayn, Alex (2015). The Revenue Growth Habit: The Simple Art of Growing Your Business by 15% in 15 Minutes Per Day. New Jersey: John Wiley & Sons.

Goleman, D. (1996). Emotional Intelligence. Why It Can Matter More Than IQ. London: Bloomsbury Publishing Plc.

Goodman, John C., and Dolan, Edwin G. (1985). Economics of Public Policy. Minnesota: West Publishing Company.

Gorton, Gary B., (2012). Misunderstanding Financial Crises: Why We Don't See Them Coming. Oxford University Press.

Green, M. Richard Jr., (1966). Business Intelligence and Espionage. Illinois: Dow Jones – Irwin, Inc.

Green, Duncan (2016). How Change Happens. Oxford: Oxford University Press.

Green, Lorraine, and Clarke, Karen (2016). Social Policy for Social Work. Cambridge: Polity Press.

Green, Lorraine (2017). Understanding the Life Course: Sociological and Psychological Perspectives. Cambridge: Polity Press.

Greenspan, A. (2008). The age of turbulence: Adventures in a new world. New York: Penguin Books.

Greenway, John D H., Blacknell Andy, and Commbe, Andy (2018). Lead: 50 Models for Success and Life. Sussex: John Wiley and Sons.

Gregory, Dan, and Flangan, Kieran (2015). Selfish, Scared & Stupid. Australia: John Wiley and Sons.

Gregory, J., & Crispin, L. (2014). More Agile Testing: Learning Journeys for the Whole Team. New Jersey: Addison-Wesley Professional.

Gugerty, Mark Kay, & Karlan, Dean (2018). The Goldilocks Challenge: Right-fit Evidence for the Social Sector. New York: Oxford University Press.

Guillén, Mauro F. (2015). The Architecture of Collapse: The Global System in the 21st Century. New York: Oxford University Press.

Guthrie, Graeme (2017). The Firm Divided: Manager-Shareholder Conflict and the Fight for Control of the Modern Corporation. New York: Oxford University Press.

Habermas, Jurgen (1976). Legitimation Crisis. Cambridge: Polity Press.

Hadfield,Gillian K. (2017). Rules for A Flat World: Why Humans Invented Law and How to Reinvent it for A Complex Global Economy. New York: Oxford University Press.

Hagenbuch, W. (1959). Social economics. Cambridge: James Nisbet and Company Ltd.

Harmel, Gray, and Prahalad, C. K. (1996). Competing for the Future. Massachusetts: Harvard School Press.

Hands, D. Wade, (2004). Introductory Mathematical Economics. Oxford: Oxford University Press.

Hands, D. Wade (1985). Karl Popper and Economic Methodology: A New Look. Economics & Philosophy, 1(1), 83-99.

Hansen, Alvin, (1953). A Guide to Keynes. New York: McGraw-Hill Book Company.

Harari, Yuval Noah (2015). Sapiens: A Brief History of Humankind. London: Vintage Books.

Harford, Tim, (2007). Undercover Economist: On the Move. London: Financial Times.

Harford, Tim (2009). Dear Undercover Economist: Priceless Advice on Money, Work, Sex, Kids, and Life's Other Challenges. London: Random House.

Harford, Tim (2010). The Undercover Economist. London: Penguin Books.

Harford, Tim (2015). The Undercover Economist Strikes Back: How to Run or Ruin an Economy. London: Penguin Books.

Harper, Richard; Randall, Dave; & Sharrock, Wes. (2016). Choice. Massachusetts: Polity Press.

Harvey-Jones John (1988). Making It Happen: Reflection in Leadership. London: Williams Collins.

Harvey, R., & Gayer, T. (2013). Public finance. New York: McGraw-Hill Higher Education.

Hatch, Mary Jo (1997). OrganizationBudget: Modern, Symbolic, and Postmodern Perspective. New York: Oxford University Press.

Haught, J. F. (2003). Deeper than Darwin: The Prospect for Religion in the Age of Evolution. Oxford: Westview Press.

Hay, Colin, & Payne, Anthony (2015). Civic Capitalism. Massachusetts: Polity Press.

Heckscher, Charles (2015). Trust in a Complex World: Enriching Community. New York: Oxford University Press.

Heilbroner, Robert L., and Thurow, Lester, (1975). The Economic Problem. New Jersey: Prentice-Hall, Inc.

Heilbroner, Robert L., (1980). The Worldly Philosophers: The Lives, Times and Ideas of the Great Economic Thinkers. New York: Simon and Schuster, Inc.

Heilbroner, Robert L., and Thurow, Lester, (1994). Economics Explained: Everything You Need to Know About How the Economy Works and Where it is Going. New York: Simon and Schuster, Inc.

Helder, Chris (2018). Cut the Noise: Better Results Less Guilt. Australia: John Wiley and Sons.

Heller, Walter Wolfgang (1966). New Dimension of Political Economy. Boston: Harvard University Press.

Heller, Walter Wolfgang (1968). Taxation – Dollars and Sense. New York: Norton.

Henderson, James. W. (2012). Health Economics and Policy (With Economic Applications). Connecticut: Cengage Learning.

Henbderson, Michael (2014). Above the Line: How to Creat A Company Culture that Engages Employees, Delights Customers and Delivers Results. Australia: John Wiley and Sons.

Hendry, D. F., & Ericsson, N. R. (Eds.). (2003). Understanding Economic Forecasts. Massachusetts: MIT Press.

Herrick, Bruce, & Kindleberger, Charles. P. (1983). Economic Development. 4-th Edition. Singapore: McGraw-Hill.

Hertel-Fernandez, Alexander (2018). Politics at Work: How Companies Turn Their Workers into Lobbyists. New York: Oxford University Press.

Hick, Laurel; Thompson, George T.; Lowman, Michael R.; and Cochran, George C. (1995).

American Government and Economics: In Christian Perspective. Florida: Beka Book Publications.

Hollingworth, P. (2016). The Light and Fast Organisation: A New Way of Dealing with Uncertainty. Australia: John Wiley & Sons.

Holt, Robert. T., & Turner, John. E. (1966). The Political Basis of Economic Development: An Exploration in Comparative Political Analysis (Vol. 8). New Jersey: Van Nostrand Company.

Honig, Dan (2018). Navigation by Judgment: Why and When Top-Down Management of Foreign Aid Doesn't Work. New York: Oxford University Press.

Hoover, K. D. (2011). Applied Intermediate Macroeconomics. New York: Cambridge University Press.

Horney, Karen (2013). Self-Analysis. New York: Routledge.

Howlett, Michael, & Tosun, Jale (2019). Policy Styles and Policy-making: Exploring the Linkages. New York: Routledge.

Howlett, Michael (2019). Designing Public Policies: Principles and Instruments. New York: Routledge.

Hulse, Carl (April 8, 2016). No accord in Budget Talks as Policy Fights Hamper Real. The New York Times. P. A1. Archieved the Original on April 11, 2016. Retrieved April 8, 2016.

Hunt, E. K., & Lautzenheiser, Mark, (2015). History of Economic Thought: A Critical Perspective. New York: Routledge.

Ingledew, John (2016). How to Have Great Ideas: A Guide to Creative Thinking. London: Laurence King Publishing.

Jhingan, L. M., (2013). Principles of Economics. Delhi: Vrinda Publications (P) Ltd.

Johansson, P. O., & Kriström, B. (2015). Cost-Benefit Analysis for Project Appraisal. Cambridge: Cambridge University Press.

Johnson, M. (2014). Winning the War for Talent: How to Attract and Keep the People Who Make your Business Profitable. Australia: John Wiley & Sons.

Johnson, Stephen Scott (2017). Emergent: Ignite Purpose, Transform Culture, Make Change Stick. Australia: Joh Wiley and Sons.

Johnson, Tana (2017). Organizational Progeny: Why Governments Are Losing Control over the Proliferating Structures of Global Governance. Oxford: Oxford University Press.

Johnson, Chris, and Johnson, Matt (2018). Capacity: Create Laser Focus, Boundless Energy, and an Unstoppable Drive in any Organization. New Jersey. John Wiley and Sons.

Johns, Charles I. (2001). Introductıon to Economic Growth. New York: Norton and Co., Inc.

Jost, John T., and Sidanius, Jim (2005). Political Psychology. New York: Psychology Press.

Kantowitz, Barry H., Roediger, Henry L., & Elmes, David G. (2009). Experimental Psychology. (International student ed.). California: Michele Sordi.

Kaplan, Thomas; Flegenheimer, Matt (April 30, 2017). "Bipartisan Agreement Reached to Fund Government Through September". The New York Times. ISSN 0362-4331. Retrieved 2017- 05-02.

Kaplan, Thomas; Steinhauer, Jennifer (December 9, 2016). "Senators Appear to Reach Deal to Avert Shutdown". The New York Times. ISSN 0362-4331. Retrieved 2016-12-10.

Katz, Michael B. (2013). The Undeserving Poor: America's Enduring Confrontation with Poverty. New York: Oxford University Press.

Keegan, William (1992). The Spectre of Capitalism:The Future of the World Economy After the Fall of Communism. London: Vintage

Kelsey, Robert (2015). The Outside Edge: How Outsiders Can Succeed in a World Made by Insiders. Sussex: John Wiley & Sons.

Kemshall, Hazel; Wilkinson, Bernadette; and Baker, Kerry (2013). Working with Risk: Skills for Contemporary Social Work. Cambridge: Polity Press.

Kenworthy, Lane (2014). Social Democratic America. New York: Oxford University Press.

Klein, Naomi (2008). The Shock Doctrine: The Rise of Disaster Capitalism. Toronto: Vintage Canada.

Kolhatkar, Sheelah (2018). Black Edge: Inside Information, Dirty Money, and the Quest to Bring Down the Most Wanted Man on Wall Street. London: Penguin Publisher

Koop, G., & Quinlivan, R. (2000). Analysis of Economic Data (Vol. 2). Chichester: John Wiley and Sons.

Kotter, J. P. (2012). Leading Change. Massachusetts: Harvard business press.

Kottler, Jeffrey A. (2018). What You Don't Know about Leadership, But Probably Should: Applications to Daily Life. New York: Oxford University Press.

Kotz, D. M. (2015). The Rise and Fall of Neoliberal Capitalism. Massachusetts: Harvard University Press.

Koutsoyannis, A., (1977). Theory of Econometrics. London: Mcmillian Press Ltd.

Kouzes, J. M., & Posner, B. Z. (2017). The Leadership Challenge. New Jersey: John Wiley & Sons.

Kraemer, H. M. (2015). Becoming the Best: Build a World-Class Organization through Values- Based Leadership. New Jersey: John Wiley & Sons.

Kriegel, Jessica (2016). Unfairly Labeled: How Your Workplace Can Benefit from Ditching Generational Stereotypes. New Jersey: John Wiley & Sons.

Krenin, E. Mordechai, (1983). International Economics: A Policy Approach. New York: Harcourt Brace Jovanovich, Inc.

Krugman, Paul, (1994). Peddling Prosperity: Economic Sense and Nonsense in the Age of Deminished Expectations. New York: Norton & Company, Inc.

Krugman, Paul (2012). End this Depression Now! New York: WW Norton & Company.

Kubicek, Jeremie, and Cockram, Steve (2015). 5 Gears: How to be Present and Productive When There is Never Enough Time. New Jersey: John Wiley and Sons.

Kuklinski, James H., & Chong, D. (Eds.). (2001). Citizens and Politics: Perspectives from Political Psychology. New York: Cambridge University Press.

Kunreuther, Howard, & Useem, Michael (2018). Mastering Catastrophic Risk: How Companies Are Coping with Disruption. New York: Oxford University Press.

Kural, Vural (2003). Issues in Public Finance. Ankara: U-Aslac Publications

Kurlantzick, Joshua (2016). State Capitalism: How the Return of Statism is Transforming the World. New York: Oxford University Press.

Lacouture, Jean (1969). Political Leaders of the Twentieth Century: Ho Chi Minh. Middlesex: Pelican Book.

Lafley, A. G., & Martin, R. L. (2013). Playing to Win: How strategy Really Works. Massachusetts: Harvard Business Press.

Langley, Paul (2015). Liquidity Lost: The Governance of Global Financial Crisis. Oxford: Oxford University Press.

Larino, Philippe (2018). Pragmatism and Organization Studies. London: Oxford University Press.

Larsen, Randy J., & Buss, David M. (2009). Personality Psychology. New York: McGraw-Hill Publishing.

Lavelle, Jane Suilin (2018). The Social Mind: A Philosophical Introduction. London: Routledge.

Lawson, Kay, (1999). The Human Polity: A Comparative Introduction to Political Science. Boston: Houghton Mifflin Company.

Leinward, Gerald (1994). Do We Need A New Constitution?. Washington DC.: Franklin Watts Publication.

Levine, Peter (2015). We Are the Ones We Have Been Waiting for: The Promise of Civic Renewal in America. New York: Oxford University Press.

Levison, Andrew, (1980). The Full Employment Alternative. New York: Coward, Mcain & Geoghegan, Inc.

Levitsky, Sandra R. (2014). Caring for Our Own: Why There is no Political Demand for New American Social Welfare Rights. New York: Oxford University Press.

Levitt, Steven and Dubner, Stephen J., (2005). Freakonomics. New York: William Marrow and Company.

Lipietz, Alain, & Slater, Malcom. (1992). Towards a New Economic Order: Postfordism, Ecology and Democracy. Cambridge: Polity Press.

Longenecker, Clinton O., & Simonetti, Jack L. (2001). Getting Results: Five Absolutes for High Performance. San Francisco: John Wiley & Sons.

Lowndes, Vivien, Marsh, David, & Stoker, Gerry (2018). Theory and Methods in Political Science. London: Macmillan International Higher Education.

Mackenzie, I. Scott (2013). Human-Computer Interaction: An Emperical Research Perspective. Massachusetts: Moorgan Kaufmann Publications.

MacNeil, Neil, & Baker, Richard A. (2013). The American Senate: An Insider's History. New York: Oxford University Press.

Magee, Jeffrey (2015). Your Trajectory Code: How to Change Your Decisions, Actions, and Direction to Become Part of the Top 1% of High Achievers. New Jersey: John Wiley & Sons, Inc.

Malabou, Catherine (2016). Before Tomorrow: Epigenesis and Rationality. Cambridge: Polity Press.

Malley, Alex (2015). The Naked CEO: The Truth You Need to Build A Big Business. Australia: John Wley and Sons.

Malim, Tony, & Birch, Ann (1998). Introductory Psychology. London: Macmillan Press Ltd.

Mann, Prem S., (2004). Introductory Statistics. New Jersey: John Willey and Sons, Inc.

Martin, I. W. (2010). Redistributing toward the Rich: Strategic Policy Crafting in the Campaign to Repeal the Sixteenth Amendment, 1938–1958. American Journal of Sociology, 116(1), 1- 52.

Maslin, K. T., (2007). An Introduction to the Philosophy of Mind. Massachusetts: Blackwell Publishers Press.

Massumi, Brian (2015). Politics of Affect. Massachusetts: Polity Press.

Matlin, Margaret W. (1992). Psychology. Florida: Holt, Rinehart and Winston, Inc.

May, Ernest R., (1993). American Cold War Strategy. New York: St. Martin's Press.

Mayer, Colin (2018). Prosperity: Better Business Makes the Greater Good. New York: Oxford University Press.

McAlevey, Jane F. (2016). No Shortcuts: Organizing for Power in the New Gilded Age. New York: Oxford University Press.

Mckenzie, Richard B., and Tullock, Gordon, (1989). The Best of the New World of Economics. Illinois: Irwin Press.

Mcleod, Lisa Earle (2016). Leading with Noble Purpose: How to Create a Tribe of True Believers. New Jersey: John Wiley and S McQuaig, Linda (2004). War, Big Oil, and the Fight for the Planet: It's the Crude, Dude. Canada: Doubleday Canada Ltd.

McQueen, Michael (2016). Momentum: How to Build It, keep it or Get It Back. Australia: John Wiley & Sons.

Meeker, James Edward, (1975). Wall Street and the Security Markets. New York: Arno Press.

Meyer, Robert A., (1976). Microeconomic Decisions. Boston: Houghton Mifflin Company.

Michelle, Baddeley (2019). Behavioural Economics and Finance. London: Routledge.

Midler, Paul (2018). What's Wrong with China. New Jersey: John Wiley and Sons, Inc.

Miller, Roger Leroy, (1983). The Economics of Macro Issues. New York: West Publishing Company.

Mishkin, Frederic S. (20013). The Economics of Money, Banking, and Financial Markets. Essex: Pearson education.

Molinaro, Vince (2017). The Leadership Contract: The Fine Print to Becoming an Accountable Leader. New Jersey: John Wiley & Sons.

Morton, Rebecca B., & Williams, Kenneth C. (2010). Experimental Political Science and the Study of Causality: From Nature to the Lab. New York: Cambridge University Press.

Montagu, Ashley (1962). The Humanization of Man: Our Changing Conception of Human Nature. New York: Grove Press Inc.

Mooney, Michael, and Stuber, Florian, (1977). Small Comfort for Hard Times: Humanist on Public Policy. New York: Columbia University Press.

Morrow, J. D. (1994). Game Theory for Political Scientists (No. 30: 519.83). New Jersey: Princeton University Press.

Mueller, D. C. (Ed.). (1997). Perspectives on Public Choice: A Handbook. Cambridge: Cambridge University Press.

Mueller, Dennis C., (1981). Public Choice. New York: Cambridge University Press.

Musgrave, Richard A., (1959). The Theory of Public Finance. Tennessee: Southern Economic Association.

Musgrave, Richard A., and Peacock, Alan T., (1967). Classics in the Theory of Public Finance. London: St. Martin's Press.

Musgrave, Richard A., and Musgrave Peggy B. (1989). Public Finance in Theory and Practice. New York: McGraw-Hill Book Company

Newell, Allen (1994). Unified Theories of Cognition. Massachusetts: Harvard University Press.

Naím, Moises (2014). The End of Power: From Boardrooms to Battlefields and Churches to States, why Being in Charge Isn't What It Used to Be. New York: Basic Books.

Nichols, Tom (2017). The Death of Expertise: The Campaign Against Established Knowledge and Why It Matters. New York: Oxford University Press.

Nicholas, Michael (2017). The Little Black Book of Decision Making: Making Complex

Decisions with Confidence in a Fast-moving World. Sussex: John Wiley & Sons.

Nicholls, Alex; Paton, Rob, and Emerson, Jed (2017). Social Finance. Oxford: Oxford University Press.

Noll, Roger G., and Owen, Bruce M., (1983). The Political Economy of Deregulation: Interest Groups in the Regulatory Process. Washington DC.: American Enterprise Institute for Public Policy Research.

Nowak, John E., and Rotunda, Ronald D, (2010). Principles of Constitutional Law. New York: Thomas Reuter Publications.

Nowotny, Helga (2015). The Cunning of Uncertainty. Massachusetts: Polity Press.

Obe, Michael Tobin (2014). Forget Strategy. Get Results: Racdical Management Attitudes That Will Deliver Outstanding Success. Sussex: John Wiley and Sons.

O'Connor, James, (1973). The Fiscal Crisis of the State. New York: St. Martin's Press, Inc.

O'Loghlin, James (2016). Innovation is a State of Mind: Simple Strategies to Be More Innovative in What You Do. Australia: John Wiley and Sons.

O'Rourke, P. J. (1987). Republican Party Reptile: The Confessions, Adventures, Essays and (Other) Outrages of PJ O'Rourke. New York: Pan Macmillan.

O'Rourke, P. J. (1992). Parliament of Whore: A Lone Humorist Attemots eo Explain the Entire US Govement. London: Pan Books Ltd.

Orts, Eric W. (2015). Busıness Person: A Legal Theory of the Firm. New York: Oxford University Press.

Osborne, David and Gaebler, James, (1993). Reinventing Government: How the Enterprenueral Spirit is Transforming the Public Sector. New York: Pengium Group, Inc.

Osborne, David E., and Hutchinson, Peter, (2004). The Price of Government. New York: Basi Books Publications.

Paarlberg, Robert (2015). The United States of Excess: Gluttony and the Dark Side of American Exceptionalism. New York: Oxford University Press.

Papacharissi, Zizi (2015). Affective Public: Sentiment, Technology, and Politics. New York: Oxford University Press.

Park, Chan S., Kim, G., & Choi, S. (2007). Engineering Economics. New Jersey: Prentice Hall.

Parson, Talcott (1970). Social Structure and Personality. London: The Free Press.

Pearson, Gordon J. (1990). Strategic Thinking. London: Prentice-Hall Ltd.

Penney, Joel (2017). The Citizen Marketer: Promoting Public Opinion in the Social Media Age. New York: Oxford University Press.

Pérez, Efren O. (2016). Unspoken Politics: Implicit Attitudes and Political Thinking. New York: Cambridge University Press.

Perry, David E, and Haluska, Mark J. (2016). Hiring Greatness: How to Recruit Dream Team and Crush the Competition. New Jersey: John Wiley and Sons.

Peter, Thomas J., and Wterman, Robert H. (2004). In Serach of Excellence: Lessons From American Best-Running Companies. New York: HarperCollins Publishers.

Pham-Chung. (1970). Money, Banking, and Income: Theory and Policy. Pennsylvania: International Textbook Company.

Piketty, Thomas (2014). Capital: in the 21st Century. Massachusetts and London: The Belknap Press of Harvard University.

Pollitt, Christopher (2017). Public Management Reform: A Comparative Analysis into the Age of Austerity. New York: Oxford University Press.

Price, Carolyn (2015). Emotion. Massachusetts: Polity Press.

Pugh, Allison J. (Ed.). (2017). Beyond the Cubicle: Job Insecurity Culture and the Flexible Self.

New York: Oxford University Press.

Putnam, Hilary (1991). Representation and Reality. Massachusetts: MIT press.

Rancieere, Jacques (2016). The Method of Equality. Massachusetts: Polity Press.

Rank, Mark Robert; Hirschl, Thomas A., & Foster, Kirk A. (2014). Chasing the American Dream: Understanding What Shapes our Fortunes. New York: Oxford University Press.

Rein, Shaun (2014). The End of Copycat China: The Rise of Creativity, Innovation, and Individualism in Asia. New Jersey: John Wiley & Sons.

Reich, Robert B. (2010). Aftershock: The Next Economy and America's Future. New York: Vintage Books.

Reich, Robert B. (2016). Saving Capitalism: For the Many, Not the Few. New York: Vintage Books.

Rhode, Deborah L. (2018). Cheating: Ethics in Everyday Life. New York: Oxford University Press.

Rich, Roland (2017). Democracy in Crisis: Why, Where, how to Respond. Colorado: Lynne Rienner Publishers, Inc.

Richard, A., & Peggy, M. B. (1989). Public Finance in Theory and Practice. Tennessee: Southern Economic Association.

Riker, William H. (1953). Democracy in the United States. New York: The Macmillian Company.

Riler, Jason L., (2008). Let Them In: The Case for Open Borders. New York. Pengium Group, Inc.

Robertson, James, (1983). The Sane Alternative: A Choice of Future. Minnesota: River Basin Publishing Co.

Robertson, David Brain (2013). The Original Compromise: What the Constitution Framers Were Really Thinking. New York: Oxford University Press.

Roberts, Cynthia A., Armijo, Leslie Elliott, & Katada, Saori N. (2018). The BRICS and Collective Financial Statecraft. New York: Oxford University Press.

Robinson, Ken (2017). Out of Our Mind: The Power of Being Creative. Sussex: John Wiley and Sons. Roland, Gerard (2000). Transition and Economics: Politics, Markets, and Firms. Massachusetts: MIT press.

Rosen, Harvey S., and Gayer, Ted (2008). Public Finance. New York: McGraw-Hill Company, Inc.

Rosser Jr, J. B., & Rosser, M. V. (2018). Comparative Economics in a Transforming World Economy. New Jersey: MIT Press.

Rourke, John T. (2010). You Decide: Current Debates in American Politics. New York: Pearson Education Inc.

Rowlands, Mark (2012). Can Animals Be Moral? New York: Oxford University Press.

Rush, Michael (1992). Politics and Society: An Introduction to Political Sociology. Essex: Pearson Education Limited

Russett, Bruce; Star, Harvey; and Kinsella, David, (2000). World Politics: The Menu for Choice. Boston: Bedford/ St. Martin's Press Inc.

Sabine, George H., and Thorson, Thomas L., (1973). A History of Political Theory. New York: The Dryden Press.

Sachs, Jeffrey D. (2017). Building the New American Economy: Smart, Fair, and Sustainable. New York: Columbia University Press.

Safety, Adel, et al. (2006). Global Leadership. Istanbul: Istanbul University Press.

Salamon, Lester M. (2014). Leverage for Good: An Introduction to the New Frontiers of Philanthropy and Social Investment. New York: Oxford University Press.

Salanie, Bernard (2011), The Economics of Taxation. Massachusetts: The MIT Press.

Salicru, Sebastian (2017). Leadership Results: How to Create Adaptive Leaders and High-Performing Organisations for an Uncertain World. Australia: John Wiley & Sons.

Salvatore, Dominick, (2017). Managerial Economics: Principles and Worldwide Application:(Seventh Ed.). OUP Catalogue. New York: Oxford University Press.

Schiavo-Campo, Salvatore (2019). Running the Government: Public Administration and Governance in Global Context. New York: Routledge.

Shapiro, Ronald M., and Dale James (2015). The Power of Nice: How to Negotiate So Everyone Wins-Especially You! New Jersey: John Wiley & Sons.

Sheingate, Adam D. (2016). Building a Business of Politics: The Rise of Political Consulting and the Transformation of American Democracy. New York: Oxford University Press.

Schirrmacher, Frank. (2015). Ego: The Game of Life. Massachusetts: Polity Press.

Schock, Kurt (2015). Civil Resistance Today. Massachusetts: Polity Press.

Schumacher, Ernst Friedrich (1974). Small Is Beautiful: A Study of Economics as If People Mattered. London. Abacus Publication.

Schumacher, Ernst Friedrich, & Gillingham, P. N. (1979). Good Work. New York: Harper & Row.

Shapiro, Michael J. (2016). Politics and Time. Massachusetts: Polity Press.

Sharp, Ansel M., Regıster Charles A., and Crimes, Paul W. (1998). Economics of Social Issues. Boston: Irvin McGraw-Hill Co., Inc.

Shaver, J. Myles (2018). Headquarters Economy: Managers, Mobility, and Migration. New York: Oxford University Press.

Shi, David E. (2001). The Simple Life: Plain Living and High Thinking in American Culture. New York: University of Georgia Press.

Shively, W. Phillips (1997). Power and Choice: An Introduction to Political Science. New York: McGraw-Hill Co., Inc.

Shoemaker, Paul (2015). Can't Not Do: The Compelling Social Drive that Changes Our World. New Jersey: John Wiley & Sons.

Shultz, George P., & Dam, Kenneth W. (1977). Economic Policy Beyond the Headlines. New York: Norton and Company, Inc.

Silk, Leonard, (1978). Economics in Plain English: All You Need to Know About Economics – In Language Anyone Can Understand. New York: Simon and Schuster. Simmons, Annette (1998). Territorial Games: Understanding and Ending Turf Wars at Work. New York: American Management Association (AMACOM).

Smart, Jamie (2016). Results: Think Less, Achieve More. Sussex: John Wiley and Sons.

Smart, Jamie (2015). The Little Book of Clarity: A Quick Guide to Focus and Declutter your Mind. Sussex: John Wiley and Sons.

Smith, Adam. (1759). The Theory of Moral Sentiments. Scotland:"printed for Andrew Millar, in the Strand; and Alexander Kincaid and J. Bell, in Edinburgh".

Smith, Stephen (2003). Labour Economics. New York: Routledge.

Smith, Rogers M. (2015). Political Peoplehood: The Roles of Values, Interests, and Identities. Chicago: University of Chicago Press.

Smith, Charles W. (2015). What the Market Teaches Us: Limitations of Knowing and Tactics for Doing. New York: Oxford University Press.

Sorman-Nilsson, Anders (2017). Seamless. Australia: John Wiley and Sons.

Sorabji, Richard (2012). Gandhi and the Stoics: Modern Experiments on Ancient Values. Oxford: Oxford University Press.

Sowell, Thomas (1980). Knowledge and Decisions. New York: Basic Books.

Sowell, Thomas (2011). Economic Facts and Fallacies. New York: Basic Books.

Sowell, Thomas (2014). Basic Economics. London: Hachette.

Statman, Meir (2017). Finance for Normal People: How Investors and Markets Behave. New York: Oxford University Press.

Steindel, Charles (2018). Economic Indicators for Professionals: Putting the Statistics into Perspective. New York: Routledge.

Stiglitz, E. Joseph (2000). Economics of the Public Sector. New York: Norton and Company, Inc.

Suen, Wing (2010). The Structure of Economics: A Mathematical Analysis. New York: McGraw Hill Companies.

Sugimoto, Cassidy R., & Larivière, Vincent (2018). Measuring Research: What Everyone Needs to Know. New York: Oxford University Press.

Susskind, Richard E., & Susskind, Daniel (2017). The Future of the Professions: How Technology Will Transform the Work of Human Experts. New York: Oxford University Press.

Sweeney, John, & Imaretska, Elena (2015). The Innovative Mindset: 5 Behaviors for Accelerating Breakthroughs. New Jersey: John Wiley & Sons.

Sweizer, Peter, (2013). Extortion: How Politicians Extract Your Money, Buy Votes, and Line Their Own Votes. New York: Houghton Mifflin Harcourt.

Talbert, Matthew (2016). Moral Responsibility: An Introduction. Massachusetts: Polity Press.

Tasler, Nick (2016). Domino: The Simplest Way to Inspire Change. New Jersey: John Wiley & Sons.

Taylor, Ros (2017). Willpower: Discover it, Use It and Get What You Want. Sussex: John Wiley and Sons.

Tebbit, Mark (2017). Philosophy of Law: An Introduction. London: Routledge

Tenney, Matt, and Gard, Tim (2016). The Mindfulness Edge: How to Rewirrre Your Brain foR Leadership and Personal Excellence Without dding to Your Schedule. New Jersey: John Wiley and Sons.

Thaler, Richard H., & Sunstein, Cass R. (2008). Nudge: Improving Decisions About Health. Wealth, and Happiness. Connecticut: Yale University Press.

Thironx, Jacques P., and Krasemann, Keith W., (2009). Ethics: Theory and Practice. New Jersey: Princeton Hall.

Thomas, S. Evelyne, (1956). Economics. London: English University Press Ltd.

Thomasma, David C., and Graber, Glemm C., (1991). Euthanasia: Towards an Ethical Social Policy. New York: Continum Press.

Thuy, Phan; Hansen, Ellen, and Price, David (2001). The Public Employment Service in a Changing Labour Market. Geneva: Internatiomal Labour Organization.

Tileagă, Cristian (2013). Political Psychology: Critical Perspectives. New York: Cambridge University Press.

Timothy, J. Conlan; Margaret, T. Wrightson; and David, R. Beam (1990). Taxing Choices: The Politics of Tax Reform. Washington D.C.: Congressional Quarterly Inc.

Tirole, Jean, (2017). Economics for the Common Good. Princeton: Princeton University Press.

Toffler, Alvin (1970). Future Shock. New York: Random House Inc.

Tormey, Simon (2015). The End of Representative Politics. Massachusetts: Polity Press

Tønder, Lars (2013). Tolerance: A Sensorial Orientation to Politics. New York: Oxford University Press.

Toje, Asle (Ed.). (2018). Will China's Rise be Peaceful? The Rise of a Great Power in Theory, History, Politics, and the Future. New York: Oxford University Press.

Tulgan, Bruce (2016). Not Everyone Gets a Trophy: How to Manage the Millennials. New Jersey: John Wiley & Sons.

Tullock, G., Brady, G. L., & Seldon, A. (2002). Government Failure: A Primer in Public Choice. Washington D.C.: Cato Institute.

Tunguz, T., & Bien, F. (2016). Winning with Data: Transform Your Culture, Empower Your People, and Shape the Future. New Jersey: John Wiley & Sons.

Turner, Margery Austin; Wial, Howard; and Wolman, Harold, (2008). Urban and Regional Policy and its Effects. Washington DC.: Brookings Institution Press.

Turner, Paul, (1993). Modern Macroeconomic Analysis. Berkshire: McGraw-Hill Book Co Ltd. Turvey, Michael T. (2019). Lectures on Perception: An Ecological Perspective. London: Routledge

Udokang, James Cosmas, Snr., (2006). Homo Politicus. Uyo: Joe Graphics Publications.

Van Hooser, Phillip (2013). Leaders Ought to Know: 11 Ground Rules for Common Sense Leadership. New Jersey: John Wiley & Sons.

Veljanovski, Cento G. (1989). Privatisation & Competition: A Market Prospectus. London: Institute of Economic Affairs.

Viscusi, W. Kip; Vernon, John M.; and Harrington, Joseph E. Jnr., (2001). Economics of Regulation and Antitrust. Washington DC.: Library of Congress Publications.

Wagner, Peter (2016). Progress: A Reconstruction. Massachusetts: Polity Press.

Wanat, John, (1978). Introduction to Budgeting. Massachusetts: Duxbury Press.

Watson, William E., (1998). The Collaps of Communism in the Soviet Union. London: Greenworld Press.

Weber, Max (1930). The Protestant Ethic and the Spirit of Capitalism. New York: Routledge.

Wiedemer, D., Wiedemer, R. A., & Spitzer, C. S. (2015). Aftershock: Protect Yourself and Profit in The Next Global Financial Meltdown. New Jersey: John Wiley & Sons, Inc.

Weisberg, Herbert I. (2014). Willful Ignorance: The Mismeasure of Uncertainty. New Jersey: John Wiley and Sons.

White, Khadijah Costley (2018). The Branding of the Right-Wing Activism: The News Media and the Tea Party. New York: Oxford University Press.

Wilson, Brad (2013). Do More, Spend Less: The New Secrete of Living the Good Life for Less. New Jersey: John Wiley and Sons.

Wolff, Richard D. (2012). Democracy at work: A cure for capitalism. Chicago: Haymarket books.

Wolff, E. (2014). Pillaging the World: The History and Politics of the IMF. Marburg: Tectum Publishing Press.

Woll, Peter (1963). American Bureaucracy. New York: Norton & Co. Inc.

Wood, David D.; Dekker, Sidney; Cook, Richard; Johannesen, Leila; Sarter, Nadine (2010). Behind Human Error. Surrey: Ashgate Publishing Ltd.

Worley, C. G., Zardet, V., Bonnet, M., & Savall, A. (2015). Becoming Agile: How the SEAM Approach to Management Builds Adaptability. New Jersey: John Wiley & Sons.

Wright, Val (2016). Thoughtfully Ruthless: The Key to Exponential Growth. New Jersey: John Wiley and Sons.

Yetiv, Steve A. (2015). Myths of the Oil Boom: American National Security in a Global Energy Market. New York: Oxford University Press.

Yule, George (1998). Pragmatics. New York: Oxford University Press

Zahavi, Dan, & Gallagher, S. (2008). The phenomenological mind. London: Routledge.

Zahavi, Steve (2019). Phenomenology: The Basics. London: Routledge.

Jacob, Herbert (1986). Law and Politics in the United States. Boston: Little Brown and Company.

Raul, John (1971). A Theory of Justice. Cambridge: Howard University Press.

Gramlisch, Edward M. (1981). Benefits-Cost Analysis of Government Programs. New Jersey: Princeton-Hall Inc.

Baker, Ross K. (1995). House and Senate. New York: Norton and Co. Inc.

Leinward, Gerrard (1994). Do We Need A New Constitution?. New York: Harper and Row Publishers.

Schlesinger, Arthur M. (1990). The Federal Government: How it Works. New York: Chelsea House Publishers.

Macy, John W; Adams, Bruce; Walter, J. Jackson (1983). American Unelected Government: Appointing the President's Team. Cambridge: Ballinger Publishing Co.

Vineyard, Dale (1968). Congress. New York: Charles Scribner's and Sons.

Casebook on Ethical Standards of Psychologists (1967). Washington: American Psychological Association, Inc.

Cunliffe, Marcus (1987). The Presidency. Boston: Houghton Mifflin Company.

Herbert, Ray Eldon; Spritzer, Carlton E. (1968). The Voice of Government. New York: John Wiley and Sons Inc.

Nelson, Michael (1984). The Presidency and the Political System. Washington DC: Congressional Quarterly Inc.

Elliott, Robert H. (1985). Public Personnel Administration: A Value Perspective. Virginia: Prentice Hall Company.

O'Connor, James (1973). The Fiscal Crisis of the State. New York: St. Martin's Press.

Breger, Loni's (1974). From Instinct to Identify: The Development of Personality. New Jersey: Prentice Hall Inc.

Lee, Robert D. Jnr. (1987). Public Personnel System. Pennsylvania: Aspen Publication.

Dolan, Edward F. (1995). Your Privacy: Protecting It In A Noisy World. New York: Cobblehill Books.

Sylvester, Robert (1995). A Celebration of Neurons: An Educator's Guide to the Human Brain. Virginia: Ronald S. Brandt Publication.

McAvoy, Paul W. (1970). The Crisis of the Regulatory Commissions: An Introduction to A Current Issue of Public Policy. New York: Norton.

Buchanan, Patrick J. (2004). Where the Right Went Wrong: How Neoconservatives Subverted the Regan Revolution and Highjacked the Bush Presidency. New York: Martin's Press.

White, Morton (1957). Social Thought in America: The Rovolt Against Formalism. Boston: Beacon Press.

Staats, Arthur W. (1975). Social Behaviorism. Illinois: The Dorsey Press.

Flanigan, William H.; Zingale, Warny H. (2006). Political Behavior of the American Electorate. Washington: CQ Press.

Sowell, Thomas (1987). A Conflict of Visions: Ideological Origins of Political Struggles. New York: CQ Press.

Government and Current Events Literature and Thoughts (2013). The three Branches of Government. Washington, DC: Perfect Learning Press.

Bernstein, Richard B. and Agel, Jerome (1993). Amending America. New York: Random House Inc.

Davidson, Roger H.; Oleszek, WalterJ.; Lee Francesa E.; Schruder, Eric (2014). Congress and It's Members. Washington DC: Sage Publication.

Digeser, Peter (1995). Our Politics, Ourselves: Liberalism, Identity and Harm. New Jersey: Princeton University Press.

Wald, Kenneth D. (1992). Religion and Politics in the United States. Washington: Congressional Quarterly Inc.

Jacob, Herbert (1986). Law and Politics in the United States. Boston: Northwestern University Press.

Meltzer, Bernard N. and Manis, Jerome G. (1967). Symbolic Interaction: A Reader in Social Psychology. Boston: Allyn and Bacon, Inc.

Leinward, Gerrard (1990). Freedom of Speech: American Issues. New York: Philip Leif Group, Inc.

MacMahon, Arthur W. (1953). Administration in Foreign Affairs. Alabama: University of Alabama Press.

Spencer, Steven J. and Myers, David G. (2006). Social Psychology. New York: McGraw-Hill Ryerson.

Gudden, Anthony (1979). Beyond Left and Right: The Future of Radical Politics. Cambridge: Polity Press.

Franklin, Daniel P. and Baun, Michael J. (1995). Political Culture and Constitutionalism: A Comparative Approach. New York: M. E. Sharpe Inc.

Bennet, W. Lance and Entman, Robert M. (2001). Meditated Politics: Communication in the Future of Democracy. Cambridge: Cambridge University Press.

Aron, Henry J. (1990). Setting National Priorities: Policy for the Nineties. Washington DC.: The Brookings Institution.

King, Gary; Lehman, Schlozman; Kay, Leyman; Nice, Norman H. (2009). The Future of Political Science: 100 Perspectives. New York: Routledge.

Cowell, Frank A. (1990). Cheating the Government. Massachusetts: The MIT Press.

Downs, Anthony (1957). An Economic Theory of Democracy. New York: Harper Collins Publishers.

Phelps, Edmund S. (1965). Private Wants and Public Needs. New York: Norton & Company Inc.

Tullock, Gordon; Littlechild, Stephen C.; muford, A. P. L.; Seldon, Arthur; Budd, Allan; Rowley, Charles K. (1979). The Taming of Government. Sussex: The Institution of Economic Affairs.

Coombs, H. M. and Jenkins, D. E. (1991). Public Sector Financial Management. London: Chapman & Hall.

Marini, John (1992). The Politics of Budget Control: Congress, The President, and the Growth of the Administrative State. Washington DC: Crane Russak.

Pierce, Lawrence C. (1971). The Politics of Fiscal Policy Formation. California: Goodyear Publishing Company Inc.

Mikesell, John L. (2007). Fiscal Administration: Analysis and Applications for the Public Sector. Indiana: Thomson and Wandsworth.

Lewis, Alan et al. (1995). The New Economic Mind: The Social Psychology of Economic Behavior. New York: Harvester wheatsheaf Publications.

Brandstatter, Herman & Guth, Werner (1994). Essay on Economic Psychology. New York: Springer-Verlag Publication.

Lewis, Alan; Webley, Paul; Furnham, Adrian (1995). The New Economic Mind: The Social Psychology of Economic Behavior. New York: Harvester Wheatsheaf Publications.

Granger, Clive W. J. (1999). Empirical Modeling in Economics: Specification and Evaluation. Cambridge: Cambridge University Press.

Beylan, Thomas A. and O'Gorman, Paschal F. (1995). Beyond Rhetoric & Realism in Economics: Towards a Reformation of Economic Methodology. London: Routledge.

Curtis, Herbert (2000). Game Theory Evolving: A Problem-Centred Introduction to Modeling Strategic Interaction. New Jersey: Princeton University Press.

Dutta, Prajit K. (1999). Strategies and Games: Theory and Practice. Massachusetts: The MIT Press.

Skousen, Mark & Taylor, Kenna C. (1997). Puzzles and Paradoxes in Economics. Cheltenham: Edward Elgar Publishing.

Robinson, Marshal A.; Morton, Herbert C.; Galderwood, James D. (1956). An Introduction to Economic Reasoning. Washington DC: The Brookings Institution.

Mishan, E. J. (1970). 21 Popular Economic Fallacies. New York: Preager Publishers.

Mayer, Thomas(1993). Truth Versus Precision in Economics. Vermont: Edward Elgar Publishing Company.

Blanchfield, William C., and Oser Jacob (1973). Economics: Reality Through Theory. New York: Harcourt Brace Jovanovich, Inc.

Boardman, Anthony E.; Greenberg, David H; Vining, Adam R.; Weiner, David L. (2011). Cost-Benefit Analysis: Concepts and Practices. New York: Prentice Hall.

Adams-Webber, J., & Mancuso, J. (1983). Applications of Personal Construct Theory. Toronto: Academic Press.

Aranda, G., & Finch, E. (2003). Using repertory grids to measure changes in risk-taking behavior. Journal of Construction Research, 4(1), 101-114.

Baker, S. (2002). Laddering: Making sense of meaning. In D. Partington (Ed.), Essential skills for management research (pp. 226-253). Lonndo: Sage.

Bannister, D., & Fransella, F. (1971). Inquiring Man: The Theory of Personal Constructs. London: Penguin.

Bannister, D., & Fransella, F. (1986). Inquiring man: The psychology of personal constructs (3 ed.). London: Routledge.

Basu, K., & Palazzo, G. (2008). Corporate social responsibility: A process model of sensemaking. Academy of Management Review, 33, 122-136.

Berger, P., & Luckmann, T. (1966). The social construction of reality. New York: Anchor Books.

Burr, V. (1995). In introduction to Social Construction. London: Routledge.

Butt, T., & Parton, N. (2005). Constructuve social work and personal construct theory. British Journal of Social work, 35, 793-806.

Campbell, J. (2007). Why would corporations behave in socially responsible ways? An institutional theory of corporate social responsibility. Academy of Management review, 32, 946-967.

Charvet, S. (1997). Words that change minds: Mastering the language of influence. Dubuqe, Iowa: Kendall/Hunt Publishing.

Christiansen, C. (2006). Sense-making and entrepreneural coalition building: A case of competing interests, cultural barriers, and interorganizational relations in a non-profit health plan. International Journal of Public Administration, 29, 501-515.

Cooper, C. (1998). Individual differences. London: Arnold.

Cromby, J., & Nightingale, D. (1999). What's wrong with social constructionism? In Social Constructionist Psychology: A critical analysis of theory and practice. Buckingham: Open University Press.

Crotty, M. (1998). The foundations of social research: meaning and perspective in the research process. Thousand Oaks, CA: Sage.

Crotty, M. (2003). The foundations of social research: Meaning and perspective in the research process (2 ed.). Thousand Oaks: Sage Publications.

Daft, R., & Weick, K. (1984). Toward a model of roganizations as interpretation systems. Academy of Management Review, 9, 284-295.

Easterby-Smith, M., Thorpe, R., & Jackson, P. (2008). Management Research (3 ed.). London: Sage.

Fontaine, J., & Fransella, F. (1988). PCT: Still radical thirty years on. In F. Fransella, & L. Thomas (Eds.), Experimenting with personal construct psychology (pp. 26-35). Routledge and Kegan Paul.

Fox, R. (2001). Constructivism examined. oxford Review of Education, 27(1), 23-35.

Fransella, F. (1988). PCT: Still radical thirty years on. In F. Fransella, & L. Thomas (Eds.), Experimenting with Personal construct psychology (pp. 26-35). London: Routledge & Kegan.

Freedman, J., & Combs, G. (1996). Narrative therapy: The social construction of preferred realities. New York: Norton.

Gaffikin, M. (2006). The Critique of Accounting Theory. Australia: University of Wollongong.

Gergen, K. (1994). Realities and relationships: soundings in social construction. Cambridge: Cambridge University Press.

Gergen, K. (1999). An invitation to social construction. London: Sage Publication.

Gergen, K., & Davis, K. (1985). The social construction of the Person. (K. Gergen, & K. Davis, Eds.) New York: European Journal of Business and Management www.iiste.orgISSN 2222-1905 (Paper) ISSN 2222-2839 (Online) Vol.10, No.10, 2018 115 Springer-Verlag.

Gioia, D., & Chittipeddi, K. (1991). Sensemaking and sensegiving in strategic change initiation. Strategic Management Journal, 12, 433-448.

Gioia, D., & Thomas, J. (1996). Idenity,image, and issue interpretation: sense-making during strategic change in academia. Administrative Science Quarterly, 41, 370-403.

Goffin, K. (2002). Repertory grid technique. In Essential skills for management research (pp. 199-225). London: Sage.

Hatch, M. (1997). Organization theory: Modern, symbolic and postmodern perspectives. Oxford: Oxford University Press.

Hines, R. (1988). Financal accounting in communicating reality, we construct reality. Accounting, organizations and society, 13(3), 251-262.

Hopwood, A. (. (1989). Accounting and the Pursuit of Social Interests. In W. Chua, T. Lowe, & T. Puxty (Eds.), In Critical Perspectives in Management Control (pp. 141-157). London: The Macmillan Press Ltd.

Houston, S. (2001). Beyond social constructionism: Critical realism and social work. British Journal of Social Work, 31, 845-861.

Kakabadse, A. (1991). The wealth creators: Top people, top teams and exective best practice. London: Kogan Page.

Kelly, G. (1955). The Psychology of personal constructs. New York: Norton.

Laird, J. (1993). Building knowledge from the study of cases: A reflective model for practitioner self-evaluation. In K. Millstein, & J. Laird (Ed.), Revisioning Social Work Education: Social Constructionist Approach. New York: The Haworth Press.

Lit, S., & Shek, D. (2002). Implications of social constructionism to counseling and social work practice. Asian Journal of Counselling, 9(1 & 2), 105-130.

Liu, C., & Matthews, R. (2005). Vygotsky's Philosophy: Construstivism and its criticisms. International Educational Journal, 6(3), 386-399.

Margolis, J., & Walsh, J. (2003). Misery loves companies: Rethinking social initiatives by business. Administrative Science Quarterly, 48(2), 268.

Marton, F., & Booth, S. (1997). Learning and Awareness. New Jersey: Lawrence Erlbaum Associates.

Mills, J., Weatherbee, T., & Colwell, S. (2006). Ethnostatistics and sensemaking: making sense of universities and business school accreditation and rankings. Organizational Research Methods, 9(4), 491-515.

Morgan, G. (1983). Beyond Method. Beverly Hills CA: Sage.

Newman, J. (2004). Constructing Accountability: Network Governance and Managerial Agency. Public Policy and Administration, 19(4), 17-33.

Nijhof, A., & Jeurissen, R. (2006). Editorial: A sensemaking perspective on corporate social responsibility: introduction to the special issue. Business Ethics: A European Review, 15(4), 316-322.

Ogborn, J. (1997). Constructivist metaphors of learning science. Science and Education, 6(1-2), 121-133.

Parrot, R. (1996). A women-centred "sense-making" approach to communicating about women's reproductive health. In R. Parrot, & C. Condit (Eds.), Evaluating Woman Health Messages (pp. 414-425). Thousand Oaks, CA: Sage Publications.

Piaget, Jean. (1954). The Construction of Reality in the Child. London: Routledge.

Porac, J., Thomas, H., & Baden-Fuller. (1989). Competitive groups as cognitive communities: The case of the Scottish Knitwear industry. Journal of Management Studies, 15, 397-416.

Reed, M. (2005). Reflections on the "Realist Turn" in organization and management. Journal of Management studies, 42(8), 1621-1644.

Reger, R., & Huff, S. (1993). Strategic groups: A cognitive perspective. Strategic Management Journal, 14, 103-123.

Ring, P., & Rands, G. (1989). Sensemaking, understanding, and committment: Emergent interpersonal transaction processes in the evolution of 3M's microgravity research program. In A. Van den Ven, M. Poole, & H. Angle (Eds.), Research on the management of innovation: The minnesota studies (pp. 337-366). New York: Ballinger.

Rogers, B., & Lynette, R. (2007). Use of repertory grid to access the underlying realities in key accounts relationships. International Journal of Market Research, 49(5), 595-612.

Rudes, J., & Guterman, J. (2007). The value of social constructionism for the counselling profession: A reply to Hansen. Journal of Counselling & Development, 85, 387-392.

Rutherford, B. (2002). The social construction of financial statement elements under private finance initiative schemes. Accounting, Accountability and Auditing Journal, 16(3), 372-396.

Sinclair, A. (1995). The chameleon of accountability: forms and disclosures. Accounting, Organizations and Society, 20(2-3), 219-237.

Stewart, V., & Mayes, J. (2002). Enquire within. Wellington, New Zealand: Enquire Within Developments Ltd.

Tan, F., & Hunter, G. (2002). The repertory grid technique: A method for the study of cognition in information systems. Management Information Systems Quarterly, 26(1), 39-57.

Thomas, J., Clark, S., & Gioia, D. (1993). Strategic sensemaking and organizational performance: linkages among scanning, interpretation, action and outcomes. Academy of Management Journal, 36, 239-270.

Walsh, J. (1994). Managerial and organizational cognition: Notes from a trip dowm memory lane. Organization Science, 6, 280-321.

Watkins, M. (2000). Ways of learning about leisure meanings. Leisure Sciences, 22(2), 93-107.

Weick, K. (1995). Sensemaking in organizations. Thousands Oaks: Sage.

Wittgenstein, L. (2001). Philosophical Investigations (3 ed.). UK: Blackwell Publishing.

Kolibri 360 GmbH
Ferdinand-Jühlke-Straße 7
99095 Erfurt, Deutschland
produktsicherheit@kolibri360.de

Druck:
CPI Druckdienstleistungen GmbH
im Auftrag der
Kolibri 360 GmbH
Ferdinand-Jühlke-Str. 7
99095 Erfurt